PUBLISHING WOMEN'S LIFE STORIES
IN FRANCE, 1647–1720

Publishing Women's Life Stories in France, 1647–1720

From voice to print

Elizabeth C. Goldsmith

Ashgate

Aldershot • Burlington USA • Singapore • Sydney

Published by
Ashgate Publishing Limited
Wey Court East
Union Road
Farnham
Surrey, GU9 7PT
England

Ashgate Publishing Company
110 Cherry Street
Suite 3-1
Burlington
VT 05401-3818
USA

Ashgate website: http://www.ashgate.com

British Library Cataloguing-in-Publication data

Goldsmith, Elizabeth C.
    Publishing women's life stories in France, 1647–1720: from voice to print. – (Women and gender in the early modern world)
    1. Autobiography – Women authors – History and Criticism
    I. Title
    809.9'9287

Library of Congress Control number: 2001086888

Transferred to Digital Printing in 2011

ISBN 978-0-7546-0370-2

MIX
Paper from
responsible sources
FSC
www.fsc.org
FSC® C004959

Printed and bound in Great Britain
by Printondemand-worldwide.com

Contents

Acknowledgements

Material from chapter three originally appeared as "Mothering Mysticism: Madame Guyon and her Public", in Donna Kuizenga and Colette Winn, eds., *Women Writers in Pre-Revolutionary France: Strategies in Emancipation* (New York: Garland Publishing, 1997), 127–39.

Material from chapter four originally appeared as "Publishing the Lives of Hortense and Marie Mancini", in *Going Public: Women and Publishing in Early Modern France*, eds. Elizabeth Goldsmith and Dena Goodman (Ithaca: Cornell University Press, 1995), 31–45.

A part of chapter five originally appeared as "Secret Writing, Public Reading: Madame de Villedieu's *Lettres et billets galants*", in *A Labor of Love: Critical Reflections on the Writings of Madame de Villedieu*, ed. Roxanne Lalande (Madison: Farleigh Dickinson University Press, 2000), 111–26.

A grant from the National Endowment for the Humanities in 1995–96 made it possible for me to take a year-long sabbatical leave from Boston University to research this study. A Boston University Humanities Foundation grant in 1994 facilitated my access to material relating to the life of Jeanne des Anges in the Cornell University Witchcraft Collection. My visits to the Colonna Archive at the Biblioteca Statale Santa Scolastica in Subiaco, Italy, and the Biblioteca Apostolica Vaticana in Rome were subsidized by an award from the American Philosophical Society in 1998. Conversations with Dom Romano di Cosmo, Lorenzo Smerillo, and Natalia Gozzano were immeasurably helpful while I was in Rome and Subiaco working on Marie Mancini. I am grateful for the gracious assistance provided by the librarians at the Jesuit Archives in Vanves and the Saint-Sulpice Archives in Paris for my research on the manuscripts and letters of Jeanne des Anges and Jeanne Guyon. The expert staff of the Houghton Library at Harvard University has consistently provided me with valuable assistance on all aspects of this project.

Among the many people who have read all or parts of this book as it has evolved over the last six years, I wish especially to thank Abby Zanger, Patricia Cholakian, Erika Harth, and George Hoffmann. Erika Gaffney of Ashgate has been a model editor, whose conversation I always appreciate.

To my husband Art and daughter Emily I owe much of what is worthwhile in my work. Their support, good humor, and love renew and sustain me.

List of Figures

Women and Gender
in the Early Modern World

Series Editors: Allyson Poska and Abby Zanger

In the past decade, the study of women and gender has offered some of the most vital and innovative challenges to scholarship on the early modern period. Ashgate's new series of interdisciplinary and comparative studies, 'Women and Gender in the Early Modern World', takes up this challenge, reaching beyond geographical limitations to explore the experiences of early modern women and the nature of gender in Europe, the Americas, Asia, and Africa. Submissions of single-author studies and edited collections will be considered.

Titles in the series include:

Maternal Measures
Figuring caregiving in the early modern period

Edited by Naomi J. Miller and Naomi Yavneh

Marie-Madeleine Jodin 1741–1790
Actress, philosophe and feminist

Felicia Gordon and P.N. Furbank

The Political Theory of Christine de Pizan

Kate L. Forhan

Introduction

In the opening words of her memoirs, published in 1681, Madame de la Guette claims her place as one of a small group of women who have made the decision to tell their lives in print:

> Ce n'est pas une chose fort extraordinaire de voir les histoires des hommes, qui par leurs beaux faits, ou par leurs vertus eminentes se sont rendus recommandables à la postérité, ou qui ont été élevés ou abaissés selon les caprices de la fortune; mais il se trouve peu de femmes qui s'avisent de mettre au jour ce qui leur est arrivé dans leur vie. Je serai de ce petit nombre ...[1]

> (It is no extraordinary thing to see the stories of men, who by their grand actions or their eminent virtues have recommended themselves to posterity, or who have been elevated or brought down by the whims of fortune; but there are few women who choose to expose to the world what has happened in their lives. I will be of this small number ...)

La Guette fully expects, as she indicates, that her readers will be familiar with memoirs by men testifying to history and their place in it, describing military exploits and the contributions of their family in the public realms of government and diplomacy, peacemaking and war. That her readers may also have read a few memoirs by women is suggested in her preface, but their inclusion is exceptional and requires justification at the outset. In La Guette's case, the events of her life included participation in military action and negotiation, repeated occasions in which she successfully disguised herself as a man, and a strong attraction to "masculine" endeavors.[2] Her bookseller, in his own preface to the reader, identifies the author as a woman with the "heart" of a man:

> ... je l'appelle femme bien qu'elle ait une humeur entièrement opposée à celle de son sexe, puisque je lui ai ouï dire plusieurs fois, que qui pourrait voir son coeur à nue le trouverait tout viril, et y remarquerait une générosité qui n'est pas ordinaire aux femmes. (n. pag.)

> (I call her a woman even though she has a disposition entirely opposed to that of her sex, as I have heard her say many times that whoever might see her exposed heart would find it completely virile, and would notice a generosity of spirit that is not common in women.)

Just as she perceives as historically worthy those parts of her life in which she has played a male role, so it is La Guette's masculine self-image that authorizes her to print them. In grounding her authority to publish her memoirs in her

1

participation in public life, La Guette is strategically linking herself with a publishing tradition of long standing. To write and circulate one's memoirs was to produce a public document testifying to a historical period or event. Male authors of memoirs laid claim to a privileged vantage point with respect to the period of history in which they lived. They were participants, for example, in the military campaigns they recorded, or they were courtiers who had both observed and influenced affairs of state. The typical memorialist was impersonal and self-effacing, or at least worked at seeming so. Authors of memoirs often referred to themselves in the third person, as if to stress the objectivity of their accounts, and alluded to their personal role in the events they were recounting only to sustain their claim to legitimacy as keepers of the historical record.

La Guette writes her memoirs with this traditional strategy in mind, hoping to claim patronage for her family as well as posterity's recognition of their historical importance. She presents herself as a warrior even in her domestic life, fighting her father's injunction against her chosen marriage, doing battle at her husband's side during the Fronde, and eventually, as a widow and Huguenot exile in Amsterdam, assuming the task of re-establishing her family and negotiating marriages for her children. Yet, while La Guette carefully inserts herself in this tradition of memoir writing that is gendered male, she is aware of another type of autobiographical voice, gendered as female, and from which she wishes to distance herself. Her narrative voice suggests her resistance to the type of voice her readers might associate with women's memoirs, the voice that betrays secrets ("quoique je sois une femme, un secret est fort bien entre mes mains") or that breaks down when confronted with disaster ("Je regardais toutes ces choses d'un sang-froid et sans émotion").[3] Taking on the male roles of soldier, diplomat, and head of family, she also projects in her writing a particular perspective on what legitimates her decision to write her memoirs, a perspective that she and her bookseller describe as male. Implicitly contrasting with this perspective is a type of female voice that her readers might expect to find in her book, but which, she tells us, we will not find in her narrative.

La Guette's memoirs are built on a careful blending of rhetorical approaches to the tasks of writing and publishing one's life story, a project that was increasingly undertaken by women during the second half of the seventeenth century. As she seems so clearly aware, at issue for a woman writer of memoirs is not only the fact that their lives are not normally built on the sort of public action that can bring glory and a place in history to a family name, but the fact that a woman would even want to display her life to the public is likely to cast doubt on her motives. Even if male memorialists, typically writing from exile or disgrace, had always been read with the understanding that they were making a case for themselves, their right to make that formal presentation was never questioned. Memoirs, growing out of the aristocratic traditions of property and military glory, were intimately associated with the masculine realm. La Guette's identification with this realm she sees as a kind of passport to acceptance by her different reading publics: in the short run, the potential patron to whom she addresses her text, and, ultimately, future readers who will judge her.

Other women writers took up the challenge differently. Faith Beasley's study of the representation of history in seventeenth-century memoirs and fiction shows that women writers, beginning with Marguerite de Valois, whose memoirs were published in 1628, argued for a new purpose to the genre and a new definition of historical truth.[4] These women contributed to a major shift in the idea of history, unmasking the traditional rhetorical pose of the memoir as an objective, historical document. They attempted instead to bring to light the more polemical motives of memoirs, emphasizing the author's investment in gaining the reader's sympathy for one particular and personal version of events. They also began to stress the more private side of historical accounts of families or noble houses that were typically the focus of memoirs. By the end of the seventeenth century, memoir accounts were promulgating a new definition of aristocratic identity de-emphasizing political power and stressing instead a more elusive notion of superiority based on personal style and self-presentation.[5]

Women writers were leaders in the development of new types of life-writing, from memoirs to private letters to fictionalized autobiographical narratives. The new attentiveness to "particular" history at the expense of accounts that treated the family name or house as a single unit determining both the reputation and individual worth of its members, encouraged women to write of their personal experience. Most of the women who circulated their life stories in the early modern period were writing in part to record and justify an experience of separation from their household, although the reasons for this separation were wide-ranging. Some of them had left their homes as the result of a religious conversion – this was the case for Marie de l'Incarnation, Jeanne des Anges, Jeanne Guyon, and Antoinette Bourignon. On the other hand, Marie-Catherine d'Aulnoy, Anne-Marguerite du Noyer, Hortense Mancini Mazarin and Marie Mancini Colonna, wrote and published their life stories after leaving their husbands and seeking to establish themselves in foreign courts. Their memoirs highlight the authors' private lives and those of well-known public figures. Even La Guette, while legitimating the publishing of her memoirs by featuring herself as a woman who has moved freely in the male public sphere, in the telling of her story attempts to redesign her personal reputation as a woman who has suffered for her defiance of father and king.[6] Her claim to participation in public history disguises, thinly, a more subversive and personal agenda. She presents to her public a private reconstruction of her family's role in contemporary events, and her own personal stake in it.

The monumental version of history traditionally buttressed by collections of aristocratic memoirs gradually gave way to a more fragmented, personalized and speculative body of writing called "particular history" or *histoire de cabinet*.[7] Writers like Saint-Réal and Desjardins de Villedieu, critical of the exclusive attention of historians to battles and royal genealogies, called for more penetrating revelations about the personal motives for political events. Even writers who viewed their projects as following in the older tradition of historical memoirs departed from some of the more ostentatious rhetorical practices of their predecessors, writing, for example, in the first person and inserting private conversations into their texts. Bussy-Rabutin, composing his memoirs after his exile in 1666 from the court of Louis XIV, turns first to the records he had kept of his military campaigns, but finds that the more engaging records of his life are from his private journal and letter correspondences.[8] He slowly constructs a hybrid text made up of letters and other documents interspersed with his own narrative, which he sends in installments to his friends in Paris, and to which they contribute with their written replies. Unwilling to assume the traditional pose of resigned *exilé*, who gains spiritual strength from observing society at a distance, Bussy-Rabutin makes of his memoirs an ongoing conversation with a world from which he hopes he is only temporarily absent.[9] Mademoiselle de Montpensier, too, who as a member of the royal family fallen out of favor, in 1653 undertook to write her memoirs from her country estates, develops a narrative style that resembles a conversation with her absent friends and integrates into her text their responses to her writing project as it evolves over time.[10] Her writing project was intimately related to the architectural project of restoring her damaged properties, and thus the writing of her memoirs progressed in tandem with the building renovations. Her memoirs are rich with references to the places she was reconstructing while drafting her autobiographical text. Her family's ancestral property of Champigny, which received her most obsessive attentions, also required the most extensive rehabilitation. To this chateau she added a room which became her favored place to write and plan her new designs, a *cabinet* which came to represent the ideal space from which to reconstruct and continue her conversations with a world from which she had been separated.

The term *histoire de cabinet*, designating a new and more private form of history, was a metaphor derived from a new architectural space, suggesting behind-the-scenes secret conversations that came to be designated as the true motors of power and public action. It was also a space that was perceived as predominantly female.[11] While the new types of memoir writing were not practiced exclusively by women, they were particularly congenial to women writers who could not or did not wish to claim, as La Guette did, that they had lived, and thus could write, like a man. The *cabinet* was also an enclosure that came to be seen as a place of escape, not only from official history but from all forms of public interaction, escape to a more authentic encounter of the individual with an inner life.[12] Even Madeleine de Scudéry, that consummate theorizer and practitioner of salon sociability, would evoke in 1680 the necessity of retreat from public conversation to solitary reflection: "Quand on a tant de choses à penser, qui valent mieux que ce que l'on entend dire; il faut demeurer dans son cabinet à s'entretenir soi-même ..."[13] (When one has so many things to think about that are worth more than what one hears being said, it is necessary to stay in one's *cabinet* to converse with oneself.)

Writers of a more religious bent describe the urge to retreat from social conversation to the privacy of one's own thoughts as an opportunity to commune with God. Like Scudéry's suggested auto-conversations, these spiritual interactions were unfamiliar but appealing. They had to be practiced, learned, and even cultivated. Emerging from the voluminous literature advising readers on the techniques of public sociability was a new form of guidebook advising readers how to be alone, how to "talk with God". Michel Boutauld's *Méthode pour converser avec Dieu* (1679) is one such text outlining a method for self-reflection that invokes a God who alternately inhabits a public and a private sphere:

> ... les soins de Dieu dans le Ciel, et sur le Trône de son empire, sont de penser aux Anges et aux Bienheureux, et aux grand desseins de sa Sagesse et de sa Sainteté: mais chez vous, et dans votre cabinet, son unique soin est de penser à vous, et toute l'application de sa Providence et de son Amour ne regarde que vos intérêts particuliers.[14]

> (... God's tasks in Heaven and on the Throne of his empire must be to think about the Angels and the Blessed, and the great plan of his Wisdom and Sanctity: but in your home and in your *cabinet*, his sole task is to think about you, and all the effort of his Providence and Love concerns only your particular interests.)

While Scudéry advises conversation with oneself as an antidote to the boredom of sociable interaction, Boutauld advises conversation with God as an antidote to both annoyance and pleasure:

> La conversation avec Dieu est exempte de ces deux dangers; il ne s'y trouve point ni de péchés, ni d'ennuis: l'innocence et la joie sont les deux parties qui composent cette félicité spirituelle. (p. 8)

> (Conversation with God is exempt from these two dangers; it contains neither sins nor troubles: innocence and joy are the two elements that make up this spiritual happiness.)

Linked to the discovery of a new kind of prayer, the project of writing one's "spiritual conversations" was a new method of cultivating the inner self. A profusion of spiritual memoirs were written in the seventeenth century, emerging from the practice of mental or silent prayer.[15] Committed to writing, the practice of auto-conversation would become a form of autobiography.

This new authorization of unmediated forms of prayer, conducted in solitude and in a private space, had particular consequences for women. Not only were they encouraged, by the Catholic Reform movements, to cultivate and examine their souls via reflection and "interior conversations", their very lack of theological training was thought to give them an advantage over men in their pursuit of an "inner way" to God.[16] The female voice, in prayer, was privileged by its perceived simplicity, or, in the secular realm of conversation, by its "naturalness".[17] As Linda Timmermans has observed, this created a climate in which a woman "had a better chance of being heard if she accepted, or even accentuated the marks of her difference".[18] The valorization of female speech had the paradoxical effect of actually facilitating the passage into print of women's private writing. Religious advisors or "spiritual directors" encouraged their protégées to write and circulate their written works.[19] With the assistance of editors and printers interested in marketing women's writing, women published their personal testimony, often presenting it to the public as a kind of conversational interaction with the world.

The process by which they saw their books into print was not simple, nor were their steps into the public arena taken lightly. A woman publishing her personal life story had to justify by what authority she had chosen to write, and then circulate, her singular, private voice.[20] In their memoirs early modern women tried to mitigate the inevitably adverse consequences of public exposure. They approached this challenge rhetorically, in careful justifications of their decision to go public. At the same time they were attentive to the practical realities of publication, which required them to collaborate and interact with others involved in the production, distribution, and reception of their stories.

The question of the addressee or public to whom a life story is presented is particularly important in the French literary tradition, in which a formative moment for women's writing has its origins in the salon and the culture of sociability.[21] The classic works on the autobiographical genre, as Felicity Nussbaum has pointed out, either define the preconditions for autobiography according to a modern idea of individuality and personal autonomy, or they define the genre in such a way that most of the seventeenth and eighteenth centuries offer no examples worthy of discussion.[22]

Studies of early women's autobiography have concentrated on the pre-dominantly Protestant English and American traditions, originating in private diaries. Some critical studies of modern female-authored autobiographies have noted the distinctive rhetorical positions taken by women writers who view themselves, for example, relationally, in terms of a connection to a chosen other, or as fragmented, discontinuous beings.[23] In these examinations of the gender-marked features of autobiography the focus has been on the point of view taken by the writer on both herself and her writing. Little attention has been paid to the role – implied or explicit – of the readers of a woman's autobiography, which in the early modern period is a complicated and crucial issue. For Post-Tridentine Catholicism, the notion of personal development is inextricable from the practice of intimate conversation with another person – a religious director who is capable of mediating and instructing the penitent in her "conversations" with God. In France, the first women to circulate their life stories were engaged from the outset with a community of readers. They presented their stories to the public because they wanted a larger role in the shaping of their own identity, which they understood from the beginning to be an interactive process. Whether the point of departure for the circulation of these stories was a "command" to write coming from a spiritual director, or a public scandal making it imperative that the testimony of a particular woman be heard, women circulated and published their autobiographies to contribute and respond to other forms of public discourse.

Changes in literary taste, in the cultural and religious functions of personal testimony, and in the composition of the reading public paved the way for women's private voices to make their way into print. Three of the writers I will study in the following chapters – Jeanne des Anges, Marie de l'Incarnation, and Jeanne Guyon – were religious figures whose autobiographies received considerable publicity in the seventeenth century. For each of them the decision to write the story of their "private" lives was closely linked to their awareness of themselves as already "public" figures who had broken free of the isolating female spaces of convent and household. Jeanne des Anges wrote her life story as a pendant to Joseph Surin's accounts of the Loudun witchcraft affair of the 1630s in which Jeanne had been the most dramatically affected of the "possessed" nuns. Marie de l'Incarnation was the first female member of a religious order to join the foreign missions in Canada. Her son, the Benedictine monk Claude Martin, was her principal collaborator in the publication and circulation, in France, of her autobiographical writings and letters. Jeanne Guyon was the spiritual leader of the revivalist Catholic "Quietist" movement which was ultimately condemned by the church in 1699 after a lengthy published debate between Bossuet and Fénelon, Guyon's follower and defender. Guyon's autobiography was printed after her death, but she and Fénelon had circulated it during her lifetime, and it was a central target of Bossuet's *Relation sur le quiétisme* attacking her doctrine.

The other three writers I will examine form a cluster of what could be called "worldly" writers, as contrasted with the spiritual ones: Hortense Mancini Mazarin, Marie Mancini Colonna, and Marie-Catherine Desjardins or Madame de Villedieu. Their autobiographical works were all published within a five-year period (1672–77), and have strong intertextual links to one another. The first of these to appear in print, Villedieu's *Mémoires de la vie de Henriette-Sylvie de Molière*, is a fictional memoir inspired by the lives of contemporary women who had fled unhappy private lives and found themselves ultimately fleeing the consequences of their public exposure. The first French woman writer to write and publish fiction under her own name, Villedieu never produced her own autobiography, but she did publish her life in other ways, and worked skillfully to control her public image both in collaboration with and in opposition to her printer Claude Barbin, who dominated the marketing of female-authored texts at the end of the century. Hortense Mancini, a friend and benefactor of Villedieu, published her own life story in 1675. In many respects Hortense's real life adventures resemble those of the fictional Henriette-Sylvie: in 1668 she escaped her fanatically devout husband to seek protection outside of France, eventually settling at the English court where she was a mistress of Charles II and an influential figure in the French expatriate community. Marie Mancini's memoirs were first published in 1677 in Madrid, where, like her sister, she had fled an unhappy marriage. Nieces of Cardinal Mazarin, both sisters were already dramatically public figures (Marie had been forced to end her liaison with Louis XIV in order to facilitate his Spanish marriage) when they decided to take the step, unprecedented for women, of producing their own printed accounts of their private lives.

These are only a few of the women who wrote and circulated memoirs in the 80-year period I am discussing. My choice of texts is selective, but not arbitrary. I have opted to explore in detail each web of written relations woven by a small number of influential writers, rather than limit my study to a more categorical discussion of a broad number of integral memoir texts. The six writers that I have selected, however, are representative of different choices that an individual woman writer might make in seeing her life story into print. Their writing practices were imitated or echoed in the works of a number of their contemporaries. Jeanne Guyon, for example, experimented in voicing her most childlike self in writing, and her commitment to the simplicity of the child echoed the "primitive" Christian voice advocated by Antoinette Bourignon (1616–80), who eluded ecclesiastical censure and wrote, printed, and disseminated her personal mystical experiences.[24] Both Guyon and Bourignon understood, too, that a woman wishing to publicize her life story could find protection in her avowed state of innocence, against charges of heterodoxy, coming from the church, or simply female impropriety, coming from the world at large. In the secular realm, Desjardins de Villedieu's ironic speculation on the mutual contamination of memoirs and fiction elicited responses in the memoirs of Madame de Nemours (1709) and the fictional journal of Madame de Lussan (1725).[25] Following Villedieu's lead, these writers suggest that irony and self-deprecation can provide a measure of freedom to writers who wish to tell their own stories while also recognizing the inevitable distortions that these stories will undergo by being read, circulated, and retold.

In considering the autobiographical writing of a core group of writers I have insisted on the importance of taking into account the different forms that this writing took – not only in their memoirs, but also their written correspondences, which in most cases have never been printed but have been preserved in archives, as well as the statements they circulated about their lives in other public forums: trial transcripts, testimonials that were published as part of other authors' works, written self-portraits that were circulated among friends. The body of material I study here includes life-writing that was circulated in a multiplicity of forms: autograph, manuscript copy, and print. I will examine the presentation and reception of early modern women's voices as they followed an uncharted passage into print, their exposure to the world by their first editors, and their reception by subsequent generations of readers and critics. In the case of Madame de Villedieu, I will explore how the female experience of "going public" was anticipated by her as having particular consequences for the development of women's autobiographical writing.

In all of these instances of self-publication, the writer's decision to launch her story into the world initiates a complex series of responses from different readers, who validate, interpret, or oppose what Janet Gunn has described as the writer's act of connection with the world, a "gesture of resistance to mutilation".[26] While the writers themselves are naturally committed to imposing their own interpretation on their readers, they also display an extraordinary sensitivity to the cultural contingency of their efforts, to the inevitable fact, as Roger Chartier notes, that "without fail, reception invents, shifts about, distorts".[27] They perceive and present their lives as mediated, and the essential nature of their writing, like their speech, as determined by its performance in the world.

Notes

1. *Mémoires de Madame de la Guette, écrits par elle-même*, (La Haye: Adrian Moetjens, 1681), pp. 1–2.
2. As she declares in a self-portrait: "Je sais fort bien que ma démarche/ Tient un peu trop du masculin;/ Mais je dis que le féminin/ Ne fut jamais ce qui m'attache" (*Mémoires* 149–50). (I well know that my conduct/ Is a bit too masculine/ But I will say that the feminine/ Was never to my liking.) All translations are my own.
3. "although I am only a woman, a secret is very safe in my hands"; " I watched all these things calmly and without emotion" (109, 130).
4. See her *Revising Memory: Women's Fiction and Memoirs in Seventeenth-Century France* (New Brunswick and London: Rutgers University Press, 1990).
5. On this point see René Démoris, *Le Roman à la première personne, du classicisme aux lumières* (Paris: Armand Colin, 1975), pp. 72–4.
6. See Carolyn Lougee's subtle analysis of La Guette's construction of a social identity in "Reason for the Public to Admire her: Why Madame de la Guette Published her Memoirs", in *Going Public: Women and Publishing in Early Modern France*, ed. Elizabeth C. Goldsmith and Dena Goodman (Ithaca: Cornell University Press, 1995), pp. 13–29.

7. See Beasley, pp. 10–71; and Démoris, pp. 59–89.
8. "Lorsque mon père me mena à l'armée, j'écrivis mes campagnes pour me faire mieux retenir les choses qui s'y passaient. J'ai continué jusqu'à présent d'en user ainsi; et sans autre vue que de m'amuser, j'ai même écrit mes moindres occupations." *Mémoires*, ed. Ludovic Lalanne (Paris: Marpon et Flammarion, 1857), p. 3. (When my father took me to the army, I wrote of my campaigns to make myself better retain the things that happened in them. I have continued up to the present to do the same; and with no other view than to amuse myself, I even wrote down my most minute occupations.)
9. See the chapter on Bussy-Rabutin in Elizabeth C. Goldsmith, *Exclusive Conversations: The Art of Interaction in Seventeenth-Century France* (Philadelphia: University of Pennsylvania Press, 1988), pp. 77–109.
10. On this point see Jean Garapon, "Mademoiselle à Saint-Fargeau: la découverte de l'écriture", *Papers on French Seventeenth-Century Literature*, **XXII**, 42 (1995), pp. 37–47.
11. On how the *cabinet* and other architectural spaces were gendered in the seventeenth century see Erica Harth, *Cartesian Women: Versions and Subversions of Rational Discourse in the Old Regime* (Ithaca: Cornell University Press, 1992), 15–33. Malina Stefanofska has also written perceptively about the symbolic significance of the space of the *cabinet* and the *galerie* in the memoirs of Retz and Saint-Simon. See, for example, "Strolling through the Galleries, hiding in a Cabinet: Clio at the French Absolutist Court", *The Eighteenth Century, Theory and Interpretation*, **35**, 3 (1994).
12. Bernard Beugnot discusses the linkage between the development of this architectural space and the discourses of solitude and separation in *Discours de la retraite au XVIIe siècle* (Paris: Presses Universitaires de France, 1996), 90–96. See also Orest Ranum's chapter, "The Refuges of Intimacy", in Roger Chartier (ed.), *A History of Private Life*, vol. 3 (Cambridge, MA: Harvard University Press, 1989), pp. 207–63.
13. From "De parler trop ou trop peu", in Phillip J. Wolfe (ed.), *Choix de Conversations* (Ravenna: Longo Editore, 1977), p. 38.
14. *Méthode pour converser avec Dieu* (Paris: Ch. Amat, 1899), p. 16.
15. For a perceptive discussion of this literature, see Nicholas D. Paige, *Being Interior: French Catholic Autobiographies and the Genesis of a Literary Mentality, 1596–1709* (PhD dissertation, University of Pennsylvania, 1996), pp. 1–31.
16. Several recent studies have explored this historical phenomenon. The most comprehensive survey of the literature debating the authenticity of the female voice in religion is Linda Timmermans, *L'Accès des femmes à la culture, 1598–1715* (Paris: Champion, 1993), pp. 593–813. Suggestive discussions may also be found in Yvan Loskoutoff, *La Sainte et la fée: Dévotion à l'enfant Jésus et mode des contes merveilleux à la fin du règne de Louis XIV* (Geneva: Droz, 1987), pp. 75–144; and Michel de Certeau, *La Fable mystique: XVIe–XVIIe siècle* (Paris: Gallimard, 1982), pp. 216–330.
17. On the esthetic of naturalness in female speech and writing, see Elizabeth C. Goldsmith, "Authority, Authenticity, and the Publication of Letters by Women", in Goldsmith (ed.), *Writing the Female Voice: Essays on Epistolary Literature* (Boston: Northeastern University Press, 1989), pp. 46–59.
18. *L'Accès des femmes à la culture (1598–1715)*, p. 615. My translation.
19. Michel de Certeau has examined this practice in the case of Jean Joseph Surin and his circle. See, for example, his introduction to Surin's *Correspondance* (Paris:

Desclée de Brouwer, 1975). See also Paige, pp. 22–51, and Timmermans, pp. 539–55.

20. The stigma of going into print, and how early modern women circumvented it, has been extensively explored. An excellent analysis is Ann Rosalind Jones, "City Women and Their Audiences: Louise Labé and Veronica Franco", in Margaret W. Ferguson, Maureen Quilligan and Nancy J. Vickers (eds), *Rewriting the Renaissance: The Discourses of Sexual Difference in Early Modern Europe* (Chicago: University of Chicago Press, 1986), pp. 299–316. For discussions of this issue in the cases of a number of women writers from the seventeenth and eighteenth centuries, see Goldsmith and Goodman (eds), *Going Public*.

21. See Joan DeJean, *Tender Geographies: Women and the Origins of the Novel in France* (New York: Columbia University Press, 1991), pp. 17–71; and Harth, pp. 15–64. On the model of conversation in seventeenth-century literature see Elizabeth C. Goldsmith, *Exclusive Conversations: The Art of Interaction in Seventeenth-Century France* (Philadelphia: University of Pennsylvania Press, 1988).

22. *The Autobiographical Subject* (Baltimore: The Johns Hopkins University Press, 1989), 5; pp. 226–27.

23. Mary Mason, "The Other Voice: Autobiographies of Women Writers", in B. Brodski and C. Schenck (eds), *Life/Lines: Theorizing Women's Autobiography*, (Ithaca: Cornell University Press, 1988), and Estelle Jelinek's introduction to her edited collection, *Women's Autobiography: Essays in Criticism* (Bloomington: Indiana University Press, 1980), pp. 1–20.

24. Bourignon's autobiographical account was published after her death by Pierre Poiret (who would later become a follower and editor of Jeanne Guyon), and titled *La Vie de Damoiselle Antoinette Bourignon, écrite partie par elle-même, partie par une personne de sa connaissance ...* (Amsterdam: Jean Riewerts et Pierre Arents, 1683).

25. Marie d'Orléans Longueville de Nemours, *Mémoires de M.L.D.D.N.* (Cologne, 1709), and Marguerite de Lussan, *Histoire de la Comtesse de Gondez*, vol. XII of *Bibliothèque de campagne ou amusements de l'esprit et du coeur* (La Haye: Cramer et Philibert, 1749; 1st edition 1725).

26. *Autobiography: Toward a Poetics of Experience* (Philadelphia: University of Pennsylvania Press, 1982), p. 28.

27. *The Order of Books* (Stanford: Stanford University Press, 1994), p. x.

CHAPTER ONE

Discovering New Worlds:
Marie de l'Incarnation and the
Process of Autobiography

The initial expression of the spiritual is nothing but the decision to leave.

Michel de Certeau

mon coeur dans un cloître et mon corps dans le monde.

Marie de l'Incarnation

The disparate writings that make up the work of Marie de l'Incarnation are all in some way inspired by the author's desire to narrate the story of her life's renewal that began with her departure for the unknown world of Canada in 1639. Most of what she wrote can be said to be autobiographical in that she wrote either to relate her own life and inner development (as in the memoir she titled her *Relation* and in her correspondence), or to document a specific occasion in which she had been involved (as in her notes from retreats, readings, and teachings). By the time of her death in 1672 her place in French history was secure. Her narratives of life in the newly established missions of Canada were widely read in France in the letters she regularly sent home for circulation and in her contributions to the regular accounts produced collectively by missionaries and sent to France, the Jesuit *Relations*. As the first female member of a religious order to become a missionary in New France, Marie was a well-known spiritual leader in her lifetime. After her death her life story was presented to generations of Catholic schoolgirls as an exemplary tale of feminine virtue and religious devotion.

The text that Marie de l'Incarnation produced in 1634 and revised in 1654 in the form of a memoir is in part a conversion narrative that traces the spiritual itinerary of an ordinary woman whose life was transformed by a series of mystical revelations leading her to shed her worldly ties and embrace monastic life. It was edited and published in revised form immediately after her death, in 1672, by her son Claude Martin, who titled the work *La Vie de la vénérable mère Marie de l'Incarnation*. In this form her life story was read by a public grown familiar with the genre of spiritual autobiography, a genre that eventually came under heavy criticism at the end of the century when Bossuet produced a condemnation of mysticism that included an attack on the practice

La Venerable Mere *Marie de L'Incarnation* Premiere Superieure des Vrsulines de la
Nouuelle France; qui apres auoir passé trente deux Ans dans Le Siecle, en des penitences extra-
ordinaires; huict ans au Monastere des Vrsulines de Tours, dans la pratique d'vne tres exacte
Observance; et trente trois ans en Canada, dans vn Zele incroyable pour la Conuersion des
Sauuages, est decedée a Quebec en odeur de Saintete le dernier d'Auril 1672, âgée de 72 Ans,
six mois, 13 Iours.   P. Mariette ex.

Fig. 1.1   Marie de l'Incarnation

of spiritual life-writing. Marie de l'Incarnation, though, was the only woman autobiographer (except for the sainted Teresa of Avila) who escaped Bossuet's disapproval. Indeed, he held her up as an exemplary writer, despite the fact that on matters of doctrine and theology her concept of mysticism and spiritual growth through prayer is indistinguishable from that of many religious writers who were condemned by the church during the Quietist controversies. Thus, while most of the other early modern women who wrote spiritual memoirs were condemned by the Gallican church as "false mystics", Marie de l'Incarnation was never charged with heterodoxy, or even the sin of vanity, for her decision to write and circulate her life. Literary and religious historians have been inclined to explain Marie's special status by suggesting, as Henri Brémond does, that she was simply a superior writer, better able than her contemporaries to convince her examiners that mysticism posed no threat to the progressively more rationalized Catholic institutions.[1] But Marie's successful evasion of censorship was not only due to the arguments she presented in defense of mysticism. Her position as an officially approved writer of spiritual auto-biography seems to be explainable for reasons due in part to her manner of writing, the personal voice that comes out in her life writing, and even more to the conditions under which her writing was circulated, edited, and printed.

Moreover, when we read her autobiographical *Relation de 1654* with her epistolary writing, which both she and her son treated as a single work, we can appreciate how she was able to satisfy the narrow definition of spiritual memoirs as authorized by the Church, and at the same time serve as a model to other women of her time who undertook a less orthodox approach to publishing their lives. Marie's autobiographical voice, and the way in which it was edited by her son and interwoven with his own commentary, which he called "the filial echo" of her voice, would serve as a guide to other women who made the decision to write their life stories and who hoped to receive an approval from readers comparable to the response that Marie's story had enjoyed.

The trajectory of Marie Guyart's life that would lead her to a position of prominence in the history of Canada and of Catholic spirituality would have been difficult to predict when, in 1616, at the age of 17, she married the silk merchant Claude Martin in the provincial city of Tours. At 19 she was widowed and left alone with her infant son to help manage her brother's family business. But an intense period of spiritual self-questioning followed, and within two years of her abrupt initiation into the world of trade Marie was secretly yearning for the refuge of a convent. Finally, at the age of 30, she managed to see her dream realized, and over the strenuous objections of her family (including her young son's poignant pleas) she entered the Ursuline convent as a novice. Barely two years later she was professed as a nun.

Marie's initial "departure" from the world into the circumscribed space of conventual life was the first in a series of leavetakings that she would come to see as patterning her life. The urge to quit her worldly life and focus on what she calls the "interior" life was also what precipitated, or facilitated, Marie de l'Incarnation's entry into the world of writing. For Marie the act of writing seems always to have been fraught with an attendant anxiety about the vanity of any kind of verbal self-expression. But paradoxically, by moving out of the secular world and committing herself to religious life, in which the rule of modesty and silence would presumably be most strong, Marie found a freedom to write "from the heart" that she had not known before. This paradoxical "inner freedom" provided to women by cloistered life has been explored in recent years by scholars studying the writings of nuns from the middle ages to the eighteenth century.[2] Established in France in the early seventeenth century, the Ursuline order promoted an approach to apostolic faith that was particularly congenial to a blending of the active and the contemplative life. Many Ursuline communities favored the taking of a special vow to promote Christianity through the teaching of young girls.[3] Ursuline spirituality and the manifestations of mystical experience as described by Ursuline nuns were to incorporate the apostolic mandate of the order, just as that outward mission was to give heavy weight to the teachings of spirituality or the "inner way" to God.[4]

Writing and spiritual direction

In truth, Marie's "coming to writing" may be traced to earlier influences in her life, and specifically to encounters with religious directors who encouraged her in her practice of mental prayer and reflection. Like many women of her generation, Marie was first exposed to the new practices of private devotion through reading François de Sales's *Introduction à la vie dévote*. As a young woman she had listened raptly to the sermons of visiting *prédicateurs*, and been overwhelmed with the urge to speak about what she heard with others in her household.[5] But describing her early religious education, Marie states that although her family was pious, she received no guidance in the "*vie intérieure*" until reading François de Sales (*R* 192). Then, in 1620, an incident occurred whose importance for her future development is marked in Marie's *Relation* by its precise dating. The date would also become the inspiration for her choice of name in religion:

> Après tous les mouvements intérieurs que la bonté de Dieu m'avait donnés pour m'attirer à la vraie pureté intérieure, en laquelle je ne pouvais entrer de moi-même, n'ayant eu jusqu'alors aucun directeur, ... sa divine Majesté voulut enfin elle-même me faire ce coup de grâce: me tirer de mes ignorances et me mettre en la voie où elle me voulait et par où elle me voulait faire miséricorde: ce qui arriva la veille de l'Incarnation de Notre-Seigneur, l'an 1620, le 24e de mars. (*R* 181)

(After all the inner promptings which the goodness of God had granted me to draw me to true purity of soul, which I could not reach through my own efforts, not having had any director until then, his divine Majesty himself wanted to deliver the *coup de grâce*. He pulled me from my ignorance and placed me on his chosen path, taking pity on me: this happened on the eve of the Incarnation of Our Father, in the year 1620, on the 24th of March.)

Walking in the street she is overwhelmed by a sense of her own culpability, and she wanders as though in a trance, until she finds herself in front of the chapel of the Feuillant Fathers, where she enters and pours out her soul to a startled priest:

Après que j'eus tout dit, je vis que ce bon Père avait été grandement surpris de la façon de m'annoncer et de lui dire ainsi tous mes péchés, et de ma façon, qu'il connut n'être pas naturelle mais extraordinaire. Il me dit avec une grande douceur: "Allez-vous-en, et demain me venez trouver dans mon confessional." (*R* 184–5)

(When I had finished I saw that the priest was astonished by the way I had introduced myself and poured out my sins in this unusual way, and by my manner which he knew was not normal but out of the ordinary. He spoke to me very gently, saying, "Go home now and come back to see me tomorrow in my confessional.")

Thus Dom François de Saint-Bernard became Marie's first religious director, and his "regulation" of her confessions gave form to her inner explorations, convincing her most importantly of the necessity of dialogue as a means of spiritual advancement. This account is paradigmatic for the historian, dramatizing as it does one individual's discovery of the power of private confession, at a moment in French history when this practice was just beginning to be widespread.[6] Marie situates the point of origin of her religious conversion and spiritual identity in this initial turning to a private space for intimate confession (beginning with Dom François's directing her to the confessional). The space of the confession-box was in fact a new configuration in Catholic ritual practices at the beginning of the seventeenth century, and Marie took to the new practice of the guided *examen de conscience* with a zeal that was remarkable to her religious directors.[7]

Marie's spiritual directors quickly expanded their demands on her substantial talents for self-expression. After Dom François, she was assigned to another Feuillant monk, "homme grandement spirituel," she writes, "et experimenté en la conduite des âmes ... Il m'interrogea sur ma façon de vie, et généralement il me voulut connaître à fond" (*R* 193). Versed in new methods of spiritual direction, it was Dom Raymond who first asked Marie to account for herself in *writing*, in the form of regular letters addressed to him.[8] Like her account of discovering the attraction and relief of private confession, Marie's account of her initiation to the practice of the written examination of conscience provides a valuable historical example. Many pious women were similarly drawn to reflect on their lives in writing during the first part of the seventeenth century, to a point that was alarming to certain clerics who would later publish arguments against the circulation of confessional and spiritual writings by women.[9]

Marie was at times a more enthusiastic apprentice than her director would have wished. At one point Dom Raymond had to dissuade her from a determination to sharpen her humiliation by posting a signed, confessional letter on the door of the church, "à ce que tout le monde sache qu'elle [mon âme] a été si déloyale à son Dieu" (R 212). And though Dom Raymond had commanded her to "tell him everything" (R 193), it appears that he sometimes got more than he bargained for. Some of her letters respond to his criticism of what he saw as Marie's excessive desire to tell all:

> ... un désir comme le mien ne peut long-temps garder le silence; il se réitère sans cesse et j'ai toujours de nouvelles choses à dire ...
> Mortifiez-moi donc tant qu'il vous plaira, je ne cesserai point de vous déclarer les sentimens que Dieu me donne, ni de les exposer à votre jugement ...[10]

> (... a desire such as mine cannot long remain silent; it repeats itself endlessly and I always have new things to say ... Mortify me then, as long as you like, I will not stop telling you of the feelings God gives me, nor will I stop exposing them to your judgment ...)

But at times, too, in a move that was not unusual in relations between directors and their protégées, it was Dom Raymond who seemed to be the follower and Marie the giver of spiritual advice.[11] Dialogues with her directors seem to have given Marie an outlet for her urge to proselytize as well as her desire to be guided. When in 1631 she entered the Ursuline convent, she was given the responsibility of teaching the younger novices. In her life story she notes the facility with which she was able to do this, and the pleasure that it gave her to express herself in teaching. Her director told her to write down her thoughts on religious instruction (later, these were published by her son under the title L'Ecole sainte). In these encounters early in her career, the role played by her directors was in no way limited to an instructional one, with Marie as pupil. Marie quickly assumed an active role in forming and shaping these connections that she saw as so crucial for her spiritual advancement. When Dom Raymond was called away from Tours in 1638, she decided that she wanted a Jesuit for her next director, and upon hearing the sermons of the Jesuit priest Georges de la Haye, she asked her superior for an introduction. Their first conversation had an immediate effect:

> Lorsqu'il m'eut entendue, il m'obligea de lui écrire la conduite de Dieu sur moi dès mon enfance et enfin tout ce qui s'était passé dans le cours des grâces qu'il avait plu à la divine Majesté de me faire. J'eus permission de ma supérieure; mais il me vint une répugnance de le faire, si je n'écrivais aussi tous mes péchés et imperfections de toute ma vie ... à ce que, par ce moyen, il jugeât mieux de ma

disposition. J'eus permission et le fis avec [la] plus grande fidélité qu'il fût possible, puis je mis le tout entre les mains dudit R.P., lequel ensuite m'assura que ç'avait été le Saint-Esprit qui m'avait conduite … (*R* 298)

(When he had heard me, he asked me to write to him about God's direction of me since childhood, and about all that had occurred during the series of blessings that it pleased his Divine Majesty to bestow on me. I had the permission of my superior; but it repelled me to do it if I did not at the same time write of all my sins and imperfections during my life … so that in this way he would be better able to judge my state. I received permission and did this with the utmost fidelity, then I gave the whole piece to the said Reverend Father, who since told me that it had been the Holy Spirit who had guided me …)

Thus Marie came to draft the first account of her life, written, as was true for other spiritual autobiographies of her day, on the "command" of a religious director, while at the same time she makes it clear that the precise nature of this command was shaped by her from the outset.[12]

The prompting by her early Jesuit directors to account for herself in writing seems also to have nourished Marie's enthusiasm for teaching, and encouraged her to rely on her own knowledge and the private practice of prayer as sources for her apostolic authority. She measured her success in self-expression by the gratifying responses of her first pupils:

J'avais une très grande simplicité pour produire mes pensées, et mes soeurs qui étaient tout étonnées de m'entendre ainsi parler, une … me dit: "prêchez-nous un peu, soeur Marie" … J'avais toute ma vie un grand amour pour le salut des âmes … Or, comme je ne pouvais pas courir par le monde pour dire ce que j'eusse bien voulu, pour tâcher d'en gagner quelques-unes, je faisais ce que je pouvais au noviciat, m'accommodant à la capacité de chacune … Elles me pressaient de plus en plus de poursuivre … (*R* 289; 307–8)

(I had a great simplicity for producing my thoughts, and my sisters were most surprised to hear me speak thus. One said to me: "preach to us a little, sister Mary" … All my life I had a great love for the saving of souls … Since I was not able to travel about the world to say anything I wanted, in order to convert a few I did what I could during my novitiate, adjusting myself to the abilities of each sister … they increasingly pressed me to continue …)

Encouraged in her writing and preaching by both directors and students, Marie soon found herself consumed with a new desire to expand her mission beyond the confines of the convent. She recounts the urgency of this need to spread the word and she recollects her early prayers for the strength to carry out this mission which as yet had no specific object: "… je suis assez savante pour l'enseigner à toutes les nations; donnez-moi une voix assez puissante …" (*R* 310–12) (I am wise enough to teach it to all nations; give me a voice that is powerful enough). It was her director Jacques Dinet, she writes, who told her that the mysterious land of which she had been dreaming was Canada.[13] One of her son's teachers, also a Jesuit, wrote to report that he had joined the missions in New France, suggesting that she make the voyage, and sent her a Jesuit Relation describing life there (*R* 314–15). Marie became obsessed with the idea of her calling, and worked strenuously to enlist patrons for the project of founding a teaching mission for girls in Canada. By the time she was preparing to join the mission herself, Marie had worked with a number of religious directors, so that when her assigned director Father Salin attempted to check her proselytizing fervor, she was able to call on the support of others through letters, and rely on her conviction that God was directing her to pursue her dream.

Like her secular counterpart Madame de la Peltrie, Marie chose her confidants.[14] In her *Relation* she is quite specific on the subject of the patronage network that enabled her in the end to pursue her ambition. In this auto-biographical narrative which is otherwise remarkable for its discretion and elliptical style when it comes to describing personal relationships, the compli-cated series of human interactions that finally resulted in her boarding the ship at Dieppe is carefully foregrounded. Present and past spiritual directors seem to recongregate around their pupil, taking position according to whether they supported or opposed her mission. The few letters we have by Marie from the period leading up to her departure for New France echo the narrative in the *Relation*, while providing evidence that the plotting and scheming of all involved was more complex and unpredictable than what Marie described in retrospect. Her later account lays out the preparations for departure as a more rational sequence of exchanges with patrons and supporters, leading steadily to the permission she received to leave France. When she finally steps onto the ship the moment represents for her a break with these contacts as well as a launching toward a new world where, she hopes, her inner direction will no longer depend so heavily on exterior, human contacts.

In her *Relation* Marie writes that the first years in Quebec were marked by long periods of spiritual despair, aggravated by her loneliness, isolation, and the lost ability to express her inner thoughts to others. Yet she soon retrieved her former sense of inner strength, and with it an enriched capacity for expression. The enormity of the communication project she had undertaken reveals itself to her as a challenge rich with possibilities for finding new forms of expression. The daunting goal of learning the languages of the Amerindians and actually preaching in Algonquin or Huron suddenly seemed attainable to her. The project of communicating with France and somehow conveying the realities of missionary life in Canada to those who were helping to sustain it financially was an activity she assumed with incredible energy (sending hundreds of letters, for example, with the annual ships returning to France). She describes her spiritual dialogues as changing, too, away from human interaction and toward more exclusive conversations with God.

The voyage out

Marie's first "departure" from the world had been her entrance into the convent. It had been a wrenching leave-taking, for with this move she abandoned her child and forfeited all claim to any inheritance that might have supported him. She made her profession against the wishes of all of her family members. The scenario of leave-taking was to be played out again and again in different forms in Marie's life and in her writing of it, most dramatically, of course, in her departure for Canada. Marie described her move toward religious conversion from its beginnings as the desire to travel or move away, to break from the distractions of a too familiar world. Detailing her early yearnings for the refuge of religious life she recounts how she would want to "flee" ordinary interaction to be alone with God:

> ... me trouvant en une compagnie ou l'on disait quelque-chose d'un peu trop libre, que prudemment je ne pouvais reprendre, ni me séparer, en en parlant à mon divin Epoux, il me pressait de quitter et m'en aller avec lui dans ma chambre ... (*R* 267)

> (... finding myself in the company of people who were saying something a bit too freely, and unable to either reply or leave, in speaking of it to my Divine Husband he would press me to leave and go away with him to my room.)

Wanting to commit herself fully to religious life, but still unready to abandon her child (and not yet permitted to by Dom Raymond), she describes herself as split, inhabiting two spaces at once: "mon coeur dans un cloître et mon corps dans le monde" (*R* 29) (my heart in the cloister and my body in the world).

The physical move into the world of the cloister, however, did not end her yearning to "depart":

> mon corps était dans notre monastère, mais mon esprit qui était lié à l'Esprit de Jésus, ne pouvait être enfermé. Cet esprit me portait en esprit dans les Indes, au Japon, dans l'Amérique, dans l'Orient, dans l'Occident, dans les parties du Canada et dans les Hurons ... (*R* 310).

> (my body was in our monastery, but my spirit, linked to the Spirit of Jesus, could not be contained. This spirit took me in my mind to the Indies, Japan, America, the Orient, the West, and to parts of Canada and Huron territory ...)

It is as though her first wrenching break with the world carried with it its own momentum, compelling Marie to seek meaning at greater distances, and making it difficult for her to find inspiration in human actions that were too close to her: "... j'avais plus l'esprit dans les terres étrangères pour y considérer en esprit les généreuses actions de ceux qui y travaillaient et enduraient pour Jésus-Christ, qu'au lieu ou j'habitais" (*C* 185). (I was spiritually more present in foreign lands, where I could consider the noble actions of those who worked there and suffered for Christ, than I was in the place I inhabited.)

When the idea of actually joining the Jesuit missions in Canada was presented to her, this goal immediately became her exclusive focus of attention. Upon learning that Dom Raymond was planning to join the missions, she wrote him seeking advice about her own great desire to go, suggesting to him that his own planned departure may be a sign that she too was meant to be a missionary (*C* 24–8). When, after encouraging her commitment, he then arranged to leave for Canada without her, she wrote him an anguished reproach: "Quoi, vous partez, mon très cher Père, et vous partez sans nous? ... Où allez-vous, mon Père, sans vos filles? Avez-vous peur qu'elles souffrent ce que vous allez souffrir? ..." (*C* 33). (What, my most dear Father, you are leaving, and without us? ... Where are you going, Father, without your daughters? Are you afraid that they may suffer what you will suffer?)

Acting on her own behalf and for the group of Ursuline sisters who had also pledged their intent to join the New France missions, Marie helped to finally arrange for this unprecedented departure. She worked with Madame de la Peltrie to assure its approval by the powerful Company of 100 Associates in Paris, hid her plans from her sister's family until just days before her departure, received the personal blessing of Anne of Austria, and on 4 May 1639 was waiting at the port of Dieppe to embark on the boat that was to take her to Quebec.

Marie rode in the coach on her way to the docks as though in a trance:

> Pendant tant d'allées et de courses que nous avions faites depuis notre partement de Tours, mon esprit et mon coeur n'étaient pas où mon corps était. ... Madame la Gouvernante de Dieppe nous fit l'honneur de nous venir prendre en son carrosse, pour nous mener au bord de la mer. Nous étions de tous côtés entourées de monde, et cependant mon esprit était si fortement occupé, qu'à grand'peine pouvait-il se divertir de son attention et entretien avec le suradorable Verbe Incarné. L'on n'eût pas jugé cela à me voir à l'extérieur, lequel faisait tout ce qui était convenable, avec une façon [qui] semblait dégagée. Lorsque je mis le pied en la chaloupe qui nous devait mener en rade, il me sembla entrer en paradis, puisque je faisais le premier pas qui me mettait en état et en risque de ma vie pour l'amour de lui, qui me l'avait donnée. (*R* 353–4)

> (During all the comings and goings that had absorbed us since our departure from Tours, my spirit and my heart were not where my body was. ... Madame the Governor of Dieppe honored us by fetching us in her carriage to take us to the seaside. We were surrounded by people on all sides, and yet my spirit was so intensely occupied that it could barely separate itself from its attention to and conversation with the most adored Word Incarnate. One would not have known this by observing my outer self, which was doing everything appropriately and in a way that seemed effortless. The moment I put my foot into the boat that was to ferry us to the ship I felt as though I was entering paradise, because I was taking the first step toward risking my life for the love of he who had given it to me.)

In this passage Marie recalls the moment of her departure for Canada as an instant that enabled her to reintegrate her divided self: the acts of spiritual and physical leave-takings converge as she sets her foot into the boat. Canada would continue to figure in her writing as an "icy" paradise because of the opportunities for martyrdom that it offered her adventurous soul. From her first brush with death on the transatlantic voyage, as their boat narrowly missed hitting an iceberg, to the freezing winters that threatened every year to put an end to the fragile community, Marie describes Canada as a land which both tested and expanded her spiritual strength. It is a place, moreover, where her errant spirit was destined by God to finally settle and realize its "particular vocation", as she would explain in a letter to her son Claude:

> Dieu commence souvent par la générale, puis il arrête le coeur dans le lieu où il l'appelle – soit pour y être actuellement, soit pour se faire prier pour les âmes de ce lieu là, ou pour leur faire du bien en d'autres manières. ... J'ay été plusieurs années sans sçavoir où arrêter mon esprit; voilà la vocation générale. Puis, très évidemmment Dieu me fit connoître que c'estoit en Canada qu'il voulait servir de moy ... (*C* 270)

> (God often begins with a general thought, then brings the heart to a halt in the place where he wants it to be – either to actually be there, or to pray for the souls in that place, or to do them some good in other ways. ... I spent many years not knowing where my spirit should rest: that was a general vocation. Then very clearly, God let me understand that it was Canada where he wished to use me.)

Marie thus describes her personal discovery of the "New World" as a place where her spirit can "settle", and it becomes a vantage point from which she can reconcile her erstwhile competing desires for separation from the world and interaction with it. The project of converting the Indians is closely tied in her imagination with the idea of her own awakening spirituality.[15] Freezing temperatures, always a threat to the survival of the missionary community, also provide a compelling metaphor to describe the long lost souls of the "savages".[16] The Huron girls who came into the Ursuline convent were first scrubbed clean of their forest "grease", and then instructed by the nuns. This constituted a kind of preaching, which, unlike at home, as Marie writes, in Canada was not a forbidden or "dangerous" activity: "Il n'y a point de danger de dire à nos sauvages ce que l'on pense de Dieu. Je fais quelquefois des colloques à haute voix en leur présence, et ils font de même" (*C* 125). (There is no danger in telling our savages what one thinks of God. I sometimes give speeches out loud in their presence, and they do the same.) Talking, persuading, preaching, exchanging talk with the inquisitive Indian girls who came to live with the nuns were all necessary to Marie's apostolic design. Thus, while the first project of the nuns upon their arrival was to build the cloister walls that would contain them, their enclosure in Canada afforded a different sort of separation from the world than the life to which they had committed themselves in France. Marie saw the convent in Quebec as a space from which to reach out to the new world around her, a territory marking out new experiences which she was eager to communicate to those remaining in France. From this crowded shelter Marie was to orchestrate a complex network of conversations with her old world, in the process refining her knowledge of the different languages necessary for any meaningful human interaction in her new home.

In the early years of her life in Canada Marie was enthusiastic about the mission's successes. She embraced the project of learning Indian languages, and took some pleasure in the equalizing effect that the common ignorance of the nuns and priests had on their community:

> Nous faisons nos études en cette langue barbare comme font ces jeunes enfans qui vont au Collège pour apprendre le Latin. Nos révérends pères quoique grands docteurs en viennent là aussi bien que nous, et ils le font avec une affection et une docilité incroyable. (*C* 108)

> (We are studying this barbarous language just as young children study Latin in school. Our reverend fathers may be grand doctors but they do it just like us, and with an incredible docility and affection.)

Equally urgent was the need to cultivate her rhetorical skills to communicate with interested patrons in France, upon whom the missionary community relied for its survival. Letters home carried the hope of assuring not only news of home but supplies, money, and official approval for projects on the return voyage. Responding to the "command" of her Jesuit superiors, Marie was soon a regular contributor to the published *Relations* that were shipped back to France. Her reports stress the difficulty of adequately describing the extraordinary life she and her sisters were leading:

> Je vous envoie quelques petites remarques pour satisfaire à l'obéissance. J'ai eu de la difficulté à m'y résoudre, pour ce que si on voulait dire toutes les choses qui peuvent donner de l'édification dans les actions de nos filles, ce ne serait jamais fait … (*C* 146)

> (I am sending a few remarks in obedience to your wishes. I had difficulty resolving to do it, because if one wanted to recount every edifying feature of our girls' actions, one would never be able to finish …)

In her private letters she frequently supplemented the narratives of the Jesuit *Relations*, which were destined for a wider public: "Béni soit donc l'auteur des merveilles que nous voyons: la relation en sera toute pleine, encore qu'il ne soit pas possible d'y mettre tout ce qui en est; aussi aurait-on de la peine à le croire" (*C* 103). (Blessed be the author of the marvels that we are witnessing: the relation would be filled with them, but it is not possible to put everything in, and besides, people would have difficulty believing it.)

Despite her professed reticence about seeing her accounts circulated and read, Marie took care to have a hand in the distribution of her writing. Whether describing the activities of the missionaries for the published *Relations* or writing a personal letter, Marie was sensitive to the different readers and types of publics her accounts would have. Certain epistolary *récits* she clearly intends for circulation beyond their primary addressee, as we see in a letter to her son: "Je supplie notre Réverende Mère Françoise de Saint-Bernard de vous envoyer une copie du récit que je lui fais du progrès de notre séminaire" (*C* 132). (I beg our Reverend Mother Françoise de Saint-Bernard to send you a copy of the account I am sending her of the progress of our seminary.) In her life story, Marie frequently expresses a certain anxiety about writing and a desire that she not be thought of as a self-conscious author or one who takes personal responsibility for her words. Instead she reminds her readers that she is writing at the command of another (her director, her son), and that she is being guided by God:

> Je pourrais peut-être me tromper si j'apportais des comparaisons pour m'exprimer autrement que je fais. Je dis simplement ce que je crois être selon la vérité et, comme j'ai dit, ce que l'Esprit qui me conduit me presse de dire. (*R* 250)[17]

> (I might possibly make a mistake if I were to make comparisons, in order to express myself in a different way. I say what I believe to be true, simply, and as I have said, only what the Spirit guides and presses me to say.)

But her letters, less guarded, show a clear awareness of the rhetorical imperatives involved in her new communication with the world. Hoping to inspire her readers to support the mission in New France, Marie sees a new purpose to authorship. She takes up the challenge of writing a good story that will be circulated to readers who might reciprocate with money, as in this letter "to a lady of quality":

> Voila, Madame, un petit récit de l'état présent de notre Séminaire, qui comme vous voyez est dans la pure providence de Dieu. Comme vous êtes visitée de plusieurs personnes puissantes, je vous supplie de le leur vouloir recommander, et si la divine majesté touche le coeur de quelques-uns, Monsieur de Bernières qui s'est chargé de nos affaires, et qui nous envoie nos nécessitez, est celui à qui il faudrait s'adresser. (*C* 99)

> (There, Madam, is a little account of the current state of our Seminary, which, as you can see exists purely by God's providence. As you are visited by many powerful people, I beseech you to commend it to them. If God's majesty touches some of their hearts, the person to contact is Monsieur de Bernières, who has taken charge of our affairs and who sends us what we need.)

Writing this way, from a distance, and with the exigencies of her mission authorizing a bolder positioning of herself as an "authority" on life there and an important player in its ongoing success, gave a new measure of freedom to Marie as a writer. Life in this new and foreign landscape, of which she had dreamed even before putting a name to it, gave shape to her writing, imposing challenges to communication that influenced the way she perceived and described her world. The enormous obstacles to interaction presented by the strangeness of Indian language and culture, on the one hand, and the geographical and temporal distance separating her from France, on the other, for someone like Marie, who yearned for the difficult, were challenges that could not fail to inspire. Communication at a distance could mean that one could choose what one wanted to hear or convey to others. In 1642, even after she had heard from De Bernières that the funds for her new convent had run out, Marie continued her construction projects and the reporting back of the mission's mounting debts.[18] A letter could always be lost, or a message poorly conveyed, so that the frustrations of delayed communication could be turned to one's advantage, at the very least allowing one to prolong hope: "... quelque pressées et importantes que soient les affaires, il faut attendre un an pour en avoir la résolution; et si on ne les peut faire dans le temps que les vaisseaux sont en France, il en faut attendre deux" (C 268). (... no matter how important and urgent things are, one must wait a year in order to have them resolved, and if this cannot be done during the period when the ships are in France, then one must wait for two years ...) In a more private register, writing from a distance lent a new rhythm and its own style of intimacy to verbal exchange. Letters replaced conversations, and letters that could be sent only once each year required an intensive communicative effort.

From Canada, Marie wrote not only to correspondents with whom she had communicated by letter before, but to everyone, including those with whom she had lived in close physical proximity, such as Ursule de Sainte Catherine, the Superior of the Ursulines at Tours. To these correspondents Marie wrote her secret thoughts: "Je ne sçay ce que je vous dis l'année dernière touchant mes sentiments intérieurs et secrets. Puisque vous voulez que je recommence, j'aurai de la complaisance à vous les dire" (C 139). (I don't know what I said to you last year regarding my inner feelings and secrets. As you want me to begin again, I will please you by telling you.)

In letters to her son, whom she had dramatically abandoned forever when she set foot on the boat that was to take her to Canada, Marie discovers the possibilities of spiritual reconciliation through writing:

Le coeur sacré de mon Jésus tient le milieu entre le vôtre et le mien, et son divin esprit est le lien de notre petit commerce: Car c'est avec lui que je traite de tout ce qui vous touche, et de tout ce qui me regarde. Je ne fais qu'une seule affaire des vôtres et des miennes ... (C 269–70)

(The Sacred Heart of Jesus holds the center between us, and his divine Spirit is the link of our little commerce. For it is with him that I speak of everything which touches you and everything which concerns me. I make only a single subject of yours and mine.)

The voyage in

From the earliest phases of her commitment to religion, Marie saw her advancement as a kind of inner voyage, a moving away from the "tracas du monde" to a secretive, inner space where she could converse with God. In the beginning, freeing herself spiritually meant disguising her practice of mental prayer and learning to present to the world a kind of "cover" for her meditations: "devant le monde, j'aimais mieux, lorsque je ne pouvais pas prendre un ouvrage pour occuper mon extérieur, prendre un livre que de donner à connaître que je faisais ou pâtissais l'oraison" (R 259). (in the presence of others, when I could not take up some handiwork to occupy my outer self, I would take up a book rather than let it be known that I was engaged in or undergoing prayer.)

Marie's *examen de conscience* was both symbolically represented and literally facilitated by epistolary dialogue with her directors. The practice of mental prayer had a symbolic analog in silent reading.[19] Attitudes toward silent reading in the early modern period are strikingly congruent with discussions about mental prayer, particularly when applied to women. Both practices seem to have created great anxiety in early observers. Both suggested a kind of sneaking away of the self to a new inner territory of the imagination, protected and untouchable from the outside. Both practices also were first conceived as conversations. Spiritual progress meant teaching the soul to retreat from interactions with the outside world and move to a separate, imaginary *cabinet* permitting more intimate interaction, as Marie explains in a letter to her son:

> L'âme étant parvenue à cet état, il lui importe fort peu d'être dans l'embarras des affaires, ou dans le repos de la solitude; tout lui est égal ... Dans la conversation et parmi le bruit du monde elle est en solitude dans le cabinet de l'Epoux, c'est à dire, dans son propre fond ou elle le caresse et l'entretient, sans que rien puisse troubler ce divin commerce. (C 4)

> (Having achieved this state, the soul cares little whether it is caught up in business matters or in the repose of solitude; all is the same ... In the conversation and noise of the world, the soul is alone in the Husband's cabinet, that is, in its own depths, where it can caress and speak with him without anything troubling this divine commerce.)

In her new life in Canada, it seemed to Marie that the difficulty of achieving this required inner retreat from the world was in one sense much greater than it ever had been in France. Living in tight quarters under conditions that required the nuns to engage in strenuous physical labor along with the men, preoccupied with the daily challenge of inventing new approaches to their teaching mission and organizing a community of nuns and priests from different religious orders, the *tracas* of life in New France would seem not to permit the sort of growth toward mystical understanding that was Marie's consuming desire. But in her letters we see Canada represented as a better world, where a higher order of spiritual growth was attainable. In part this is precisely because of the increased physical difficulties of life there – they mortified the body and challenged the spirit: "Il est vrai, les sens ne soutiennent point en Canada; l'esprit laisse la nature dans les pures croix qui s'y retrouvent ..." (*C* 151). (It is true, the senses cannot sustain one in Canada; the spirit leaves nature in the pure sufferings that are found there.) The 'opportunity' for martyrdom is regularly evoked as an exhilarating reality of life in the missions. Even the large scale and strangeness of the landscape, the huge "forest" to which her Indian charges would suddenly and inexplicably return, is a powerful symbol of the enormity of the task they had assumed and their own miserable inadequacy. In such an environment, religious contemplation took on a new drama and intensity:

> Il en est de même du spirituel: Car je voy que ceux et celles que l'on croyait avoir quelques perfections lorsqu'ils étaient en France, sont à leurs yeux et à ceux d'autruy très-imparfaits, ce qui leur cause une espèce de martyre. Plus ils travaillent, plus ils découvrent d'imperfections en eux-mêmes. Et la raison est que l'esprit de la nouvelle Eglise a une si grande pureté, que l'imperfection pour petite qu'elle soit lui est incompatible; ensuite de quoi il faut se laisser purifier en mourant sans cesse à soi-même. (*C* 353)

> (It's the same with spiritual life: For now I see those who were thought to have some perfections when they were in France who to themselves and in the eyes of others are very imperfect, which causes them great suffering. The more they work, the more they discover their own imperfections. This is because the spirit of the new Church has such purity that imperfection, however small, is incompatible. One must let oneself be purified through this ceaseless dying of the self.)

Involved in Marie's private discovery of the new world of Canada, then, was a parallel inner voyage toward a more perfect union with God, a voyage which she describes in the regular rhythm of epistolary communication with those of her correspondents with whom she is most intimately connected – her Ursuline sisters, her directors, her son. In a letter to Claude she writes of her continual struggle to free her spirit for conversation with God:

> Pour moi quand je me vois dans cette impuissance, je tâche de me perdre en lui: je fais mon possible pour m'oublier moy-même afin de ne voir que luy, et si mon coeur en a le pouvoir, il traite avec luy familièrement. Pour vous parler ingénuement, ma vie est d'entretenir continuellement ce commerce. (*C* 270)

> (When I see myself failing thus, I try to lose myself in him: I do all I can to forget myself in order to see only him, and if my heart has enough strength, it talks to him in a familiar manner. To speak frankly, my life is to continually sustain this commerce.)

Not long after her arrival in Canada, her religious director advised Marie that she was not worthy of "conversing" with God in such a way, that the intimacy of these conversations was condemnable. Marie recalls in the *Relation* how difficult it was for her to accept this reproach. Retreat to mental prayer and what she called her "tender exchanges" with her "chaste love" was a form of devotion that she felt compelled to practice. Soon after her confrontation with Father Lallemant she learned how to accommodate his directives in a new way, accepting her obligation to obey, but recognizing that certain commands were beyond her capacity to respect. Her last reference in the *Relation* to her directors, seems to signal her new autonomy as well as a new stage in her progress toward closeness with God: "Pour les lumières extraordinaires, je pourrais avoir des connaissances que la Divine Majesté voulût ces choses [de moi]. Je le déclare à mon directeur, je le laisse juger et ensuite me tiens en repos, s'il l'approuve ou non" (*R* 420). (For extraordinary illuminations, I might have some knowledge that the Divine Majesty wanted these things of me. I tell this to my director and leave it to him to judge, then I keep myself at peace whether he approves or not.)

But while her departure from France and her embracing of the Canadian adventure also launched Marie down the vertiginous path of spiritual alienation, renewal, and "commerce" with God, the restrictions and rhythms of interaction with the outside world that life in Canada imposed also helped give a particular shape to Marie's expression of her spiritual adventure and her sharpened sense of self. Communicating her life to a public was an urgent task in Canada for reasons having to do with the survival of the community. Her Jesuit superiors not only invited but "commanded" her participation in the important project of writing the *Relations*. Her supporters in France relied on her accounts to gain the ecclesiastical and secular authorizations necessary for the maintenance of the missionary colony. And her more personal correspondents were both fascinated and nourished by her accounts, and pressed her to reveal her most private thoughts in her letters. Marie does not always seem eager to comply (though the sheer volume of her epistolary output belies her hesitancy!), but she learned that the disadvantages of the great distance separating her from her correspondents could be turned to her profit. Her yearly messages were both urgent and necessarily limited; she could choose what to reveal and what not; she could decide which questions to answer, which of her "secrets" to unveil, and to whom. The possibility of a lost or intercepted letter could always be invoked: "La distance des lieux et le danger que les lettres ne soient interceptées, ne me permet pas d'en dire davantage à ma très-chère Soeur, et même ce que je viens de dire est seulement pour luy obéir, ne m'étant pas possible de luy rien refuser" (*C* 353). (The distance between places and the danger that letters might be intercepted do not permit me to say more about it to my dear Sister. Even what I have just told is only to obey her, since I can refuse her nothing.)

Or the imminent departure of a ship could impose closure on the exhausting and exhilarating annual frenzy of writing:

Mon bon et très cher Fils, voilà qu'on va lever l'ancre. Je ne puis pas vous dilater mon coeur selon mon souhait. Je suis extrêmement fatiguée de la quantité de lettres que j'ay écrites. Je croy qu'il y en a la valeur de plus de deux cens: il faut faire tout cela dans le temps que les vaisseaux sont icy ... (*C* 240)

(My good and very dear son, the ships are about to lift anchor. I cannot open my heart to you as I would like. I am extremely tired because of the number of letters I have written. I think it amounts to more than two hundred: one must do all this while the ships are here ...)

Because of the distance separating Marie from France, because of the need to communicate regularly with the motherland in order simply to convey the radically different life she is leading as well as the need to attract patrons for the missionary project, because of her obligation to contribute to the Jesuit *Relations* and to create written materials for the convent school, Marie de l'Incarnation's life in all its aspects in Canada was perpetually echoed by her written reenactments of it. Hers is also, she realizes quite early, a life that will be read. Marie herself had first put a name to her mysterious longings to travel when she read about the Canadian missions, and once in Canada she understood that it would be her own testimony that would be shipped back to France to satisfy both devout and simply curious readers. Events occur to sharpen this awareness, and cause her to reflect on her legacy: in 1650 the Ursuline convent in Quebec burned to the ground, destroying precious books and papers belonging to the nuns, including Marie's first manuscript, written in 1634, narrating her spiritual life (which she had specifically refused to save from the fire), and in 1652 occurred the first death among the original party of nuns that had embarked with Marie from Dieppe. The task of writing the deceased's biography and sending it to France for circulation was assigned to Marie, who herself had reached the age of 50, an event which makes her reflect in a letter to her son:

... il est temps que je pense sérieusement à l'Eternité, car encore que je sois d'une bonne constitution et que j'aye la santé bonne, il me semble néanmoins que depuis qu'on est arrivé à l'âge de cinquante ans, il faut croire que la vie ne sera plus guère longue. (*C* 390)

(... it is time for me to think seriously about eternity, for although I have a strong constitution and good health, I think that when one reaches the age of fifty one must believe that life will not go on much longer.)

It was at this stage in her life that she undertook to respond to requests that her son Claude had been making for years, that she write her life story as a gift to him.

In two letters sent to Claude in the years 1653 and 1654, Marie describes how she came to write a new *Relation*, and the difficulties that it posed for her. As is typical in her letters, she stresses the importance of the material conditions of the writing, the fact, for example, that she decided she could not write it in the winter because in that season she could not work alone and out of sight of others:

> J'ai fait ce qui m'a été possible pour vous donner cette satisfaction; je vous diray que l'on écrit icy en hiver qu'auprès du feu, et à la veue de tous ceux qui sont présans: Mais comme il n'est nullement à propos que l'on ait connoissance de cet écrit, j'ay été obligée contre l'inclination de mes désirs d'en différer l'exécution jusques au mois de May. (*C* 515)

> (I have done what I can to give you this satisfaction; I will say that here, in the winter, one only writes by the fire and in sight of all present. But as it is not at all appropriate for this writing to be known to others, I was obliged against my wishes to defer it until the month of May.)

She is troubled, too, about sending this text to her son until her director approves, even "orders" her to finish the task, thereby relieving her mind and facilitating her writing (*C* 516). With a 1653 letter Marie sends a detailed outline of her project, stressing its ambitious nature, the difficulty that she will have in writing it, and praying for guidance in the authoring of it. She envisions her task as not simply a record of a spiritual journey but also an account of the "outer" dimensions of her life. She wants to thus draw a fuller picture of herself:

> Dans le dessein donc que j'ay commencé pour vous, je parle de toutes mes avantures, c'est à dire, non seulement de ce qui s'est passé dans l'intérieur, mais encore de l'histoire extérieure, sçavoir des états ou j'ay passé dans le siècle et dans la Religion, des Providences et conduites de Dieu sur moy, de mes actions, de mes emplois, comme je vous ay élevé, et généralement je fais un sommaire par lequel vous me pourrez entièrement connaître, car je parle des choses simplement et comme elles sont ... Priez le Saint Esprit, qu'il luy plaise de me donner la lumière et la grâce de le pouvoir faire ... (516, 521).

> (In the task that I have thus begun for you, I speak of all my adventures, that is, not only of that which has taken place in my inner being, but also of the outer story, of the stages I have passed through in our time and in my religious life, of God's providence and guidance of me, of my actions, of my occupations, of how I raised you, and in general I am constructing a summary from which you will be able to know me completely. I speak of things simply, as they are ... Pray the Holy Spirit that it may please him to give me light and the grace to be able to do it ...)

Though she stresses in these letters accompanying both the outline and the manuscript of her *Relation* that the text is intended for her son, it is clear that she also is aware of the work's potential passing out of Claude's hands. Paul Le Jeune, the Jesuit Superior of the Canadian mission, had recently intercepted another manuscript Marie had written, the biography of Mère Marie de Saint Joseph, and published excerpts from it in the Jesuit *Relations*, citing Marie's authorship (*C* 521). Father Lallemant's role in the creation of Marie's *Relation* was not only that of a director commanding her to write her spiritual life. He also was an admiring reader of her writing, who insisted, for example, that she have a copy made of the manuscript before committing it to the risks of the sea voyage to France (*C* 532). In the months following the shipment of her text, Marie would write more letters to Claude reflecting on her sense of guilt about having written it and her worry that it should fall into the wrong hands. Wanting to assure herself that he will receive not only the manuscript but also her instructions as to its disposition, she sends the same message in different letters on different ships setting sail for France.[20] In these letters she reminds Claude of his promise that the manuscript be kept secret and she instructs him to burn or return it to her if he should fall ill or otherwise risk relinquishing control of the text:

> Mon très cher et bien-aimé Fils. L'amour et l'affection que j'ay pour vous, et la consolation, que je ressens de ce que vous êtes à Dieu m'ont fait surmonter moy-même pour vous envoyer les écrits que vous avez désirés de moy. Je les ay faits avec répugnance, et les envoye avec peine … je ne désire pas que qui que ce soit en ait la communication et la connoissance que vous. Je me confie que vous me garderez la fidélité que je vous demande, et qu'après vous avoir accordé ce que vous avez demandé de moy, vous ne me refuserez pas ce que je désire de vous. (*C* 548)

> (My dear and beloved Son. The love and affection that I bear you and the consolation that I feel from your belonging to God have made me overcome my own self to send you these writings that you have desired of me. I wrote them with great reluctance and send them to you with difficulty … I want no one but you to have knowledge or hear of them. I trust that you will keep the faith I ask of you, and that after I have granted you what you asked of me, you will not refuse me what I desire of you.)

Constructing Marie as author: Claude Martin's (auto)biography

Claude Martin did not keep his promise. Immediately after his mother's death in 1672 he set about completing his collection of her writings and preparing them for publication. Initially he intended to write a biography of Marie de l'Incarnation, but according to his own account he was dissuaded from this project by friends who argued for the publication of Marie's life in her own words. Claude's preface to the resulting book is a fascinating document. In it he lays out his reasons for publishing his mother's text and also explains and justifies his final decision to make of himself a co-author, by adding explanations of her thought, editing her prose, and supplementing her accounts with lengthy excerpts from her letters and other writings. The part of the book dealing with her life after 1654 is made up of fragments of letters written to her son, which he arranged to create the impression of a continued narrative.

In outlining his reasons for letting Marie speak for herself in his book, Claude stresses two points. First, he writes, he was persuaded by the argument

LA VIE
DE LA VENERABLE
MERE MARIE
DE
L'INCARNATION
PREMIERE SUPERIEURE
DES URSULINES
DE LA NOUVELLE FRANCE.

Tirée de ſes Lettres & de ſes Ecrits.

Sicut qui theſauriʒat , ita qui honorificat matrem
ſuam. Eccli. 3. 5.

A PARIS,
Chez Loüis Billaine, au ſecond pillier de la
grande Salle du Palais, au grand Ceſar.

M. DC. LXXVII.
AVEC APPROBATION ET PRIVILEGE.

Fig. 1.2   Title-page from Marie de l'Incarnation's *Life*, edited by Claude Martin

that the simplicity of Marie's style would more effectively touch readers than a more erudite exposition of her thought that he might provide:

> Mais plusieurs personnes de science et de piété ayant vu la relation de sa vie sur laquelle je me proposais de travailler, m'ont conseillé de la donner au public en la manière qu'elle est sortie de sa plume, et m'ont représenté que sa simplicité avec laquelle elle est couchée édifieroit sans comparaison d'avantage, que si l'on y méloit des pensées sublimes et recherchées qui seroient plus capables d'éblouir l'esprit que de toucher le coeur: que par mes pensées et par mes paroles, je pourrois à la vérité luy donner plus d'éclat, mais aussi que j'en pourrois diminuer l'onction et peut-estre la sincérité; ...[21]

> (But many learned and pious people, having seen the account of her life that I was intending to work on, advised me to give it to the public exactly as it came from her pen. They argued that the simplicity with which it is written would be much more edifying than if I were to add sublime and cultivated thoughts that would be more likely to impress the mind than to touch the heart; that with my thoughts and words I could in fact make the life more impressive, but I might also diminish its humility and perhaps its sincerity.)

The first argument for publishing Marie's work, then, is that her own words, communicated directly to the reader, carry the added authority of humility or sweetness (*onction*) and sincerity. Here Claude invokes honesty or naturalness as both a religious and an esthetic value, comparing his glosses to a kind of ornament or cosmetic and his mother's writing to beauty unadorned. He continues:

> ... que la vertu ne paroit jamais plus belle que quand elle se montre avec son visage naturel, et qu'elle ne se fait jamais tant aimer que quand elle paroist sans fard et sans déguisement: que d'y changer quelque chose, ce seroit vouloir corriger le saint Esprit, qui après luy avoir fait faire tant d'actions saintes et héroiques a conduit sa main pour les coucher sur le papier, car il est évident que ce n'est point un discours premédité, et il est facile de croire que cet Esprit saint en a voulu faire son Ouvrage propre ... (XVII).

> (... that virtue never appears more beautiful than when it shows its natural face, and that it is never more loved than when it appears without make-up and without disguise: that to change anything in it would be like trying to change the Holy Spirit who after having brought her to so many saintly and heroic actions, drew her hand to lay them on paper. For it is obvious that this is not a premeditated discourse, and it is easy to believe that this Holy Spirit wanted to make of it his own Work ...)

After establishing the superiority of his mother's "natural" style, Claude takes a further step in constructing her self-effacement, by insisting on the truth of Marie's own often repeated disclaimer of authorship – if it was indeed, as she claimed, the Holy Spirit who was writing through her, then all the more reason not to alter her words. Claude insists on this point, citing as proof of his mother's divine inspiration the fact that she never attended to her writing style as though it were her own: "... dans l'original que j'ay entre les mains à peine se trouve-t-il une rature qui donne à connaitre qu'elle ait fait aucune reflexion sur ce qu'elle avait écrit pour y ajouter, ou retrancher, ou corriger quelque chose" (XVIII). (In the original that I have in my possession there are almost no corrections to indicate that she reflected on what she had written in order to add or cut or correct something.) Thus Claude outlines his paradoxical attempts to protect Marie from the taint of self-conscious authorship. In his preface he proceeds alternately to describe his mother as an author, whom he wishes to introduce to her readers as a person and a figure of authority ("Il est même important pour lire des Ouvrages avec plaisir et avec fruit, sur tout quand ils sont pour la piété et pour la dévotion, d'en connaître l'auteur dont le seul nom donne souvent du poids et de l'autorité aux choses qu'il avance ..." (I) [It is even important, if one is to read works with pleasure and profit, especially when they are for piety and devotion, to know their author whose very name often gives weight and authority to the thoughts he is advancing ...]), and then to undermine his own claims by reiterating that she was not engaged in traditional memoir-writing, in which an author attempts to "porter témoignage de soi-même" (V) (bear witness to himself). He reminds us that Marie wrote on the command of her director, and for his eyes alone, that she went to great trouble to prevent the circulation of her writings, that above all she had no desire to acquire a "réputation" (V).

Instead, it is Claude who assumes the role of exposing the person Marie, by inserting a lengthy *addition* or supplement after every two or three pages of text written by her, and also by significantly reworking Marie's prose.[22] In his preface he returns several times to the idea that Marie's text, standing alone, is frustratingly opaque on private matters, about which readers will naturally be most curious. Marie, he writes, has a tendency to omit the telling detail, to speak of herself and her actions in general and abstract terms rather than recounting particular incidents:

> Il serait seulement à souhaiter qu'elle eust davantage particularisé les actions de sa vie desquelles pour l'ordinaire elle ne parle qu'en termes généraux, comme quand elle dit en divers endroits, *qu'elle s'est trouvée dans les occasions de souffrir de grandes confusions et de grandes injures*. Il serait à désirer qu'elle eust dit quelles ont été ces injures et ces confusions, parce que c'est ce particulier qui touche, et qui fait paraître la vertu dans sa force et dans sa splendeur ... c'est dans ce détail que l'on reconnait combien une âme est généreuse et héroïque. (XII–XIII)

> (One only wishes that she had itemized the actions of her life, which she normally describes only in general terms, as when at different moments she says *that she has found herself in situations where she has suffered great embarrassment and injury*. One might wish that she had told us what these injuries and embarrassments were, because it is the detail that touches us and makes virtue more visible in all its force and splendor ... it is in this detail that one can recognize the grandeur and heroism of a soul.)

To fill in these missing details is the principal function, in the *Vie* as Claude presents it, of the additions from Marie's letters to him, "dans lesquelles elle m'a découvert dans une parfaite confiance ce qui s'est passé dans son interieur" (XIII) (in which she revealed to me, in perfect confidence, what happened in her interior). In this way Marie's *Vie* can be said to unveil "des profonds secrets de la vie spirituelle" to readers who are prepared to give it the attentive *"application d'esprit"* that it deserves (XVI).

This dual presentation of Marie as one who wrote but was not a writer, one with authority who was not an author, is split once again by the role that Claude devises for himself in the presentation of her voice to his readers. The book, he explains, has not one author, but two:

> Il y a plus d'un Autheur; il y en a deux, et l'un et l'autre étaient nécessaires pour achever l'Ouvrage. Cette grande servante de Dieu y a travaillé elle-même, et son fils y a mis la dernière main, en sorte neanmoins qu'il n'y parle que comme un écho qui répond à ce qu'elle dit par ses propres paroles, et qui explique par elle-même ce qui pourrait être trop obscur à ceux qui n'auroient pas assez de lumière pour pénétrer les secrets de la vie sublime où Dieu l'a élevée. (II)

> (There is more than one Author; there are two, and each was necessary to complete the work. This great servant of God worked on it herself, and her son put the final touches to it, but he speaks only as an echo responding to what she is saying using her own words, explaining herself what might seem too obscure to those who may not have enough insight to penetrate the secrets of the sublime life to which God elevated her.)

With this remarkable image Claude describes the unusual step he has taken in his manner of presenting this text to the public. As "echo" he will enhance the voice presented by Marie in her account of her life as written in the *Relation* of 1654, by adding pieces to the story taken from her own letters and other writings. When, a few pages later in the preface, Claude returns to this metaphor, he adds another layer of meaning to it, namely the idea that it is his own voice, too, that is constituting an "echo" to his mother's. What he means by his playing the role of "echo" is that he is adding to Marie's voice by reproducing additional fragments of it, thus making of himself a co-editor as much as co-author of her printed persona. This echo is a kind of supplement to Marie's text, continuing after her death and working to expand and clarify her words for her new readers:

> Voilà les sentiments avec lesquels elle a écrit sa vie: Mais elle n'a pas été seule à la composer, j'ay dit que son fils y a encore travaillé comme un Echo. L'on peut bien certes luy donner icy cette qualité, puisque l'Echo est le fils de la voix, et comme un supplément qui l'étend au delà de sa propre activité, lors meme qu'elle n'est plus. J'y ay donc travaillé avec elle … (VIII)

> (There are the sentiments with which she wrote her life: But she was not alone in composing it, as I said, her son also worked on it like an Echo. One might well characterize him thus, for the Echo is the son of the voice, and like a supplement

that spreads it beyond its own enactment, even when it no longer exists. I thus worked with her ...)

In this role of mythical Echo, as both editor and co-author Claude seems to see his purpose as an explicator of Marie's often elliptical and discreet voice as well as an articulator of secrets which she herself could never have been expected to reveal.

For the history of women's life narratives, Claude Martin's preface is an enlightening document. The intensity of Claude's personal involvement with his subject inspires him to reflect at length and in print on the problems involved in publishing the life writing of a virtuous woman. In the process he works out for himself, and submits to his readers, an exposition of his idea of what a woman's published life should be, of why and how it should be committed to print, and how it should be read. Claude Martin's motives for the project are personal, but he sets up a model for publishing a woman's voice that we will find repeated in the editorial history of female autobiographies and letters through the seventeenth and eighteenth centuries. Claude insists on Marie's submissive relationship to another individual who had commanded her writing. This deferential stance is one that Marie herself had indeed proclaimed, but which in reality had been far more complex, as we have seen. In the particular cast he gives his own role as editor/son, and in his practice of directing readers as to the manner in which they should read Marie's text, Claude provides his public with guidelines as to how to read, interpret, and evaluate the private writings of a woman. In deciding to publish his mother's story "in her own words", but at the same time layering her text with his own editorial colorations in order, ostensibly, to render her voice more "true", Claude hit upon a formula that was to prove immensely appealing to other editors of women's memoirs and letters. This paradoxical presentation of a woman as a writer but not an author, as an individual from whom readers learn the most to the extent that they are not being directly addressed, sets up a relationship between writer, editor, and reader that manages to draw the reader into an intimate knowledge of the woman writer's secret self while at the same time sustaining the reader's belief in that author's modesty or reserve, and in the male hegemony over the printed text.

In the particular case of Claude Martin's concern with the public reception of his mother's work, there was also the question of the official Church position on mysticism as it had been developing in the last years of Marie's life. A Benedictine monk, and to some extent a mystic himself, Claude was preoccupied with the question of how private forms of religious experience could most effectively be articulated in order to promote acceptance by the church fathers.[23] By 1677, when he published the *Vie de la vénérable Mère Marie de l'Incarnation*, Claude was aware of the controversies over new mystical doctrines such as Quietism, and he was concerned to protect Marie de l'Incarnation from critical attack.[24] He buttressed his edition with three laudatory letters from ecclesiastical censors, thus granting the book both "approbation" and "privilege", as indicated on the title-page. The letters also point readers toward a particular way of receiving the text and conceiving of its authorship, giving even more weight than Claude himself had to the idea that he, and not Marie, was the author of the book. The longest of the official approbatory statements compares Marie's letters to her son to mother's milk which nourished Claude's spiritual growth. Claude's additions to Marie's *Relation* (both the letters she wrote him and his own explicatory supplements) in a sense thus "belong" to Claude, though they "emanated" from his mother or ultimately, from God:

L'Auteur du Livre est irréprochable ... C'est un fils qui fait l'éloge de sa Mère, corporelle et spirituelle, d'extraction et de religion, qui ne lui a pas seulement donné le lait de ses mammelles, avec ses soins et ses Voeux durant son enfance, mais depuis sa vocation et dans tous ses âges, s'est plue par ses lettres très fréquentes, de verser dans son coeur les sentiments que Dieu lui inspirait pour sa gloire, et n'ayant point d'autres biens à lui laisser que les spirituels, l'a rendu Légataire universel, de ses communications intérieures, pour y participer comme son fils, et pour en juger comme comme son Père. Aussi a-t-il été uniquement capable d'y réussir, ... n'ayant perdu aucun fragment des écrits de cette fidèle intérprète de son état et de sa conduite, l'onction du saint Esprit, l'ayant toujours enseignée, et lui ayant fourni des paroles pour ses pensées, et des pensées pour ses paroles, que le monde ne connait pas, et ne produit pas. (XXXIII)

(The Author of the book is irreproachable ... He is a son eulogizing his mother, both corporal and spiritual, of extraction and of religion, a mother who not only gave him the milk of her breasts, with her care and blessings during his childhood, but since his vocation and throughout his life, in her frequent letters she took pleasure in pouring into his heart those sentiments that God had inspired in her for his glory. Having only spiritual goods to bequeath him she made him her sole legatee of her inner communications, so that he might participate in them as her son and judge them as her father. And he was the only one capable of achieving this, having lost not a single fragment of the writings of this faithful interpreter of her state and direction, the sweetness of the Holy Spirit having always guided her and furnished her with words for her thoughts and thoughts for her words that the world can neither know nor produce.)

Loisel concludes his letter of approbation with a guarantee of the author's orthodoxy, and anticipates possible criticism of Claude Martin's presentation of "particular experiences" by suggesting that his added texts naturally belong with the "body" of his mother's work: "... il contient des eclaircissemens comme des rayons qui se répandent dès leur source et se joignent utilement au corps de l'ouvrage, qui mérite en toutes ses parties d'être lu, relu, et pratiqué ..." (XXXIII) (... it contains clarifications that enlighten like rays that spread from their source and are usefully added to the body of the work, which merits reading, rereading, and application in all of its parts ...).

Thus Marie's *Relation* is the maternal body of the *Vie*, and Claude's additions are presented as achieving a reuniting of the sun's rays with the sun, of son with mother. Like Claude's image of the voice and its echo, Loisel's metaphor presents the text of Marie's life as a natural phenomenon, which to be appreciated requires work on the part of Claude as "observer," collector, and composer.[25] Both Claude and Marie are thus spared the taint of self-conscious authorship, but Marie more importantly than Claude, for as both woman and mystic (and paradoxically, as a writer reflecting on her own life) her credibility depends most heavily on her freedom from self-consciousness.[26]

Perhaps the most revealing testimony to the success of Claude Martin's editorial approach in assuring not only publication but ecclesiastical approval for his mother's printed life-writing came some 20 years after the first edition of the *Vie* was produced, in the midst of the quarrels over Quietism. While writing his manifesto against Quietism Bossuet was to read the work of many female mystics, but only Marie's writing gained his approval as a description of the controversial "inner" way to God. From Bossuet's commentary it is clear that his approbation derives largely from Claude Martin's particular recomposition and presentation of his mother's text.[27]

Even so, Bossuet had reservations about the capacity of women to recognize for themselves the mystical experience of unity with the divine for which some religious figures were arguing women had a superior capacity. In a letter he wrote responding to a list of questions from one of his pupils, Bossuet commented on Marie de l'Incarnation's descriptions of her "perpetual union with divine majesty" and on her notion of continuous mental prayer. If she was able to recognize this state in herself, he asserts, then she had not fully achieved it: "Si sa disposition avait été un acte direct et continu, elle aurait dû ignorer son état: car ce ne peut être que par réflexion qu'on sait tout ce que cette Mère démêle ici."[28] (If her disposition had been a direct and continuous act, she should have been unaware of her state: for it is only on in reflecting that one understands all that this Mother explains here.) Indeed, what Claude's presentation of his mother's spirituality had tried to preserve her from was the implication that she had thought about it, either at the moment she was experiencing it most intensely or upon reflection later. This model for "true" insight – that it involves no reflection or intellectual construction – he extended to apply to all of his mother's private revelations of herself. It was through his, not her, "reflections" that Marie's words were to be communicated to her public. It was via his mediating and admiring "echo" that we were intended to hear her voice. Marie's conversations are presented as having enhanced value to the extent that they were overheard. Marie's autobiographical voice is presented as a voice recorded in intimate conversation, and the reader is positioned as a listener unbeknownst to the speaker, but authorized by her original interlocutor.

Notes

1. Brémond argues that Marie was a particularly convincing defender of mysticism,
    and calls her writings a prolonged "apologie des mystiques": "Nul peut-être
    n'aura mieux montré que la quiétude n'a rien qui doive épouvanter les amis de
    l'intelligence; rien non plus, et encore moins, qui menace d'énerver la volonté;
    rien qui ne ruine les fausses prétentions des illuminés ..." in *Histoire littéraire du
    sentiment religieux en France* (Paris: Bloud et Gay, 1926), VI, 175–6. (Perhaps no
    one will have better shown how there is nothing in quietude to frighten the friends
    of intelligence, nothing either, even less, that is threatening to the will, nothing that
    wouldn't ruin the false pretensions of visionaries.)
2. For example, Jo Ann Kay McNamara, *Sisters in Arms: Catholic Nuns Through
    Two Millennia* (Cambridge: Harvard University Press, 1996).
3. See Elizabeth Rapley, *The Dévotes: Women and Church in Seventeenth-Century
    France* (Montreal: McGill-Queen's University Press, 1990), pp. 48–60.
4. Linda Leirheimer discusses the Ursuline notion of the reciprocal influences of
    mysticism and the active life in her "Female Eloquence and Maternal Ministry:
    The Apostolate of Ursuline Nuns in Seventeenth-Century France", Princeton PhD
    dissertation, 1994, pp. 94–110.
5. *Relation de 1654*, in Marie de l'Incarnation, *Ecrits Spirituels et Historiques* ed.
    Dom Albert Jamet (Paris: Desclée de Brouwer, 1930), vol. II, 162–9. Subsequent
    page references to this edition will be indicated in the text preceded by the letter *R*.
6. Natalie Zemon Davis discusses this in her essay on Marie de l'Incarnation in
    Women on the Margins (Cambridge: Harvard University Press, 1995), pp. 63–139.
7. The confession-box was "invented" in 1565 by the bishop Borromeo, a figure of
    enormous importance in the Catholic Reformation. From Milan it gradually spread
    throughout Italy and France until by the end of the seventeenth century the practice
    of regular private confession and communion had replaced the social practice of
    annual public penances. See John Bossy, *Christianity in the West, 1400–1700*
    (Oxford: Oxford University Press, 1985), pp. 133–5.
8. On written confessions as a new technique of spiritual direction in the early seven-
    teenth century, see Linda Timmermans, *L'Accès des femmes à la culture (1598–
    1715)* (Paris: Champion, 1993), pp. 539–55, and Michel de Certeau. On Marie's
    correspondence with Dom Raymond, see Jamet's note, *Relation* p. 193.
9. See the discussion of this literature by Timmermans, pp. 585–91.
10. Marie de l'Incarnation, *Correspondance*, ed. Dom Guy Oury (Solesmes, Abbaye
    de Saint-Pierre, 1971), 36; 45. Subsequent references to this edition will be
    indicated in the text by the letter *C*.
11. See for example *C* 8–9.
12. This autobiography, which survives only in fragments, is known as the *Relation de
    1633*. On the practice of directors ordering their female (and male) followers to
    write their lives, see Timmermans, pp. 587–91.
13. Linda Lierheimer notes the tendency among Ursuline mystics to have visions like
    this, which incorporated images of the order's mandate to proselytize ("the content
    of their visions tended to reflect the apostolic missions of the order"), p. 104.
14. It was the bequest of Mme de la Peltrie that ultimately facilitated the founding
    of the Ursuline mission in Quebec, but in order to dispose of her money as she
    wished, Mme de la Peltrie had to engage in complicated negotiations and subter-
    fuge, including the enlisting of a *dévot* friend in staging a false marriage. For a
    description of her role in Marie's life see Natalie Zemon Davis, pp. 81–3.

15. For a discussion of Marie de L'Incarnation's particular anthropological vantage point, see Marie-Florine Bruneau, "Marie de l'Incarnation: L'Anthropologie Mystique", in Bernard Beugnot (ed.), *Voyages. Récits et imaginaire*, Paris: Biblio 17 (1984), pp. 181–98. Bruneau substantially expands this discussion in her book *Women Mystics Confront the Modern World: Marie de l'Incarnation and Madame Guyon* (Albany: State University of New York, 1998), pp. 101–22.

16. "[les miséricordes de Dieu] sont grandes et infiniment grandes dans notre Amérique, dans laquelle les âmes cédant aux froidures qui y dominent presque continuellement, avaient été toutes gelées, depuis qu'elle est habitée, jusqu'à nos jours que notre Seigneur témoigne par sa bonté en vouloir faire fondre les glaces" (*C* 181). ([God's mercies] are great and infinitely great in our America, where souls, yielding to the perpetual cold, had been frozen since the time it was first inhabited up until our own time, when our Lord in his goodness is showing his desire to make the ices melt.)

17. Jamet and other readers of Marie de l'Incarnation have cited her "natural" style and her supposed "aversion to comparisons and symbols" as a particular mark of her sincerity. See Jamet's note on this passage, for example, *R* 250.

18. See her letter to Mlle de Luynes, 29 September 1642.

19. On the distinction between mental and vocal prayer, *The New Catholic Dictionary of Catholic Spirituality* reads: "vocal prayer uses a preset formula, whereas mental prayer, if it uses words, is not tied to any set formula but, as in conversation, makes up the words as it goes along." On the earliest history of the practice of silent reading see Paul Saenger, *Space Between Words: The Origins of Silent Reading* (Stanford, CA: Stanford University Press, 1997).

20. See letters dated 9 August, 12 August, 27 September, 18 October 1654.

21. Dom Claude Martin, *La Vie de la vénérable Mère Marie de L'Incarnation, première supérieure des Ursulines de la Nouvelle France. Tirée des ses Lettres et de ses Ecrits* (Paris: Louis Billaine, 1677); facsimile edition, Solesmes 1981, p. XVII.

22. It is difficult to determine with any certainty the precise extent to which Claude edited and rewrote Marie's letters, for which most of the originals have been lost. The discovery, in the 1930s, of a copy of the *Relation de 1654* manuscript in the Ursuline convent in Trois Rivières proved, though, what many readers of Marie de l'Incarnation had always suspected: that Claude's revisions to his mother's writing were much more substantial than he had led readers to believe. The most thorough discussion of this point is by Oury in his introduction to the *Correspondance*. Lierheimer notes that one effect of Martin's additions was to "domesticate" Marie's claims to authority as a teacher and derail any potential invocations of the Church's prohibitions against public speaking (277–80). Most recently, Nicholas Paige has discussed Martin's edition as an example of a generalized trend toward increasing citation and first-person testimonial in seventeenth-century catholic (auto)biographies, in "Being Interior: French Catholic Autobiographies and the Genesis of a Literary Mentality, 1596–1709" (University of Pennsylvania PhD dissertation, 1996), pp. 71–7.

23. See Louis Cognet, "Dom Claude Martin (1619–1696) et le mysticisme français", *Revue d'Histoire de l'Eglise de France*, 43 (1957), pp. 125–49; and Henri Brémond's treatment of Dom Claude Martin in *Histoire littéraire du sentiment religieux en France* (Paris: Armand Colin, 1966; first published 1916–32), vol. VI, pp. 177–226.

24. Dom Claude's efforts to preserve Marie's works from the condemnation of the

anti-Quietist faction proved effective, as Lonsagne remarks in his introduction to the reprint of the *Vie* (15–16). She was in fact always acceptable to both factions. Madame Guyon, Fénelon and Bossuet were to cite Marie de l'Incarnation as an example of an "authorized mystic" whom they admired. On Claude Martin's involvement in discussions that were crucial to the Quietist controversy, see Louis Cognet, "Dom Claude Martin", and André Rayez, "Le 'Traité de la contemplation' de Dom Claude Martin", *Revue d'Ascétique et de mystique*, 115 (1953), 206–49.

25.   Another of the three approbatory letters, by Pirot, cites as part of the title of the manuscript he had examined: *[La Vie de la vénérable Mère Marie de l'Incarnation …] composée par le R.P. Dom Claude Martin …* (XXXIV).

26.   On the sincerity of the mystical writer as measured by a reluctance to write, see Timmermans, pp. 545–8. On this same standard applied to early women writers in the secular sphere, see Elizabeth C. Goldsmith, "Authority, Authenticity, and the Publication of Letters by Women", in *Writing the Female Voice: Essays on Epistolary Literature* (Boston: Northeastern University Press, 1989), pp. 46–59.

27.   On this point see Oury's introduction to Marie de l'Incarnation's *Correspondance*. I will discuss more fully Bossuet's role in prescribing ways of reading women mystics in Chapter 3, on Jeanne Guyon.

28.   *Correspondance de Bossuet*, ed. C. Urbain and E. Levesque (Paris: Hachette, 1920), vol. XII, p. 188 (letter to Mme de la Maisonfort, 1 May 1700).

CHAPTER TWO

Public Sanctity and Private Writing: The Autobiography of Jeanne des Anges

In France, by the seventeenth century, ... a good way for a woman of achieving public, influential, vocal sanctity was by means of a good possession disguised as, or sometimes combined with, a diabolic one.

D.P. Walker, *Unclean Spirits*

l'orgueil ... est le plus dangereux démon qui vous peut posséder.

Saint-Jure to Jeanne des Anges, 31 October 1643

In the 1630s, when Marie de l'Incarnation was beginning to think about establishing an Ursuline mission in Canada, the Ursuline order was gaining notoriety in France in quite another manner. The case of Jeanne des Anges, a nun belonging to the order in Loudun, 40 kilometers southwest of Marie's hometown of Tours, and the prolonged "diabolic possession" of which she was the principal victim, was the most publicized witchcraft episode of its day. Visitors traveled from all over Europe to Loudun to observe the public exorcisms of the nuns and decide for themselves on the authenticity of the case. On 18 August 1634, the Jesuit priest Urbain Grandier was burned alive in the town square after having been convicted of witchcraft in connection with the nuns' possession. His case became a *cause célèbre* among the more progressive and cartesian-minded in France and England, and inspired a flurry of printed works debating this late chapter in the "witch craze" that had infected Europe since the early part of the sixteenth century.[1]

Marie de l'Incarnation and Jeanne des Anges met each other on one occasion in 1638. Their encounter was memorable for Marie, as she tells it in her *Relation de 1654.* Her description seems to sum up the extreme differences in character in the two women, and foretell their contrasting styles of self-presentation. For a number of years, Marie writes, she was periodically troubled by nightmare visions of the devil, visions that had begun when she first heard about the Loudun possessions. In 1638, she had a conversation about these visions with Jeanne des Anges, who by this time was "cured" and was being held up to the public as a spectacular example of successful dispossession. Marie writes that when she told Jeanne of her visions, Jeanne replied that often the devil had provoked similar dreams in her exorcists.

42

Shocked, Marie abruptly closed the subject of the conversation, noting simply for her readers that the dreams "never happened again".[2] It is noteworthy that Marie does not claim to have been *freed* of her visions by Jeanne, at a time when Jeanne was in fact touring the country and effecting dramatic public "cures". Instead, she presents the moment simply as a turning point, almost as though the simple thought of the devil giving her these visions was enough to make her stop having them, enough to make the determinedly practical Marie muster all her strength to turn away from the hallucinatory and terrifying voyage that her Ursuline sister had taken. Marie de l'Incarnation's sober and modest character, her single-mindedness and ability to reject the darker side of spiritual experience simply by an impressive effort of will, may go a long way toward explaining the approval that her written life has always enjoyed among literary and religious historians. Jeanne des Anges, on the other hand, is universally regarded with more than a small amount of skepticism. And well she might be, perhaps – for it is difficult to imagine how a woman of her day could have found a way to attract more attention to herself. In an age when, in Hortense Mancini's famous phrase, "a woman's good reputation consists in her not being spoken of", Jeanne des Anges was a prime candidate for bad publicity.

"A little notebook of things past"

Jeanne des Anges began writing her autobiography in 1644, ten years after the death of Urbain Grandier and seven years after her triumphant public pilgrimage across France to the grave of Saint François de Sales, where the last of her demons left her.[3] By this time she was already, to put it mildly, familiar with the experience of being in the public eye. She had been received by Richelieu, Anne of Austria, and Louis XIII, and put on display to masses of spectators eager to see and touch the body that had been the site of a spectacular battle between God and the devil. In 1644 Jeanne was back in the convent in Loudun, of which she was now prioress, somewhat out of the spotlight, but part of an active community of religious and political figures who were still debating the events of her recent past. Jeanne's spiritual director for most of the previous decade had been the well-known Jesuit mystic Jean-Joseph Surin, but in 1644 Surin was incarcerated in an asylum for melancholics, overwhelmed by his own devils and unable to communicate with the world. A few years earlier he had entrusted Jeanne with his manuscript account of their joint battle against "the powers of hell" entitled *Triomphe de l'amour divin sur les puissances de l'Enfer*, telling her that he intended to finish it when he regained his strength. Jeanne first conceived of her autobiography as providing this continuation, as an extension and revision of the story of her life that had already been written, and that had already been presented to the public in many forms.[4]

Like Marie de l'Incarnation, Jeanne des Anges was drawn to the practice of life-writing through letters. She first brought up the idea of writing her own life story in a 1643 letter to Jean-Baptiste Saint-Jure, a prominent Paris Jesuit who had recently assumed the role of her spiritual director.[5] She had initiated a correspondence with Saint-Jure, whom she knew by reputation but had never met, and invited him to be her director via epistolary contact.[6] Though somewhat perplexed by this request from a person he had heard of but was unlikely ever to meet, Saint-Jure eventually agreed after Jeanne explained to him that his name had come to her in prayer. Jeanne's past history interested him, as did her ongoing experience of the supernatural – her regular contacts with a guardian angel and her miraculous visions and conversations with souls in purgatory had been publicized. After some initial jockeying in their first few letters, they settled into a reciprocal pattern of exchange – he guiding her in the difficult process of self-examination, repentance, and renewal, and she interceding for him with her blessed "Saint Ange".[7]

At the time she began her correspondence with Saint-Jure, Jeanne was not inexperienced in the practice of spiritual direction, and was accustomed to being both the person directed and the director. She herself was responsible for the guidance of many of the nuns in her charge, and was often solicited for advice by members of both secular and religious communities who knew her by reputation. But her relationship with Saint-Jure was the first one with a director which was purely epistolary – she was never to meet him in person, their conversations taking place exclusively in writing. Her earliest letters to him reveal her fascination with this experience of expressing her most intimate thoughts in a palpable, written form. In his first letter to her, Saint-Jure sets up their relationship as a bargain, promising her confidentiality and asking for complete openness in return:

> Et pour cela je vous promets le secret, la sincérité, le soin et la vraie charité chrétienne à votre bien. Mais aussi je demande de votre côté le secret et la parfaite franchise, parce que, aux circonstances, ignorer ces choses si difficiles et si subtiles, comme sont les spirituelles, pourrait beaucoup nuire et tirer de nous de mauvaises réponses.[8]

> (For this I promise you secrecy, sincerity, care and true Christian charity for your good. But also I ask on your part both secrecy and absolute openness, because, in the circumstances, to be in ignorance of such subtle and difficult matters as are matters of spirituality, could do grave damage and draw poor responses from us.)

In the same letter Saint-Jure provides Jeanne with a detailed outline of the topics she will need to cover in informing him about herself,[9] and as further assurance of confidentiality he directs her not to sign her letters. In her reply, Jeanne enters willingly into the bargain, even pressing her examiner to deal harshly with her avowals, and produces a lengthy accounting of her youth and first years in the convent, apologizing at the end for having gone on longer than he might have wished.[10] Soon, though, Jeanne is writing her confessional narrative on her own schedule, without waiting for Saint-Jure's replies. He agreed to this change, apparently recognizing that it would encourage her to write more freely. Jeanne describes her satisfaction at being able to write to him daily, thus transforming her letters into a kind of diary:

> Je ne veux plus attendre que vos lettres m'ayent été rendues à vous écrire, afin de pouvoir satisfaire à répondre aux choses que vous me demandez d'un voyage à l'autre ... Et à l'avenir de jour en jour je vous écrirai ce que je remarquerai dans mon intérieur ... je vous dirai que j'espère avec la grâce de N. Seigneur de répondre peu à peu à tout ce que vous désirez de moi, quoi que je sois très paresseuse à écrire, néanmoins le désir que j'ai que vous connaissiez bien mon intérieur me fera diligente, et notre bon Dieu me donna une grande liberté vers vous, et fait que tout ce que vous me dites s'imprime fort dans mon esprit et m'apporte paix ... (*L* 14 janvier 1644)

> (I no longer wish to wait for your letters to reach me before writing you myself, so that I can manage to respond to the things you ask me from one voyage to the next ... And in the future I will write you daily of the things I note in my inner life ... I will say that I hope by the grace of Our Father to gradually respond to everything you ask of me, although I am very lazy about writing. Nonetheless, the desire that I have that you know my inner thoughts will make me diligent and impress upon my spirit all that you tell me, bringing me peace ...)

When Jeanne suggests that Surin's unfinished *Triomphe de l'amour divin* might help Saint-Jure understand the process by which she had fallen under the control of the devil, he replies immediately that he wants to see it and any other papers by Surin that she might be able to obtain for him. Surin's account thus becomes part of Jeanne's autobiography, she describes his text as her unfinished story. She reports that she will try to procure the relevant texts for him (she refers to Surin's narrative and their letters as "our" letters and papers) and in the same breath suggests to Saint-Jure that she might write a continuation:

> J'écris au Rd Père Jacquinot suivant ce que vous m'ordonnez pour lui demander nos lettres et papiers, s'il les renvoye vous en ferez à qu'il vous plaira. Je ne manquerai à l'avenir, autant que ma mémoire me le fournira, de vous mander ce que je pourrai des choses passées, ou, si vous jugez à propos, sans les insérer dans mes lettres, je vous en ferai un petit cahier à loisir ou je travaillerai peu à peu. ... Je vous remercie très humblement mon père de la charité que vous m'avez fait de m'avertir des fautes que je fais en mes lettres. Je tacherai d'y prendre garde, c'est un effet de ma promptitude. (*L* 7 avril 1644)[11]

> (I am writing to Reverend Father Jacquinot as you command me, to ask him for our letters and papers. If he sends them back you may do with them what you wish. I will be careful in the future, as my memory permits, to send you what I can about past events, or, if you deem it appropriate, rather than include them in my letters I will make you a little separate notebook at my leisure, at which I can work bit by bit ... I humbly thank you, father, for the kindness you show me in pointing

out the mistakes I make in my letters. I will be careful to watch for them, it is because of my hastiness.)

This suggestion elicited Saint-Jure's approval, although he was careful to describe what she will be writing simply as "what Surin left out": "J'approuve votre pensée d'écrire dans un cahier à part et à votre loisir, sans pourtant perdre de temps, les choses passées que le P. Surin a omises ..." (*L* 16 avril 1644). (I approve your plan to write in a separate notebook, at your leisure, without however wasting time, about the past events that Father Surin left out ...) Like the Jesuit advisors of Marie de l'Incarnation, Saint-Jure encourages Jeanne to write what she has witnessed, implying that she has an obligation to testify to her experience. But in Jeanne's case what she has witnessed are the torments of her own soul. The world she is called upon to map is her own physical body; the adventure she is asked to document is her body's possession. Saint-Jure reminds her precisely of what issues seem to remain to be discussed at the end of Surin's narrative, and directs Jeanne to take these up in her own:

> Vous savez bien où il en est demeuré, à savoir à quelques combats, qui restent encore après celui des aises, de l'attache des créatures, de l'orgueil et de la paresse; ce qu'il voulait encore déduire, et après venir au don de contemplation. (*L* 16 avril 1644)

> (You well know where he left off, for example with the struggles that remain after those with one's physical comforts, the attachment to the creatural, pride, and sloth; all of which he wanted still to divest himself so as to achieve the gift of contemplation ...)

Jeanne's letters to Saint-Jure during this period describe her troubled mental state; she finds herself in a spiritual "night" and the process of writing her life is apparently what begins to bring her out of her depression. Saint-Jure was eager to see her "continuation" of Surin's memoir, and he persisted in asking her for it in every letter he wrote to her during the spring of 1644.[12] He solicited other narratives from her, too, of events that were "already public", that he directed her to produce on separate paper rather than in the context of her letters, so that he might circulate them.[13] When in early July she finally sent him the first sections of what she called "my past state", he responded encouragingly, urging her to continue and instructing her to entrust the material only to him. She has given him, he writes, exactly what he needs to be able to help her become "what she should be":

> J'ai lu votre papier qui est bon et nécessaire et vous ne faites pas bien de plaindre le temps que vous y avez mis. Ces choses passées sont fort utiles pour bien conduire les présentes et je trouve que de là vous pouvez tirer des sujets très puissants pour vous humilier, pour vous confondre, pour espérer en Dieu et pour l'aimer. Il me semble que vous n'êtes pas, après tout cela, maintenant, ce qui vous devriez être. L'ordre que vous avez gardé est bon. Je vous renverrai votre papier par M. de Laubardemont, ... (*L* 8 juillet 1644)

(I read your paper; it is good and necessary, and you are not right to complain about the time you spent on it. These past things are very useful in order to conduct those of the present, and I find that you can draw some very powerful subjects from them to achieve humility, to confound yourself and to put your faith and love in God. It seems to me that you are not now, after all that, what you should be. The order you have kept is fine. I will send you the paper back via M. de Laubardemont ...)

Thus during this first year of their correspondence Saint-Jure presses Jeanne to begin and then continue her writing project, repeating his instructions as to how to proceed, attempting to reassure her when she tells him of the difficulty of writing, reiterating the importance of the text in enabling him to fulfill his role as her director, and reminding her to give him exclusive reading rights.[14] He repeats his request to see the developing manuscript in subsequent letters, but after Saint-Jure's reading of the first installment, and despite his urgent claim that the project was "much more important than you realize" (*L* 19 août 1644), she never sent him any more. Eventually, years later, she would show parts of it to Surin, but in the meantime she had chosen to retain this piece of work as her own, entrusting it with her other papers only to her intimate friend Madame du Houx, who annotated and preserved the manuscript copy that we have today.

It is not clear from her correspondence why Jeanne did not give the finished manuscript of her life narrative to her new religious director. What is clear, though, is that the autobiography does not follow the outline he had suggested to her. Though she had not objected to Saint-Jure's description of the project as a continuation of Surin's memoir, the actual organization and presentation of her account followed neither Surin's model nor her new director's suggested outline.[15] Surin's *Triomphe de l'amour divin* had been written as a historical account of the possessions, and of Surin's particular approach to Jeanne's cure or "dispossession". It had ended with a promise to describe how Jeanne had finally arrived at "peace".[16] Surin's memoir is written in the third person, enhancing its sober, documentary and impersonal tone. The author and Jeanne are the principal mortal figures in the account, but the main character is neither "le Père" nor "la Mère", but rather the devil, and "les puissances de l'Enfer". In undertaking her continuation of Surin's story Jeanne shifted the focus dramatically onto herself, writing in the first person, and enlarging the temporal framework to include a narrative of her childhood. And even in her opening paragraph, when she declares that her writing is an act of obedience, she describes the story she will tell as a story about her liberation from servitude to the voices of her demons:

A la plus grande gloire de Dieu et pour satisfaire à l'obédience qui m'a été donnée, je vais écrire avec simplicité les miséricordes qu'il a plu à la divine bonté exercer sur mon âme, depuis neuf ans, ça pour la retirer des vices et imperfections où elle se laissait emporter. Je dirai aussi les divers mouvements que sa bonté me

donnait de temps en temps pour me convertir à lui et pour quitter mes attaches aux
créatures qui me rendaient leur esclave (*A* 53–4).

(To the greater glory of God and to satisfy the obedience given to me, I am going
to write simply the blessings that it has pleased divine goodness to grant my soul
for the last nine years, in order to draw it from the vices and imperfections where
it had led itself be led. I will also recount the diverse movements that his goodness
granted me in order to convert me to him and to break my attachment to the
creatures that were enslaving me.)

Jeanne's autobiography, then, moves the narrative begun by Surin forward to
cover the nine years that had passed in the interim, but it also sweeps backward
over the same period described by her former director and beyond, to her
childhood, thus essentially reconstructing the story of her life in her own newly
"repossessed" voice. The text moves significantly beyond the scope of the
project as directed by Saint-Jure, and Jeanne herself decided to withdraw it
from Saint-Jure's editorial control when she found that she was not adhering to
the design he had advised her to follow.

Autobiographical dialogues

Saint-Jure's request that she provide him with a further exposition of Surin's
method, in order to assist him in turn in his role as her director, gave Jeanne the
opportunity to tell the story of her possession and deliverance in the first
person, giving voice to her inner thoughts while at the same time presenting
herself as observing the vow of obedience. The story of her life that Jeanne des
Anges began to write in 1644 is a narrative that claims to be engaged in
dialogue with several different audiences. Saint-Jure, of course, is her primary
interlocutor as she starts the project, and in its early phases he plays the role of
editor as well as director. Other voices from Jeanne's past are invoked within
the narrative, principally that of Surin, whose role as a kind of co-author of
the autobiography is constituted not only by his authorship of *Triomphe de
l'amour divin*, but also by the part he had played in returning Jeanne to herself,
in making it possible for her to speak and write as the "bienheureuse" Jeanne
des Anges. In undertaking her continuation of his story Jeanne is, in a sense,
articulating her gratitude in a reciprocal effort to give voice to her former
director, who had been rendered both mute and mad by the exertion of his years
in Loudun. It had been during a brief remission in his illness that Surin had
given Jeanne his manuscript, after traveling to meet her and share in the public
acknowledgment of her "cure". His return to the Jesuit infirmary in Bordeaux
in 1637 was a dramatic interruption of a conversation barely renewed. Seven
years later, Jeanne would pick it up again on her own, in writing.

Surin had written his *Triomphe de l'amour divin* to testify to the success of an innovative approach to the task of curing Jeanne des Anges, or more precisely, as he had stated in his preface, to testify to how she had been repossessed by God.[17] His arrival in Loudun and the assignment, by his account coming from Louis XIII himself, to take charge of the exorcisms, had marked a turning point in the methods used in treating the nuns. Surin opposed the practice of public exorcisms, which dramatized the struggle between exorcist and demons, and insisted instead on the purification of the possessed woman, in private, through the practice of mental prayer and confession. Surin describes his method as a quiet but effective weapon: "c'était une affaire d'oraison et de silence, non pas de tumulte et d'action" (p. 21). (It was a matter of prayer and silence, not tumult and action.)

Jeanne's narrative, too, devotes considerable space to Surin's controversial innovations in the practice of both exorcism and spiritual direction.[18] She describes, for example, her own surprised reaction to his uncanny ability to read her thoughts and describe to her what she was feeling, when she had been silent and reserved in his presence (A 105).[19] But what in Surin's account is the exposition of a method, in Jeanne's is a crucial moment in the process of self-discovery. For Jeanne, the encounter with Surin and her discovery of the healing powers of silent prayer begins a process of recovery as she slowly begins to learn a new way of communicating with another person and with God. She contrasts this new experience of communicating "from the heart" with both her previous religious training and her social education, when she had prided herself in her skill at other kinds of conversation:

> Je m'appliquais à la lecture de toutes sortes de livres, mais ce n'était pas par un désir de mon avancement spirituel, mais seulement pour me faire paraître fille d'esprit et de bon entretien et pour me rendre capable de surpasser les autres en toutes sortes de compagnies … Je m'étudiais autant qu'il m'était possible à donner une bonne opinion de moi-même aux personnes spirituelles avec lesquelles je pouvais avoir quelque communication. (A 55–6)

> (I applied myself to reading all sorts of books, but it was not out of desire for my own spiritual advancement, but only to make me seem a witty girl, good at conversation, and to enable me to surpass the others in all sorts of company … I strove as hard as I could to create a good opinion of myself in those clever people with whom I was able to have some communication.)

Jeanne describes, by contrast with her later "conversion" to Surin's methods, the bonds she had formed in her first years at the convent, which had been based on a "exterior" impression of piety: "Pour comble de mon malheur, je me liai d'affections déréglées à certaines personnes sous prétexte de piété, et je m'y engageai si avant, que j'employais les journées toutes entières aux parloirs dans des discours fort inutiles" (A 61). (To complete my misfortune, I formed unregulated friendships with certain people in the guise of piety, and I became so involved in this that I would spend entire days in the convent parlours in useless conversations.) She recounts her failed efforts to comply with the demands of her first directors who had tried to convert her to the practice of contemplation and interior prayer (*A* 59–60), and reports that she prayed for someone "who could see to the depths of my soul" (76). Surin's arrival on the scene was an answer to her prayers: "C'était un homme très pieux et très savant; il avait de grandes communications avec Dieu; il ne m'eut pas plutôt vue qu'il connut que mon mal était aussi grand au dedans de moi qu'il était au dehors ..." (*A* 86). (He was a most pious and wise man; he had great communication with God; he had no sooner seen me that he knew that my pain was as great inside of me as it was on the outside.)

Compared to Surin's narrative, Jeanne's is remarkably free of descriptions of her possession; indeed there are long stretches of the narrative where the reader is not reminded at all of this crucial context of her relationship with Surin. Instead, Jeanne describes how Surin helped her to "acquire her freedom" by speaking unconstrainedly about herself:

> Je fis un petit narré au père Surin de l'état de mon âme, et des mouvements que Dieu me donnait de me convertir à lui. Je lui parlai du dessein que j'avais de faire une confession générale, et lui exposai les grandes difficultés que j'y ressentais ... Il s'appliqua autant qu'il put à me faire acquérir ma liberté, tant par les exorcismes que par les entretiens spirituels. (*A* 107)

> (I gave Father Surin a little narrative of the state of my soul and the movements that God had granted me to convert me to him. I spoke to him of the intention I had had to make a general confession and I exposed to him all the difficulties I felt ... As much as he could, he set about helping me acquire my freedom, as much through exorcisms as through spiritual conversations.)

Like Marie de l'Incarnation describing her first encounter with a priest versed in the new methods of spiritual direction, Jeanne des Anges marks her simultaneous discovery of prayer and true confession as a moment when she discovers the intoxicating power of her own voice. Like Marie, she signals the importance of this moment in her autobiography by noting the date, and like Marie, too, she declares that once she started speaking, she couldn't stop:

> Je commençai ma confession les premiers jours du mois de juin 1635; j'employai près de six semaines à la faire. Il me semble que Notre-Seigneur me conduisait par la main ... J'aurais déclaré volontiers mes péchés à tout le monde si l'obéissance ne m'en eût empêché. (*A* 116–17)

> (I began my confession the first days of June 1635 and it took me almost six weeks to complete it. It seemed as though Our Father was guiding me by the hand ... I would have willingly declared my sins to the whole world if obedience did not prevent me from doing so.)

Unlike Marie's, though, Jeanne's experience of conversion was inseparable from an experience of self-discovery. Describing the effects of these first efforts to prepare the way for Jeanne's deliverance, Surin had said he was communicating only with the devils, not their victim; he had quoted the voices of Leviathan, Iscaron, etc, testifying to the efficacy of his method, but Jeanne herself does not speak in his text until close to the end of his account. The most dramatic way in which Jeanne's narrative completes and complements Surin's is Jeanne's focus on her personal connection to Surin, and its effect on her awareness of herself. In Surin's account, the essence of their relationship was in his battle with Jeanne's devils, while for Jeanne, it was her conversion and awakening to a new self. Surin describes his early interactions with Jeanne as exclusive and private, unlike those she had had with other exorcists, but his method of communication was always indirect – he would, for example, pray for hours in her presence, never giving her a direct order, never speaking *to* her but only allowing his words to go "into her ear" in the hopes that his words would "reach her heart".[20] For Jeanne, who by the time of Surin's arrival had grown accustomed to an abusive and public approach to her cure, Surin's behavior must have been astonishing. Writing in the third person, Surin describes his own style as a combination of kindness and crafty misdirection:

> Le Père, non seulement en ce commencement mais encore dans toute sa conduite, garda cette pratique de ne lui rien ordonner; et quoiqu'elle fut fort obéissante et qu'il vit ce qui lui était nécessaire, il ne lui disait néanmoins jamais directement: Faites cela; et ne lui déclarait pas qu'il ne voulut aucune chose d'elle; mais quand il était question de la mettre en quelque nouvelle pratique, il la disposait de longue main, l'invitait doucement et la conduisait, sans qu'elle s'en aperçut, au point qu'il le désirait; ... (*Triomphe* 34)

> (The Father, not only in the beginning but also throughout all of his conduct, kept to the practice of not ordering her to do anything; and although she was very obedient and though he saw what she needed, he never said directly to her: Do this; and he never told her that he wanted anything from her; but when it was a question of getting her to practice something new, he disposed her to it indirectly, inviting her slowly and guiding her, without her realizing it, to the point he wanted; ...)

Jeanne's narrative attests to the effectiveness, from her side of the exchange, of this ingenious refusal to issue direct orders, a refusal to command which was all the more successful in eliciting obedience.[21] Surin's approach, in fact, had consequences that reached beyond those he had envisioned, for while his own account of the Loudun possessions keeps it carefully contextualized within the larger drama of a battle between *l'amour divin* and *les forces de l'enfer*, Jeanne's explores the personal ramifications of what he had taught her and of his bold position that it was she, and not the devil, who was the "author" of her troubles: "... on désapprouvait fort la conduite qu'il tenait sur moi, et principalement de ce qu'il ne voulait pas que je regardasse le diable comme auteur de mes troubles ..." (*A* 155). (The conduct that he had with me was much disapproved, mainly because he did not want me to consider the devil as the author of my troubles.) By assuming responsibility for her "troubles" Jeanne

will also, after first "merging her will" with her spiritual guide, eventually find the way to effect her own deliverance, and become her own author. Furthermore, at the moment she was writing the story of how she had learned to facilitate her own cure, Jeanne was thinking of her former director and of the spiritual darkness in which he was suffering. This time, she was attempting to help him retrieve his voice; in testifying to her own cure she was revealing to him a way out of his own possession.[22] Surin, who had publicly argued for the viability of women as religious directors, was now himself in need of direction, and Jeanne's text offers to him a mirror of his own teachings, a chance to resume their interrupted conversations.

"For those who might read this ..."

By the time she set about writing her autobiography Jeanne des Anges was very used to being observed and read about by a public that extended well beyond her immediate religious community.[23] And though the initial addressees of her text seem to have been her religious guides, those to whom she has been authorized to confess, her narrative quickly moves beyond these interlocutors to address a broader, more anonymous, public to whom she wants to present her version of her story, an explanation in her own words of the events that had made her famous as well as those that had not yet been narrated in print. It was important to her to be able to communicate in her own words both the experience of possession and, more importantly, the process by which she was cured. In contrast to other accounts of her possession, Jeanne's descriptions eschew many of the details of the outward manifestations of diabolic possession. These details had been recounted in the vast pamphlet literature describing the Loudun exorcisms, and had also been vividly evoked by Surin in his descriptions of Jeanne's possession as well as his own.[24]

Jeanne's narrative of the years of the possessions focuses instead on her inner thoughts, on her private reactions to crucial events like Surin's arrival in Loudun. When she describes the devils that possessed her, it is always in the context of her response to their attacks, her conversations with them, her fear of their temptations and her attempts to resist them. The most vivid and precise description of her physical torments is of the crisis that ended her hysterical pregnancy, when she attempted to kill herself and cut the "creature" out of her body. This horrific moment ends with a divine intervention, a miraculous voice shocking her out of her state.[25]

Jeanne presents these "experiences" to her readers as part of a more general exposition of how she interpreted Surin's theory of personal culpability and responsibility. She prefaces each of her personal anecdotes with a general proposition that the anecdote is supposed to illustrate. Her rhetorical purpose is instructional as well as confessional, and her intended readers include a public she does not know personally, but whom she is trying to influence. She describes her own belief, before Surin had proposed it, that the work of her devils could not have been done without her having prepared the way. This amounted to an interiorization of guilt and of responsibility for self-cure, an approach to possession that other ecclesiastics had rejected.[26] Jeanne assumes the task of instructing her readers in her own way:

> Pour mieux me faire entendre, il faut que j'en donne quelques exemples, tant en choses importantes comme en matière légère, afin que ceux qui pourront lire ceci, connaissent combien il est nécessaire que les âmes qui sont travaillées des démons se tiennent fortement à Dieu, et se défient fort d'elles-mêmes. (*A* 78)

> (In order to make myself better understood, I must give some examples of both the important and the trivial things, so that those who may read this will know how necessary it is for souls who are tormented by demons to hold fast to God, and not trust in themselves.)

Jeanne's narrative seems to turn increasingly, as her story progresses, toward a new, imagined reader, with whom she has no personal connection, but who already knows something of her story and might be receptive to her version of it. Nearly one-third of the autobiography covers the period after Surin's departure, when Jeanne's cure, not her possession, became the object of public fascination. This is the period of time not covered by the manuscript that Surin had given her, so that when she moves into this part of her narrative she is no longer weaving her own accounts into his, but rather creating a new descriptive space of her own. It was during 1637 and 1638, too, that Jeanne literally moved outside of the convent and made a processional journey across France. Beginning with her descriptions of the last of her public exorcisms, which Surin had reluctantly taken up again at the request of highly placed personages who wanted to observe them, Jeanne focuses her narrative on her relationship to her spectators, to the ever-present crowd to which she was displayed. In the two years prior to her journey there was a new wave of publications describing the "miraculous" flight of the possessing demons from the nuns' bodies. Jeanne des Anges was prominently featured in these *Relations*.[27] In her own text, Jeanne discusses a variety of reader responses to these accounts, describing for the first time the religious and political factions decrying the Loudun possessions as fraudulent, and suggesting the range of private interests that motivated the public's eagerness to view her suffering. Moving away from the reflective style that characterizes the first parts of her memoir, in this final section Jeanne assumes a more public persona. Events are carefully documented and dated, proper names and places are cited. In this phase of her adventures Jeanne had repeatedly been subjected to tests of the authenticity of the possessions and of the physical evidence of her deliverance – names that had miraculously been stigmatized on her hand, and the piece of her chemise that had been permeated with an unguent brought to her by an angel, which she said had cured her of a dangerous illness.[28] Jeanne describes these tests with a precision that is absent from her accounts of the effects of possession. It is this evidence that she wants to impress upon her readers, this picture of herself cleansed, favored by God and the powerful, even sanctified, that she presents as the completion of her story.

Jeanne decisively marks the break between the final section of her memoir and the preceding narrative by announcing her wish to recount her journey to Annecy and the tomb of François de Sales:

> Le père Surin, étant venu à bout de son entreprise en chassant Béhémoth, le dernier des démons qui me possédaient, se retira de Loudun par l'ordre du Père provincial qui le renvoya à Bordeaux ou il continua d'éprouver les opérations des démons qui l'obsédaient. Je pourrai dans la suite en dire quelques circonstances qui ont du rapport à mon état. A présent, je dirai ce qui s'est passé dans le voyage que je fis à Annecy au tombeau du Bienheureux François de Sales. (*A* 207)

> (Father Surin, having come to the end of his task by driving out Béhémoth, the last of the demons that possessed me, left Loudun on the orders of the provincial Father who sent him back to Bordeaux, where he continued to suffer the work of the demons that were obsessing him. Later I will recount some of the circumstances of this that have to do with my own state. For now, I will recount what happened on the trip that I made to Annecy, to the tomb of the Blessed François de Sales.)

A new phase of her autobiography is thus initiated by Surin's departure from the scene, and, in a sense, the transference of the remnants of Jeanne's symptoms onto him. Surin's departure signaled Jeanne's cure and her move into the public sphere, which she henceforth would orchestrate, assuming the task of obtaining the necessary authorizations both for herself and for the now incapacitated Surin.[29] It was arranged that Surin would meet her on the last leg of her journey. She left Loudun on 26 April 1638.

At each stop on her itinerary Jeanne met important personages. She carefully recorded their responses to her. With these contacts Jeanne gradually inserted herself into a new web of patronage relations, a community of prestigious interlocutors whom her readers are obliquely invited to join. In the foreground are her reports of meetings with the Archbishop of Tours, the Bishop of Boulogne, the Duc d'Orléans, etc., culminating with audiences with Richelieu, Anne of Austria, and Louis XIII, while in the background is a growing mass of unnamed spectators – first the nuns of the various convents which received Jeanne's party, then "le peuple", the thousands who came to view and touch her. At each stop along the route the same scenario is played out, beginning with a private audience with local elites who question her, and ending with a mass public display of the marks on her body:

On voulut savoir de moi les opérations que les démons qui possèdent un corps font sur les facultés spirituelles de l'âme. ... Je tâchai d'y satisfaire et la compagnie parut contente de mes réponses. ... Le bruit de l'impression de ces noms s'étant répandu par toute la ville, le peuple accourut en foule pour les voir, en sorte qu'il vint par jour quatre à cinq mille personnes pour les visiter. (*A* 209–10)

(I was asked about the workings of the demons who possess a body on the spiritual faculties of the soul ... I strove to answer satisfactorily and the company seemed happy with my responses ... Word of the impression of these names having spread throughout the city, crowds of people rushed to see them, such that every day four or five thousand people came to visit them.)

This exhausting ritual quickly created the need for Jeanne to communicate with her public by some means other than speech. She was unable to answer all of her interlocutors personally, so, as she reports, her story was put into print:

Ce qui était embarrassant est qu'on ne se contentait pas de voir ma main marquée des sacrés noms, mais on me faisait mille questions sur ce qui était arrivé en la possession et en l'expulsion des démons; ce qui obligea de faire un imprimé dans lequel on instruisit le public de ce qui s'était passé de plus considérable dans l'entrée et la sortie des démons de mon corps et sur l'impression des sacrés noms sur ma main. (*A* 217)

(What was difficult was that people were not satisfied with seeing my hand marked by the sacred names, but they asked me a thousand questions about what had happened during the possession and expulsion of the demons; which made it necessary to draw up a printed piece in which the public was informed of the most important things that had taken place during the entry and the exit of the demons from my body and concerning the impression of the sacred names on my hand.)[30]

Thus Jeanne records how her story moved from physical evidence of a miracle (the imprints on her hands) to her own oral account of her adventures, and then to another imprint in the form of a book (which was illustrated with engravings of her stigmatized hands). This part of Jeanne's story, she reminds her readers, had already made the passage from voice to print well before she decided to rewrite it once more in the fuller context of her life. For Jeanne, that her story was printed seems to be one more piece of evidence that it was judged authentic by those in power. In her autobiography she includes, as further evidence of the approval she has managed to win, detailed transcripts of her conversations with highly placed figures. Inserted verbatim in her account, the words of Richelieu and the King and Queen serve as seals of approval and authentication for the miracles that Jeanne claims had cured her. Each of these three interlocutors take on different detractors: Richelieu argues against Jeanne's ecclesiastical critics, Queen Anne sympathetically listens to Jeanne's account of the material deprivations and public scorn suffered by the nuns during the possessions, and the King chides his courtiers for their skepticism, promising support for Jeanne's continued journey and for the Loudun Ursulines. Once again Jeanne is

Fig. 2.1   Portrait of Jeanne des Anges displaying the names inscribed on her hand

put on display, but Jeanne stresses that these most prestigious admirers left her unscathed – Richelieu rejected the suggestion of one of his courtiers that he mark Jeanne's hand with his own seal, Louis held up her hand for his courtiers to see and the Queen restrained her own curiosity and allowed Jeanne to retain her relic of St Joseph – the miraculous chemise – intact. Thus Jeanne managed to leave the court not only unmutilated but with her prestige greatly enhanced, and with a model of public reception to present to her future audiences and readers.[31]

Having received the blessing of both king and pope for her continued voyage to Annecy, Jeanne proceeded on her way, retelling her story to each of her hosts.[32] Surin, still unable to speak, met her outside of Lyon for the final leg of her pilgrimage. The last few pages of Jeanne's autobiography attest to a succession of miracles effected by the unguent of St Joseph during her remaining travels – Surin temporarily recovered his speech, people who came to view Jeanne were healed and converted. In Annecy the pilgrims were received at the Visitation convent presided over by the venerated Jeanne de Chantal, close friend and disciple of François de Sales. Chantal spent long hours in conversation with Jeanne des Anges. Her endorsement of the pilgrimage was perhaps the most gratifying response that Jeanne was to receive.[33] Jeanne des Anges and Jean-Joseph Surin were thus able to pray at the grave of St François de Sales attended by the saint's spiritual heir Jeanne de Chantal, herself already beatified in the eyes of the public.

Jeanne brings her life story to a close with two narratives of spectacular cures, the first being the cure of a paralytic "young lady of quality" who came to meet Jeanne in Chambéry as she was beginning her return voyage to Loudun. This anecdote is striking because of the detail Jeanne provides – the woman is not named, but she is quoted and we are told what became of her after their encounter:

> On lui appliqua l'onction de saint Joseph sur la tête, et, dans le moment, elle se trouva fortifiée. Ses nerfs s'étendirent, [elle] marcha aisément et monta un degré. Se voyant guérie, transportée d'une grande joie et de beaucoup de reconnaissance envers Dieu, fondant en larmes, elle s'écria: "Oh! quel faveur, je suis guérie." Et, ce qui est particulier, est que cette jeune dame avait été fort mondaine, et, lors de l'application de la sainte onction, elle fut touchée de Dieu intérieurement et changea de conduite, ce qui fut confirmé par le récit qu'en fit M. le marquis d'Urfé, lorsqu'il était à Bordeaux, ayant assuré que cette dame, qui était morte depuis, avait vécu depuis ce miracle d'une manière si édifiante qu'un religieux entreprit d'écrire sa vie, ce qui fut fort bien reçu du public. (*A* 251–2)

(The unguent of St Joseph was applied to her head, and in a moment she was strengthened. Her nerves stretched, [she] walked easily up one step. Seeing herself cured and transported by great joy and gratitude toward God, bursting into tears she cried out: "Oh, what favor, I am cured." And what is striking is that this young woman had been very worldly, and when the unguent was applied to her she was touched by God inwardly and changed her conduct, which was confirmed by the account given by the marquis d'Urfé when he was at Bordeaux. He attested that this lady, who since had died, had lived since the time of the miracle in such an edifying manner that a monk had undertaken to write her life, which was very well received by the public.)

This unnamed woman resembles the young Jeanne des Anges: well bred, worldly, (Jeanne, too, had a physical infirmity, a slightly twisted torso that in her parents' judgment rendered her unmarriageable) and like Jeanne she is miraculously cured and "touched by God". The young woman's story, though, bypasses the sort of humiliation and suffering that Jeanne had undergone in Loudun, and instead is presented to the public in an edifying printed account of her life. Wishfully, Jeanne notes this manner of going public, and proceeds to close her autobiography with her second detailed description of a cure she had effected. This story is of how the St Joseph unguent enabled her own healing during an illness which struck her immediately after she returned to Loudun.

Jeanne describes how "an unbelievable crowd" gathered in the convent church on Christmas night 1638 to witness the miracle of her cure. A Jesuit priest placed the sacred relic on her head, whereupon Jeanne declared herself healed and asked permission to get up and sing high mass with the others. Her life story closes with this dramatic recovery of her voice in song, and with the "great admiration" of her public:

> Le Père s'en alla en bas, prit la chasuble pour commencer la messe, ou j'assistai, chantant la Grande Messe avec les autres sans ressentir aucun mal. Je fis la même chose à la Grande Messe de l'aube et à celle de neuf heures. Je chantai à toutes ces messes avec une grande joie de ma part, et une grande admiration du peuple qui me voyait en parfaite santé. (*A* 255)

> (The Father walked down and took the chasuble to begin the mass, in which I participated, singing High Mass with the others without feeling any pain. I did the same thing at High Mass at dawn and at nine o'clock. I sang at all the masses with great joy on my part, and great admiration from the public who saw me in perfect health.)

"In perfect health": with these words Jeanne ends the narrative, and with the image of a public admiring this rebirth, a public after which she would want all of her readers to model themselves. She knows, too, that this story will be written and printed, as it in fact already had been in many fragmented forms.[34] But in writing her own account of her life to shift its emphasis from her possession to her recovery and conversion she hopes to turn the manner of telling it in this new direction, more akin to the edifying life story of the unnamed "young lady of quality". In transmitting this narrative to her new spiritual guide, Jeanne knew that she was also launching it into a wider network of possible readers, who would compare her version to other accounts and view it as part of an ongoing discussion. Not the least important of these secondary readers was Jean-Joseph Surin, by 1638 showing signs of a possible recovery. Much later Surin would rejoin the spiritual community in which Jeanne had become an important figure. He would resume his conversations with and about her via letters and his own continuation of the *Triomphe de l'amour divin*, which he saw as both interacting with and confirming Jeanne's autobiography.[35] Surin and Saint-Jure would both serve as editors of Jeanne des Anges, as well as her spiritual directors. Surin would later write eloquently on the influence she had also exerted on him, and on the consequences of their intense relationship. Her death in 1665 closed off the possibility of the only human intimacy which had enabled him to find his own voice, as he wrote: "I will never communicate with anyone like I did with her."[36] Surin's writings about Jeanne des Anges paved the way for her own self-presentation to the public and marked the beginning of an editorial history that continues to play a crucial role in the way her readers receive her spectacular life story.

Editing Jeanne's voice

In the history of cases of witchcraft and possession that swept across France in the sixteenth and seventeenth centuries, the Loudun affair comes late. By the time she wrote her own account of the possessions Jeanne's overwhelming concern was the task of convincing skeptics. When Surin finally resumed his version of the story in 1660, he was already immersed in other debates with his Jesuit brothers and superiors, over whether it was legitimate at all to lend credence to the "demonic voices" emanating from a possessed woman, or to the physical manifestations of "divine grace" that marked the departure of those voices when the possessed person was finally cured. A lively series of letters exchanged with Claude Bastide, Surin's friend and principal adversary in these discussions, attests to Surin's increasingly isolated position and to the role Jeanne was called upon to play in the debate.[37] Bastide and others in his camp were particularly adamant in their opposition to Jeanne's new role as a kind of spiritual oracle, who with the help of her divine connection to the "angel" who had saved her was offering advice, from the convent in Loudun, to visitors and correspondents. Both men invited Jeanne to take a personal stand in their argument, but she was evasive and answered their questions only after she "heard her angel" pronounce on the subject. Matters of doctrine were not topics that she wanted to address directly, particularly if her pronouncement could jeopardize valuable patronage contacts, or call into question the authenticity of her own experience as she already had reported it publicly. Jeanne seemed to think that the only opinion she could afford to voice publicly was one based on personal experience. Her ultimate defense against critics could only be that she was simply reporting what had happened to her and what she felt. Doctrinal issues not only were more risky for her to address, but they were not the topics that most people wanted to hear her talk and write about.

Surin believed in the variety of mystical experience and in the value of publicizing and encouraging it in order to reenergize the devout life. The trend toward skepticism and rationalism in the church alarmed him; he found nothing so discouraging as the thought of young novices turning to philosophy and reason, as he wrote to Jeanne:

> Je vois que l'excès de philosophie fait une grande ruine dans le royaume de Dieu. Par la philosophie, j'entends la multitude des réflexions raisonnantes, et quand cela entre dans l'esprit des filles, c'est merveille si elles font aucun profit en vertu. (*Corr* 1059)

> (I see that the excess of philosophy is doing great damage to God's realm. By philosophy I mean the multitude of reasoning reflections, and when such thinking enters the minds of girls, it is a miracle if they make any virtue of it.)

Having convinced Jeanne that the path toward her own cure was via the exploration of the inner self, Surin became the first in a series of her listeners, as she constructed an account of her strange and exotic "*vie intérieure*". Like many other religious directors, Surin was himself enlightened by listening to Jeanne's voices. He never wavered in his defense of the authenticity of her voice and the salutary experience of listening to it. Surin's conversations with Jeanne became a laboratory for working out his own mystical thought. Many of his published writings on spirituality derive from these spoken and epistolary conversations, and from the increasingly dense network of correspondences that he maintained with other religious figures (most of them women) during the 25 years of his life following the Loudun possessions. Surin's approach to the question of whether to publish these writings went against the position taken by his superiors, and itself received much publicity. Jeanne des Anges was part of a subversive network of correspondents who circulated and saved copies of Surin's letters as well as those of his correspondents, letters that he defiantly put into circulation and directed to be read.[38] An official condemnation, in 1639, of his methods of preaching to women did not seem to diminish the curiosity of other priests who, like Saint-Jure, looked to him for guidance in the practice of spiritual dialogue.[39]

Surin's commitment to epistolary writing and to his letter conversations, which he called "*conversations spirituelles*", is an example of a notion of religious practice, new at the time, that valorized the personal over the doctrinal. Equally important for the circulation and publication of writing by women was the implicit value placed on writing in the first person. Surin's careful attention to the circulation of letters amounted to an orchestration of voices speaking in the first person singular, "testifying", as he would often term this kind of speech and writing. In his letters to Jeanne des Anges, Surin is persistent in his recommendation that she speak and write to others about her mystical experiences. In late 1660, having finally completed *Triomphe de l'amour divin*, he received from Jeanne a narrative of a ghostly vision she had had on the night of 6 November. Gabrielle de l'Incarnation, one of a few nuns from the Loudun convent who had survived the wave of possessions without herself being possessed, appeared to her, repeating her visits on two more occasions in November and December. Jeanne wrote letters to Surin describing these visions, then at his request composed a single *récit* of the three visitations and sent it to Surin to be published.

The letters they exchanged concerning the apparition and the ensuing debate over the printing of Jeanne's narrative illustrate the issues involved in understanding how Jeanne – and other women mystics of her time – were presented to a reading public. Immediately upon receiving the account, Surin had begun to have it circulated. He reported to Jeanne that he had been accused of trying to make her into a saint:

> Il y a pourtant bien des personnes qui blâment ceux qui publient semblables choses, et qui y trouvent des erreurs mêlées lesquelles j'ai grand'peine à reconnaître. On nous fait une petite persécution de ce que l'on vous prêche comme sainte, pour cela seul que nous avons franchement fait savoir cette histoire. (*Corr* 1032)

> (There are, however, many persons who condemn those who publish such things, and who find errors in them that I have great difficulty recognizing. They persecute us by saying that we are preaching you as though you were a saint, and yet all we have done is forthrightly make this story known.)

By putting into circulation Jeanne's own words, Surin can claim to be acting simply as a mediator, one who facilitates the reporting of an event, unlike the hagiographer who makes claims for the saintliness of his subject. Jeanne's authority, too, is doubly displaced in this incident, first onto the ghost of Gabrielle, from whose mouth, not Jeanne's, had come the admonitions to her sister Ursulines to correct their unvirtuous behavior, and second back onto Surin, who tells Jeanne in another letter to tell people that he had ordered her to spread this story:

> Je crois que notre Seigneur voulait que tout cela fût su, et je vous sais très mauvais gré de n'avoir pas dit à celles de toute votre communauté tout le reste que vous m'avez écrit et, si on vous en gronde, jetez la faute sur moi, car je vous conseille de leur dire le tout, disant que vous l'avez fait par ordre d'une personne à qui vous déférez. (*Corr* 1059)

> (I believe that our Lord wished all this to be known, and I begrudge you for not having told the members of your community everything that you have written me. If you are scolded about it, blame me, for I advise you to tell them everything, saying that you have done so on the order of a person to whom you defer.)

Thus nudged by her correspondent, Jeanne chooses to ignore admonishments from others to take no more credit for her most recent publication, and instead delivers an expanded, oral account of the miraculous visitation to an apparently enthralled audience. She reports the event in a letter to her friend Madame du Houx, including with her message two letters by Surin:

> Je vous envoie deux lettres du cher P. Seurin, l'une qu'il écrit à la mère Buignon, religieuse à Notre Dame de Poitiers, et l'autre à moi, que je vous supplie de me renvoyer. On revient fort de cette histoire et tout le monde, je veux dire dans les monastères, en demande des copies. On la prêche publiquement ... Pour rendre mes obéissances à ce bon père, je l'ai raconté hier en son entier à toute notre communauté ou sincèrement je remarquai universellement des coeurs bien touchés. On me fit de grands reproches de mon silence, et je leur en dis fort simplement la cause ... Les RR. PP. Seurin et Bastide en ont envoyé des copies en divers lieux. (*L* 31 janvier 1661)

> (I send you two letters from dear Father Surin, one that he wrote to mother Buignon, a nun at Notre Dame de Poitiers, and the other to me, which I beg you to return to me. This story has made a big impression and everyone, I mean in the orders, wants copies. It is being publicly preached ... To obey this good father I told the whole story yesterday to our entire community, where I honestly saw everyone universally touched by it. I was greatly reproached for my silence and I told them simply what had been the cause of it ... The Reverend Fathers Surin and Bastide sent copies around to different places.)

This little episode shows Jeanne and her circle working closely to create acceptable conditions for the publication of a woman's voice. The casual tone of the exchange between Surin and Jeanne on her observing the vow of obedience, Jeanne's specific references to the various forms in which her words are being presented to the public (from the pulpit, in her own kind of preaching to the Ursuline sisters, in manuscript copy, and in letters) and her definition of this public (monasteries, and a more vaguely named "*divers lieux*") all packed into a few lines in a letter to her friend, reveal how thoroughly she has learned the rules of the game, and how comfortable she is with the idea of the circulation of her writing. By 1661 Jeanne was not only used to being a public figure, but she was accustomed to being an author. There is even a certain pride that is communicated in these lines to Madame du Houx, and a pleasure taken in the practice and spectacle of public speaking and writing. After Jeanne's death in 1665 her network of friends continued to publicly champion the authenticity of her mystical adventures. Surin, in particular, understood how crucial the acceptance of her identity as a woman with a special capacity to communicate with God was to the acceptance of his own mystical thought and teachings.

Jeanne's autobiography continued to be copied and circulated in manuscript form among religious communities into the eighteenth century, but it was not published in print until 1886, and has not been re-edited since.[40] In many respects, her writing fared better in the editorial hands of Surin than in those of her nineteenth-century editors. In fact, Surin's warnings about the consequences of an over exuberant rationalism were dramatically born out in the scholarly apparatus prepared for the autobiography by Gabriel Legué and Gilles de la Tourette in 1886, an apparatus that is preserved intact in the 1985 reprint. The title given the text sets the scene: *Soeur Jeanne des Anges: Supérieure du couvent des Ursulines de Loudun (XVIIe), Autobiographie d'une hystérique possédée.*[41] Jeanne is presented as a medically verifiable example of a hysteric, and her narrative is overshadowed by lengthy footnotes interpreting the physiological symptoms of the Loudun possessions. The text is transformed into a textbook case, fulfilling all of the requirements for a specific medical diagnosis. The reader's eye is repeatedly drawn to the footnotes on each page citing medical literature and relevant lessons from the publications and seminars of the editors. When Jeanne's narrative opts for ellipsis, as when she characterizes some of her seizures simply as "violent", the notes restore the "missing" memory with details of other observed cases: "La grande attaque *hystéro-epileptique* ... se compose essentiellement, d'après M. Charcot, de trois périodes: ... les malades battent les assistants qui veulent les retenir, déchirent leurs vêtements, se frappent le visage et la poitrine, se mordent parfois jusqu'au sang ..." (*A* 72, n.1). (The grand *hystero-epileptic* attack ... is essentially composed, according to Mr Charcot, of three phases: ... the patients strike the attendants that are trying to restrain them, tearing their clothes, striking their own faces and chests, biting themselves sometimes to the point of drawing blood ...) Not only does this sort of presentation do violence to Jeanne's version of her life, by reducing it to the status of an illustration of editorial points, it also undermines precisely the most original feature of Jeanne's narrative, and the one that was central to her autobiographical project. The voice that Jeanne tries to project in her life story is her own, repossessed voice, a figure of self-control as well as a beneficiary of divine grace. Her modern editors relentlessly return her to the state of victim or *malade*, and when she is accorded a measure of autonomy it is only to the extent that she is "narcissistic", "manipulative", or "egocentric".[42]

This edition has continued to play a role in what seems to be a universal skepticism about the honesty of Jeanne's autobiographical voice. Modern responses to Jeanne des Anges both as historical figure and author are striking in contrast to treatments of Surin, whose work has benefited from Michel de Certeau's impressive scholarly presentation of his writings. Aldous Huxley's widely read book *The Devils of Loudun*, for example, judges Jeanne harshly, stressing her own confessions of hypocrisy and arguing that her obvious sensitivity to the psychology of spectacle and image-making was evidence of her dishonesty. He never questions the sincerity of Surin's bouts with "possession" or his belief in the supernatural evidence of the devil. The most alienated moments of Surin's religious life are treated, as they are in most accounts of Surin's mysticism, as painful episodes in a spiritual quest, and Surin's cure is viewed as a heroic return to sanity and orthodoxy, while Jeanne's confessions of her own culpable susceptibility to the devil are interpreted exclusively as signs of a personal hypocrisy or narcissism.[43]

Readings of Jeanne that dismiss her as either deluded or criminally insincere remain fixed within the limited range of interpretive options originally established by seventeenth-century diatribes against her, and continued in nineteenth-century medical discourse on hysteria. These readings isolate her, moreover, from the mystical circles in which she functioned and was taken very seriously as an advisor, spiritual director, and conduit to the divine. No one understood better than Jeanne des Anges the importance of the role played by a mediator – religious director, editor, patron or angel – in presenting one's testimony for public judgment. If we are able to look at her writings as part of an ongoing cultural dialogue, as participating in the practice, new for her time, of "spiritual conversations", then it becomes possible to read her autobiographical voice in a new way. When we read her life story in the context of the epistolary writing out of which it grew, and against the backdrop of other published accounts to which she was responding, we can appreciate its function as part of a number of circulating documents that she understood would constitute a written record of her life.[44]

Notes

1. The historical literature on the Loudun witchcraft episode is massive. The best account is Michel de Certeau's *La Possession de Loudun* (Paris, Juillard, 1970), which also includes lengthy excerpts from otherwise unpublished archival material. A more popular, but insightful account is Aldous Huxley's *The Devils of Loudun* (New York: Harper and Row, 1952). For a general discussion of witchcraft trials and the phenomenon of possession in seventeenth-century France, see Robert Mandrou, *Magistrats et sorciers en France* (Paris: Plon, 1968).

2. [Jeanne] "me dit que souvent le diable faisait chose semblable à leurs exorcistes. Jamais depuis ce temps-là, cela ne m'est arrivé" (*Relation de 1654*, in *Ecrits spirituels et historiques*, ed. Jamet, pp. 293–4).

3. The autobiography of Jeanne des Anges is available in a modern edition of the text first published in 1886 under the title *Autobiographie d'une hystérique possédée*. The 1886 edition was edited by two psychoanalysts and prefaced by Charcot, the famous theorizer of hysteria. Although the modern edition (Grenoble: Jérôme Millon, 1985) corrects some of the textual errors of the nineteenth-century one, it retains the cumbersome (though interesting for the history of psychoanalysis) scholarly apparatus interpreting Jeanne's narrative as a series of symptoms. The particular bias of this presentation has been accepted uncritically by most modern readers, as I will discuss further. Modern reader reception of Marie de l'Incarnation, by contrast, has benefited from the lucid and comprehensive editorial presentations of scholars like Oury and Jamet.

4. For a list of the printed works dealing with the Loudun possessions that are known

to have appeared between 1633 and 1639, see Certeau, *La Possession de Loudun*, pp. 268–75.

5. Until Ferdinand Cavallera researched Jeanne's correspondence with Saint-Jure in the 1920s, it was thought that Jeanne des Anges had written her autobiography in 1642, and in a more conventional manner, following the "orders" of her mother superior. As Cavallera was able to show, however, Jeanne's letters to Saint-Jure reveal not only that she wrote the text later, but that the idea was hers. See "L'autobiographie de Jeanne des Anges d'après des documents inédits", in annex to *Autobiographie d'une hystérique possédée*, pp. 323–32 (first published in *Recherches de Sciences Religieuses*, 18 (1928)). Cavallera notes, too, that a formulaic introductory sentence had been added to Jeanne's narrative by the eighteenth-century copyist, in an attempt, perhaps, to give the autobiography the authorization it would have needed to elicit the sympathy of readers. The added phrase is as follows: "La supérieure de la mère des Anges lui ayant ordonné de mettre par écrit ce qui s'est passé dans sa possession, par esprit d'obéissance, elle s'y soumit aveuglément et écrivit ce qui suit" (53). (The Superior of Mother Jeanne des Anges having ordered her to commit to writing the account of what occurred during her possession, in the spirit of obedience she blindly submitted and wrote what follows.)

6. The letters of Jeanne des Anges have not been published, although the letters addressed to her from Surin and Saint-Jure have been, as I will cite below. Manuscript copies of Jeanne's letters with replies from a number of different correspondents do exist. The one to which I will refer is housed in the Jesuit library outside of Paris (Archives SJ, Vanves), and forms part of a collection of materials under the rubric *Jean-Joseph Surin* (cote GSu 21). My own parenthetical references to these letters will be by date, preceded by the designation *L*.

7. See, for example, Saint-Jure's letters in *Revue d'ascétique et de mystique*, vol. 9, 251–7. In an informative article on Saint-Jure, Georges Bottereau notes that Saint-Jure was much sought after as a director for the Ursulines. He suggests that Jeanne des Anges would have read his favorable predisposition toward her in his published commentaries on the Loudun possessions. See "Jean-Baptiste Saint-Jure S.I., 1588–1657", *Archivum Historicum Societas IESV*, **XLIX**, 97, 161–202.

8. *Revue d'Ascétique et de mystique*, **VII** (27), 252. Designated as *RAM* in subsequent notes.

9. "… il faudra pour cela que vous m'informiez et particulièrement touchant les points suivants: Quelle est votre humeur; – quelles sont vos inclinations bonnes ou mauvaises; – en quelles fautes vous tombez plus souvent; – comme vous avez passé votre jeunesse; – si vous avez été toujours portée à la dévotion et comme vous vous y êtes prise; – quand et comment vous vous êtes donnée à Dieu; …" (*RAM*, **VII** (27), 252). (… for this it is necessary that you inform me and particularly concerning the following points: What is your humour; what are your good or bad inclinations; into which faults do you fall most often; how you spent your youth; if you were always drawn to devotion and how you took to it; when and how you gave yourself to God; …)

10. "Et puis, ce que vous demandez de moi, n'est pas à ce que je crois une narration de toutes ces choses passées. Celle-là me servit d'occasion pour me résoudre à travailler tout de bon à mon amendement et à faire pénitence de ma vie passée" (22 octobre 1643). (And then, what you ask of me, is it not, it seems to me, a narrative of all of these past things. This gave me the occasion to resolve to work hard on my improvement and make penitence for my past life.)

11. It is interesting to note that in his letters Saint-Jure does not refer to Jeanne as having had any role in the composition of *Triomphe de l'amour divin*, nor does he initially ask to see any of her writing, only Surin's. It is Jeanne who introduces the references to her own writings, as well as her own life story, as part of Surin's "work". See Jeanne's letters dated 14 janvier 1644, 24 février (to Laubardemont), 7 avril, and Saint-Jure's dated 23 janvier, 5 mars, 16 avril, in *RAM*, cited above.

12. See letters dated 7 mai, 28 mai, 26 juin.

13. As, for example, an account of her vision of St Joseph: "comme c'est un fait divulgué et public, mettez-le en papier à part. Mais faites-le à votre loisir et au long car peut-être m'en pourrai-je servir à la gloire de Dieu et le bien de quelque âme" 31 octobre 1644 (*RAM*, **VII** (27), 256). (as it is a revealed and public fact, put it on paper separately. But do it at your leisure, and at length, for perhaps I will be able to use it for the glory of God and the good of some soul.)

14. See Saint-Jure's letters dated 19 août, 11 novembre.

15. As Cavallera notes, Jeanne did not follow Saint-Jure's instructions on how to organize the narrative, and her "obedience" in writing the autobiography, was in fact "simply the formal approval of an initiative that she had been the first to undertake" ("L'Autobiographie", 328).

16. "On va rapporter maintenant comment la Mère est parvenue à cette contemplation si désirable et à cette douce paix ou l'âme reçoit de Dieu sans peine les infusions de sa lumière. Mais parce que cette façon de prier fut précédée de grands travaux, et qu'il faut un long exposé pour rendre compte des choses qui s'y passèrent, cela demande un autre chapitre", *Triomphe de l'amour divin sur les puissances de l'Enfer* (Grenoble: Jérôme Millon, 1990), pp. 69–70. (We will now recount how the Mother arrived at such a desirable contemplation and at this sweet peace in which the soul receives from God without struggle the infusions of his light. But because this way of praying was preceded by great travail, and because a long exposition is required to give an account of what happened then, it requires another chapter.)

17. "… comme quoi le divin amour, par le ministère de ce Père l'a tirée de l'effroyable captivité du Diable, pour la posséder, non seulement en la liberté de ses enfants, mais encore en la possession d'une haute grâce, faisant confusion en la maison de Nabuchodonosor par la générosité d'une fille et donnant par ce moyen un plein triomphe à son amour sur les ennemis de son royaume" (p. 9). (… how divine love, by the ministry of this Father pulled her out of the frightful captivity of the Devil, in order to possess her, not just in the freedom of his children but also in the possession of a high grace, creating confusion in the house of Nabuchodonosor through the generosity of a girl and in this way giving his love full triumph over the enemies of his kingdom.)

18. On the originality of Surin's practices and opposition to them from other priests, see Linda Timmermans, *L'Accès des femmes à la culture (1598–1715)* (Paris: Champion, 1993), pp. 595–600. Timmermans notes in particular that Surin was accused of fomenting spiritual excess among women, by treating their interior life so seriously.

19. All references are to the 1985 edition, described in note 3 above. Subsequent parenthetical references will use the letter designation *A*.

20. *Triomphe de l'amour divin*, pp. 35, 25–7, 19.

21. "… il me dit: 'Je vois bien que les exorcismes ne vous profitent pas beaucoup. Si vous entreprenez avec courage la mortification de vos passions, et si vous vous étudiez à la pratique des vraies vertus, j'espère que vous serez bientôt libre de vos

troubles ...' Dès lors, je m'abandonnais totalement à sa conduite, et pris une ferme résolution de lui obéir en tout ce qu'il voudrait de moi" (125). (... he said to me: "I see that exorcisms don't help you very much. If you try with courage to mortify your passions, and if you apply yourself to the practice of true virtues, I hope that you will be soon free of your troubles." From that time I gave myself over totally to his direction, and took a firm resolution to obey him in all that he wanted of me.)

22.   Jeanne quotes Surin: "Si vous voulez joindre votre volonté à la mienne, je vous assure que vous sortirez de l'état auquel vous êtes ..." (*A* 105–6). (If you want to join your will to mine, I assure you that you will come out of the state you are in ...) Surin's critics and some of his more skeptical superiors viewed his radical stance as a threat to the ability of the church to retain some control over extreme cases of ascetic behavior such as possession, as well as more manageable forms of mysticism. Moreover, Surin's intensely personal approach to possession was not one that many other priests were willing to risk. Curing the patient by means of such intimate identification could easily mean killing the doctor – as Surin's own extended periods of madness (what he calls "obsession", "possession", and "melancholy") demonstrated. See Certeau, "Surin's Melancholy", in *Heterologies: Discourse on the Other* (Minneapolis: University of Minnesota, 1986).

23.   In addition to the letters and manuscript accounts of the Loudun affair that were circulated throughout Europe, dozens of books were printed in the 1630s describing and debating the possessions and exorcisms as well as the trial of Urbain Grandier. Many of these included transcripts of the nuns' "possessed" voices. Michel de Certeau includes a detailed bibliography of this material in *La Possession de Loudun*, pp. 265–75.

24.   For example, a typical description from Surin's third-person account of his own suffering: "Comme il se fut retiré seul après la collation, il sentit de grands maux de coeur, qui enfin aboutirent à un grand tourment de ses membres et puissances, en sorte qu'il commença à se débattre et tordre le corps comme une personne possédée ... il avait toujours l'usage de la raison libre, mais on ne l'eut pas jugé aux actions étranges qu'il faisait. Il se portait la main à la bouche pour se mordre, il s'agenouillait avec des impressions extérieures d'une si grande violence, qu'il ne savait que devenir ..." (*Triomphe* p. 40). (Having retired alone after the meal, he felt strong pains in his heart that ultimately ended in a great torment of his members and faculties, so that he started to thrash and twist his body like a possessed person ... he still had the use of his free reason, but one would not have known it from the strange actions he did. He took his hand to his mouth to bite himself, he kneeled down with such outward violence that he didn't know what would become of him ...)

25.   "Je fus en un instant terrassée par terre avec une violence que je ne puis exprimer; l'on m'arracha le couteau de la main, et il fut mis devant moi au pied du crucifix qui était dans ce cabinet. J'entendis fort distinctement une voix qui me dit: Que penses-tu faire? Désiste de ton mauvais dessein, aie recours à ton Sauveur et te convertis à lui, car il est tout près à te recevoir" (*A* 90–91). (In an instant I was struck to the ground with a violence I cannot express; the knife was torn from my hand, and it was put in front of me at the foot of the crucifix that was in the little room. I very distinctly heard a voice saying to me: What are you thinking of doing? Desist in your bad intention, have recourse to your Savior and convert to him, for he is ready to receive you.)

26.   "[Les esprits maudits] se familiarisent avec l'esprit humain et tirent de lui par ces

petits agréments un tacite consentement pour opérer dans l'esprit de la créature qu'ils possèdent, ... Quand je parlais de cela à mes exorcistes, ils me disaient que c'était le démon qui me donnait ces sentiments afin de se cacher en moi, ... Je pense que c'est qu'ils avaient de la peine à croire que je fusse si méchante ..." (*A* 76–8)

27. See Certeau's itemization of this *littérature de triomphe* in *La Possession de Loudun*, pp. 303–5.

28. "Quelque personne proposa de laver ces noms avec de l'eau, mais les trois médecins assurèrent que l'eau n'y ferait rien pour effacer ces noms.

    Cette épreuve, ayant été divulguée par la ville, échauffa l'ardeur et la curiosité du peuple pour continuer et même pour augmenter son concours; de sorte que, les jours suivants, il venait par jour au monastère jusqu'à sept mille personnes" (*A* 211). (Someone proposed to wash these hands with water, but the three doctors stated that water would do nothing to erase these names. This test, having been revealed by the town, excited the curiosity and eagerness of the people to continue and even to increase their visits; so that in the days that followed up to seven thousand people came to the monastery every day.) See also pp. 237–40, where Jeanne describes a series of tests conducted on the stigmata at the request of Laubardemont, "pour fermer la bouche à ceux qui désapprouvaient et condamnaient ce miracle." (to close the mouths of those who disapproved of and condemned this miracle.)

29. "Je me sentis pressée intérieurement d'exécuter le voeu que nous avions fait d'aller à Annecy au tombeau du Bienheureux François de Sales. J'eus recours au père Jacquinot provincial pour obtenir de lui la permission nécesssaire au père Surin pour se rendre au rendez-vous" (*A* 208). (I felt inwardly pressed to execute the vow that we had made to go to Annecy to the tomb of the Blessed François de Sales. I had recourse to the Jesuit Father Jacquinot to obtain from him the necessary permission to have Surin come to the rendez-vous.)

30. The book to which she is referring was entitled *Représentation et sommaire des signes miraculeux qui ont esté faits à la gloire de Dieu et de son Eglise en la sortie des sept démons qui possédaient le corps de la mère prieure des religieuses ursulines de Loudun* (Rouen, D. Ferrand, [1637]).

31. Jeanne invokes Richelieu to prevent his brother the archbishop of Lyon from testing her stigmata by trying to cut into the flesh of her hand: "Il voulut effacer les noms imprimés sur ma main avec des ciseaux. ... Je m'y opposai, et lui dis: Monseigneur, je n'ai point ordre de mes supérieurs de souffrir ces épreuves ... Mr le cardinal de Richelieu, votre frère ... a eu la bonté de me recevoir avec beaucoup de douceur. Je lui demandai s'il voulait faire faire des épreuves pour reconnaître la vérité de l'impression des noms. Il m'a répondu qu'il n'avait pas jugé cela nécessaire, et qu'il ne doutait en aucune manière d'une chose si évidente (*A* 243–4). (He wanted to erase the names imprinted on my hand with scissors ... I opposed it, and said to him: Monseigneur, I have no order from my superiors to suffer these tests ... Cardinal Richelieu, your brother ... had the goodness to receive me with much kindness. I asked him if he wanted to have tests done to establish the truth of the impression of the names. He replied that he had not judged that necessary, and that he in no way doubted such an evident thing.)

32. According to Jeanne, Louis provided her with a *brevet* commanding his provincial governors and city magistrates to give any necessary assistance to the group as it made its way on the pilgrimage (*A* 240). The papal envoy visited Jeanne in Paris, and declared "qu'il s'étonnait que les Huguenots demeurassent dans leur

aveuglement, après une preuve si sensible des vérités qu'ils combattent ..." (237) (he was surprised that the Huguenots remained in their blindness after such a palpable proof of the truths they are fighting against ...).

33. As in her descriptions of her conversations with Richelieu and the royal couple, Jeanne's account of these conversations seem construed to point to *what is important* in her story, what other readers, too, should retain. Chantal, like other spectators, is interested in the accounts of the possessions, but she focuses on the story of Jeanne's deliverance: "Nous eûmes ensemble de forts longs entretiens sur tout ce qui s'était passé en la possession, et surtout, je lui fis un récit fort exact de ce qui s'était passé dans l'apparition de saint Joseph lorsqu'il me guérit miraculeusement par la sainte onction" (*A* 250). (We had very long conversations together about all that had happened in the possession, and especially, I gave her a very exact account of what had happened in the appearance of St Joseph when he miraculously cured me with the saintly unguent.)

34. It had been printed, for example, in *La Guérison miraculeuse de Soeur Jeanne des Anges, prieure des religieuses ursulines de Loudun, par l'onction de Saint-Joseph* (Poitiers, 1637).

35. See his letter to Jeanne in Jean-Joseph Surin, *Correspondance* (Paris: Desclée de Brouwer, 1965), pp. 1022.

36. Cited in Certeau, "Surin's Melancholy", p. 106.

37. See Surin, *Correspondance*, pp. 669–71, 684.

38. See Certeau's introduction to Surin, *Correspondance*, pp. 51–6; 67–71.

39. See *Correspondance*, pp. 441–3.

40. The manuscript copy of Jeanne's autobiography that is the basis for the 1886 edition (reprinted in 1985) dates from the eighteenth century, when it was prepared as part of a dossier on the Loudun episodes. It is housed in the archive of the Ursuline convent in Tours.

41. The title given the autobiography on the Tours manuscript, which may have been added by the eighteenth-century copyist, is *L'Histoire de la Possession de la Mère Jeanne des Anges, de la maison de Coze, supérieure des religieuses Ursulines de Loudun*.

42. Frank Bowman has surveyed the historiography of the Loudun affair, especially the impact of the publication of Jeanne's autobiography, in "From History to Hysteria: Nineteenth-Century Discourse on Loudun", ch. 6 (pp. 106–21) of *French Romanticism: Intertextual and Interdisciplinary Readings* (Baltimore: Johns Hopkins, 1990). "For some time," he remarks, "it would be impossible for any historian to write about Loudun without serving it up in a medical sauce" (119).

43. An interesting exception to the traditional hostility to and questioning of Jeanne's "motives" is Mitchell Greenberg, "Passion Play: Jeanne des Anges, Devils, Hysteria and the Incorporation of the Classical Subject", ch. 3 of *Subjectivity and Subjugation in Seventeenth-Century Drama and Prose* (Cambridge: Cambridge University Press, 1992), pp. 65–86. He views masochism in Jeanne's autobiography, as in other classical texts concerned with a theatrical display of the body, as having an important function in the production of a modern subjectivity based on an inner, hidden self.

44. Future research on Jeanne des Anges would benefit immeasurably not only from a new edition of her autobiography but also from the publication of her correspondence. The same is true for other women writers of the seventeenth century, many of whom were rediscovered in the nineteenth century only to be published in

fragments, in heavily editorialized formats, and have not been reedited since. On the legacy of some of these editorial practices see Elizabeth C. Goldsmith, "Authority, Authenticity, and the Publication of Letters by Women", in *Writing the Female Voice: Essays on Epistolary Literature* (Boston: Northeastern University Press, 1989), pp. 46–59.

CHAPTER THREE

Silent Communications:
The *Life* and Letters of Jeanne Guyon

Jeanne Guyon (1648–1717) has always been a controversial historical figure. Author of treatises on "the inner way" to God, biblical commentaries, several volumes of mystical poetry, and a story of her life published posthumously in 1720, Madame Guyon was read in her own lifetime by French Catholics attracted by the spiritualist movements of the seventeenth century. But after 1687 her teachings were condemned along with those of other "Quietist" figures – although she herself always denied adhering to the Quietist doctrine.[1] The official rejection of her teachings by the church was, in any event, a dramatic sign of the waning of the mystical movements of the seventeenth century. Jeanne Guyon thought of her life as participating in an established contemplative tradition when she decided, in 1680, to leave her household and travel across France as an itinerant "spiritual guide" with her friend and collaborator François de La Combe. In her autobiography she tells her readers that for her this was a decision inspired by predecessors; she was imitating a host of illustrious spiritual couples beginning with Jeanne de Chantal and François de Sales: Vincent de Paul and Louise de Marillac, Madame Acarie and Pierre de Bérulle, Jean-Jacques Olier and Mère Agnès. Each of these were already famous instances of fruitful partnerships in which a devout woman and her religious director worked together in public to teach new devotional practices or present their own lives as evidence of God's grace.[2] But Jeanne's mission, the audience she was to reach and her means of communicating with them, and most importantly her own published notion of her relationship to both her directors and her followers, all evolved in ways that distinguish her from the figures she initially was imitating. Unlike her predecessors, Jeanne was brought before an ecclesiastical court and condemned for her particular mystical vision, in a highly publicized examination in which Archbishops Bossuet and Fénelon, the two most powerful Catholic voices in France, engaged, in print, in a lengthy debate over her innocence. Just why her writing was so singled out is one of the topics I will explore in this chapter.

In 1687 Madame Guyon was enjoying both popularity and prestige. After seven years of a somewhat vagabond existence in Savoie and the cities of southeastern France, she had arrived in Paris and was at the center of a powerful

JEANNE MARIE BOUVIERES.
De la Mothe Guion. Etat 44.
Née le 13 Avril 1648. Morte le 9 Juin 1717.

A Paris chez Odieuvre Md. d'Estampes, rüe Danjou Dauphine la derniere Porte Cochere

Fig. 3.1   Jeanne Guyon

circle of *dévots* including Fénelon and Madame de Maintenon. It is no doubt in part because of her elite contacts that Bossuet singled her out as *the* representative figure of Quietism in his decisive battle with Fénelon over the doctrine of "pur amour".[3] Bossuet's *Relation sur le Quiétisme* attacked Madame Guyon's protector indirectly, via a detailed critique of Guyon's writings, and resulted in a papal condemnation of Fénelon's writings in 1699, though he himself was not arrested. Madame Guyon's writings were never condemned by Rome, but she was arrested in 1696, imprisoned at Vincennes and eventually transferred to the Bastille, where she remained for seven years. Fénelon's work was ultimately rehabilitated in the eyes of the church. Madame Guyon was not; having served as a scapegoat in the power struggle between Fénelon and Bossuet, she remains an ambiguous historical figure, treated by historians and theologians as an embarrassment to the church, more of a narcissist than a mystic.

It was not always so. In her own lifetime she was a central figure in the Catholic Reform movement. An avid member of the "Enfance de Jésus" movement, which advocated an extreme simplification of devotional practice, Guyon was instrumental in adapting its tenets to the interests of a broad public.[4] Though herself quite at ease with discussions of theological doctrine and patristic literature, in her own apostolate she stressed the belief that the way of "pure love" was not one that required learning, but was accessible to all, and in fact required a kind of dismantling of one's formal religious training, which could be an encumbrance to the desired state of childlike innocence. Her approach proved timely, and was more appealing and popular than she probably had ever imagined it would be. With the publication of her little handbook, *Le Moyen Court*, in 1685, Guyon became a celebrity, her teachings exerting a powerful and simple appeal for readers of different social backgrounds attracted by her promise of a "short and easy way" to God. For women, in particular, Guyon's way had a strong appeal, for it valorized the maternal bond as well as the superiority of childlike "naturalness": "Dieu ne demande rien d'extraordinaire, ni de trop difficile: au contraire, un procédé tout simple et enfantin lui plaît extrêmement."[5] (God demands nothing extraordinary nor too difficult: on the contrary, a simple and childlike method pleases him extremely well.)

Like other women of her time who dedicated themselves to religious devotion, as both mystic and missionary Jeanne Guyon found inspiration in the well-known lives of female saints like Teresa of Avila and Jeanne de Chantal. But, for reasons I will explore in this chapter, Madame Guyon departed from tradition in some dramatic ways. She was a public figure in a more modern sense than either Jeanne des Anges or Marie de l'Incarnation in that, after considerable struggling with this role, she came to embrace her status as an author, and to participate openly in defining her public image for posterity. Like her predecessors, Guyon designated the progressive experiences of her own life as the ultimate guarantors of her sincerity and apostolic authority. Like earlier mystical writers, she preached the authenticity of *la vie intérieure* and the superficiality of liturgical ritual. Michel de Certeau has described how, during the course of the seventeenth century, Catholicism moved away from a notion of revelation as embodied in the divine word of the Bible, to an acceptance of the diversity of personal experiences of revelation, embedded in human relations.[6] In the tradition of Catholic Reform spirituality, Guyon advocated the practice of mental prayer and explored her own spiritual growth as a constant interactive process, a series of conversations with others similarly committed to the new "way" who like her were learning how to converse with God. By the 1680s, the collaborative group consisting of a speaking woman, a listening cleric who helps her transcribe her voice, and a male editor and critical reader, was a familiar triad in the new discourse of mysticism. Jeanne Guyon's story follows this pattern, but only superficially, for she asserts a dominant role for herself as a voice of authority. Pursuing the full implications of a new notion of revelation based on personal experience, Guyon explicitly inverts the traditional power relation between director and pupil. She does this primarily by exploiting specifically female metaphors describing the experience and practice of motherhood. Moreover, in her version of mystical conversation the voice is muffled, even silenced, and writing is presented as an adequate substitute. Unlike her sanctified predecessors Marie de l'Incarnation and Jeanne de Chantal (who burned her own writings), Jeanne Guyon openly strove to preserve her written words. Guyon's discovery of the interior life did not carry with it a compelling need for marginalization or retreat. These urges, so characteristic of the mystical current in seventeenth-century Christian discourse, are not important in Guyon's descriptions of her life's progress, or rather, perhaps, they are urges expressed in new ways.[7] With the printing of *Le Moyen Court* Guyon launched her spiritual conversations into the world, and it is clear that by the end of her life she viewed herself as interacting with a public made up of readers extending far beyond the boundaries of her own personal experience.

The authority of spiritual motherhood

From what Guyon tells us of her life, it is clear that, for her, interaction with the world, beginning with her own family, did not come easily. Talking with God as well as with people was a struggle that led her to question the established norms of conversational exchange and invent new ways of communicating. In her autobiographical writings, she reflects on her place in a female spiritual and pedagogical tradition that was undergoing significant transformations at the end of the seventeenth century.[8] Guyon's *Life* and letters document both her evolving idea of a public for her words and the strategies she developed to assure herself of the existence of that public in the face of efforts to restrict the circulation of her works.

For a female spiritual leader at the end of the seventeenth century, proselytizing was a delicate business. On the one hand, the counter-reformation ideal of women in religion embraced a new connectedness with the world, rejecting the inevitability of clausura and promoting a limited teaching role for nuns. Jeanne spent much of her early life in a convent of Ursulines, the new order of nuns charged with the mission to educate girls by using their "natural talents" to lead souls to God. As Elizabeth Rapley has described, the ultimate objective of the new religious schooling for girls was to make them good mothers.[9] François de Sales and Jeanne de Chantal had originally founded another new order, the Order of the Visitation, for widows and other women not disposed to accept the traditional rigors of the cloister. The principal mission of the Visitandines was to attend to the needy in the community.

Guyon's autobiography begins with a description of her own mother's approach to the education of girls. She describes her early formative encounters with other religious figures as replacing an unsatisfactory filial bond. Guyon gives an unusually extended emphasis to a narration of her childhood, a phase of life that was typically neglected in both memoirs and biographies in her era.[10] It quickly becomes apparent that not only does Guyon regard her experience of childhood as an important force in her eventual choice of a spiritual vocation, but she also views her own mother as a counter-example to all that a mother should be. Guyon's enumeration of her mother's failings – her preference for her son, her lack of affection, her inattentiveness to the daily occupations of her children – reflects a new standard of maternal behavior that would not in fact have been predominant in Guyon's own childhood.[11] She begins her life story with an unambiguous description of her parents in which she cites her father's "saintly" family and his love for her from the moment of her birth, and her mother's open indifference to, if not dislike of, all girls, including her new daughter (20–22). Jeanne describes her early childhood as dominated by her mother's neglect of her education and her father's ineffectual but sincere affection. She makes frequent asides to the reader, pointing to the general lessons that may be drawn from her observations about good and bad mothering:

Je ne saurais ici m'empêcher de dire la faute que font les mères qui, sous prétexte de dévotion ou d'occupations, négligent de tenir leurs filles auprès d'elles, ... Qu'elles fassent leur dévotion de n'écarter jamais leurs filles d'elles: qu'elles les traitent en soeurs, et non pas en esclaves; qu'elles leur fassent paraître qu'elles se divertissent de leurs divertissements. ... O que si l'on en usait de la sorte, on romprait bientôt le cours aux désordres! Il n'y aurait plus ni de méchantes filles ni de mauvaises mères: car ces filles devenant mères, elles élèveraient leurs enfants comme elles auraient été élevées elles-mêmes. (24–6)

(I cannot help but point out here the fault of mothers who, under the pretext of devotion or other occupations, neglect to keep their daughters close to them ... Let them perform their devotion by never letting their daughters stray far from them, they should treat them as sisters, not slaves, they should let them see that they share their pleasures ... O if mothers conducted themselves like this, ... there would be no more bad daughters, no more bad mothers: for the daughters becoming mothers themselves would bring up their own children as they themselves had been raised.)

It is only after her mother's death in 1666 that Jeanne's intense interest in religious devotion takes the form of a conversion. The person who Jeanne describes as the first instrument of her conversion – Madame de Charost – appears in Jeanne's life story immediately after her mother's death, and is described as a figure whose style of piety contrasts sharply with that of Jeanne's mother. Charost was a new model for Guyon both as mother figure and a female mystic, and in both roles Charost was enacting new cultural prototypes.[12] When they first met, Jeanne was trying to imitate her mother's devotional practice of "outward" acts of charity. Charost proposed to show her pupil the new "inner way", but withdrew when Jeanne's confessor objected to such a heavy emphasis on private prayer and contemplation (70). This meeting with what Guyon was to come to view as a "good" mother figure was the first in a long chain of personal encounters shaping Jeanne's progressive discovery of mysticism. After Charost it was the Benedictine prioress Geneviève Granger, to whom Jeanne would long refer as her spiritual instructor and "mother." Granger first urged Guyon to sacrifice everything to contemplation and prayer, to ignore the more restrained advice of her confessors and instead confide her thoughts in her as to a mother: "J'avais une extrême confiance à la mère Granger. Je ne lui cachais rien ni de mes péchés, ni de mes peines: je n'aurais pas fait la moindre chose sans la lui dire" (135). (I was totally trusting of Mother Granger. I hid from her none of my sins, none of my trials. I would not have done the slightest thing without telling her). Forbidden by her husband and mother-in-law to communicate with Granger, Guyon nonetheless maintained a clandestine correspondence with her.

Granger acted as Guyon's principal teacher until a prolonged period of illness in the household in 1670. In this year Guyon's youngest son died of smallpox and she writes that at about the same time she also "lost" her other son, when he turned against her to ally himself with his father and grandmother in the divided family. Jeanne herself contracted smallpox (her mother-in-law, Jeanne writes, had forced her to remain in the infected house) and a short time later met François La Combe, a Barnabite priest who was to become her most intimate collaborator. Just as Granger had been a substitute mother for Guyon, revising the education her own mother had given her and preparing her for a new kind of maternity, so La Combe was to become a substitute son. He would be her most loyal disciple, consoling her on the death of her father and daughter in 1672, encouraging her in her resolution to leave her family after her husband's death in 1676 (an event which for her meant that God "was giving me my freedom" [174]), following her to the community of converted protestants or "New Catholics" which she joined in 1680, founding a hospital with her in 1683, and finally in 1688 suffering arrest, torture, and imprisonment as her follower.

At first Madame Guyon consciously modeled her relationship with La Combe after that of other famous "spiritual couples", most notably François de Sales and Jeanne de Chantal.[13] As a girl, she had read the biography of Jeanne de Chantal by Maupas du Tour. Chantal was a powerful inspiration for Guyon in her mission, and in the manner in which she was to conceive her relationship to her religious directors, especially La Combe and Fénelon. But in her own life story Guyon attempts to resolve the strong tension that accounts of Chantal's life describe, the tension between a mother's obligation to her children and the spiritual woman's exclusive commitment to God. Seventeenth-century hagiographies of Jeanne de Chantal went to considerable lengths to justify her abandonment of her surviving son, an episode that would scarcely have been remarked in comparable literature of the sixteenth century.[14] Prior to the sixteenth century, abandonment of one's children had not been perceived as a significant contradiction in the lives of female saints and spiritual leaders.[15] Women who left their families to follow a religious calling regarded their children as one of their worldly ties, and their sacrifice was often seen as a gesture enhancing the mother's eligibility for sainthood. Like Jeanne de Chantal and Marie de l'Incarnation, Jeanne Guyon abandoned a young son (although she took her daughter with her) when she left her home to become an itinerant mystic. In her reflections on the events leading to her departure, she implies that she was to assume a new motherly function in her apostolic life, and her biological children become dead to her, both figuratively and in reality (two of her five children had died in the 1670s). Unlike Jeanne de Chantal, Guyon left her home not to follow her saintly mentor, but to nurture his aspirations to saintliness. Her encounter with La Combe was a turning point, provoking her to modify and develop an image of herself as spiritual mother.

In her descriptions of her relationship with La Combe Guyon integrated new secular images of teaching as a form of mothering with an older Christian topos of Jesus as mother.[16] She recounts a dream in which the nature of her attachment to La Combe was revealed to her:

… Notre Seigneur me fit entendre que, sans que je le susse, il me l'avait donné, l'attirant à une vie plus parfaite que celle qu'il avait menée jusqu'alors; que c'était dans le temps de ma petite vérole qu'il me l'avait donné et qu'il m'en avait coûté ce mal et la perte de mon cadet; qu'il n'est pas seulement mon père, mais mon fils; ... (286)

(Our Lord made me understand that, without my knowing it, he had given him to me in order to bring him to a life more perfect than the one he had led up until then; that it was during the time of my smallpox that he had given him to me, and that it had cost me that illness and the loss of my youngest son; that he is not only my father, but my son; ...)

When Guyon and La Combe decided to break with the forced conversion methods of the New Catholics and retreat from the increasingly hostile Bishop of Geneva, she discovered in their mutual isolation her own powers of "spiritual mother" that she would later claim to be the unique feature of her apostolate:

Ce fut là aussi que je sentis la qualité de *Mère spirituelle*, car Dieu me donnait un je-ne-sais-quoi pour la perfection des âmes que je ne pouvais cacher au père La Combe. Il me semblait que je voyais jusque dans le fond de son âme et jusqu'aux petits replis de son coeur. ... (322)

(It was then, too, that I felt that quality of *spiritual mother*, for God gave me a special gift for the perfection of souls that I could not hide from Father La Combe. It seemed to me that I could see into the depths of his soul and even into the smallest folds of his heart.)

Even in the fairly formulaic opening paragraphs of her autobiography, where she establishes that she is writing only out of obedience, Guyon makes it clear that what convinces her to write is her conviction that the reading will benefit her addressee:

Puisque vous souhaitez de moi que je vous écrive une vie aussi misérable et aussi extraordinaire qu'est la mienne ... je veux de tout mon coeur pour vous obéir faire ce que vous désirez de moi ... Je tâcherai cependant de m'en acquitter le moins mal qu'il me sera possible, m'appuyant sur l'assurance que vous me donnez de ne la faire jamais paraître aux yeux des hommes, et que vous la brûlerez lorsque Dieu en aura tiré l'effet qu'il prétend pour votre profit spirituel, pour lequel je sacrifierais toutes choses ... (15–16)

(Since you wish me to write to you of a life as miserable and extraordinary as my own ... I want with all my heart, in order to obey you, to do what you wish of me ... I will nonetheless strive to acquit myself [of this task] as least poorly as I can, relying on the assurance you give me that you will never present it to the eyes of men, and that you will burn it as soon as God has made the use of it that he intends for your spiritual benefit, for which I would sacrifice everything ...)

Guyon reports that understanding her mission as something comparable to the sacrificial devotion of an ideal mother, a devotion that enabled her followers to rediscover the purity of childhood, was what permitted her to accept her calling to write. The metaphor of the mystic as mother was not new to religious writing at the time Guyon was proselytizing, but Jeanne's extensive and specific use of bodily metaphors of mothering was striking to her first readers, and it contributed to her being labeled first as dangerous (especially to female readers), then as mad. The role of spiritual mother was for her also one invested with great authority, comparable to that of a male *directeur de conscience*, though not following a patriarchal model. As Jean-Robert Armogathe has noted, Guyon's imagery of spiritual motherhood gives a dignity to the female body that she otherwise ritually degrades in keeping with the Christian mystical tradition.[17] She described her first written works as a kind of lactation, emanating from her despite her own violent efforts to exert some control over them. Her writing, she says, was driven by a physical need. She begins writing when she is ill, and finds that the experience literally alleviates her pain:

> Dans cette retraite il me vint un si fort mouvement d'écrire que je ne pouvais y résister. La violence que je me faisais pour ne le point faire me faisait malade, et m'ôtait la parole. ... J'étais comme ces mères, trop pleines de lait, qui souffrent beaucoup. Je déclarai au père La Combe après beaucoup de résistance la disposition où je me trouvais; il me répondit qu'il avait eu de son côté un fort mouvement de me commander d'écrire, mais qu'à cause que j'étais languissante, il n'avait osé me l'ordonner. Je lui dis que ma langueur ne venait que de ma résistance, et que je croyais qu'aussitôt que j'écrirais, cela se passerait. ... Il m'ordonna de le faire. (322–3)

> (In this retreat there came to me such a strong inclination to write that I could not resist it. The violence that I did to myself to keep from writing made me sick, and took away my speech. ... I was like those mothers who are too full of milk and who suffer much from it. After much resistance, I told Father Combe of my disposition; he answered that he, too, had felt a strong urge to command me to write, but that because of my weakened condition he had not dared to give me the order. I told him that my ailment came from my resistance and that I believed it would pass as soon as I started to write. ... He ordered me to do so.)

This passage illustrates another way in which Guyon transposed the conventional tie between female mystic and *directeur de conscience*. Seventeenth-century literature on female spiritual writing prescribed a very limited relationship between the writer and her readers.[18] As we have seen in the cases of Marie de l'Incarnation and Jeanne des Anges, women were to commit their religious experiences to paper only if directed to do so by their religious advisor, and then only in the form of a private letter to him. But Guyon's metaphor of a mother establishes a different image of mutual need to describe the connection of writer to reader.

Guyon would continue to exploit the metaphor of a nursing mother feeding "on demand" to describe her apostolic mission. Her spiritual director, she writes, plays the role of a child whose "commands" are in fact the expression of a profound dependency. After her first descriptions of having established this new, reciprocal dependency in her connection to La Combe, Guyon goes on to examine the force of the maternal metaphor from every possible angle. It becomes the filter through which she expresses her particular version of mysticism, and an image that seems to have contributed in no small part to her charismatic power over audiences. Guyon's descriptions of her itinerant preaching, from her departure for Geneva and Gex to her imprisonment in Paris in 1688, are marked by continual references to her special ways of "nourishing" her followers. She extends the conventional metaphor of her disciples as "children" to describe herself as their mother and God as their father who has "given" these children to her, each time causing her to suffer as in childbirth: "Quand il me donne quelqu'un en particulier, il me faut toujours souffrir quelque chose. O mon Dieu qu'il est bien vrai que je n'ai enfanté qu'avec douleur!" (370). (When he gives me someone in particular, I always have to suffer something. O my God how true it is that I have given birth only in pain!) Her style of communicating with her followers only in private homes and always by means of unpremeditated "free expressions" – never via preaching or even catechizing – was also a way to respect (or circumvent) the Pauline proscription against female teaching reiterated by the Catholic church after the Reformation. Increasingly, her practice with those who would come to her was to have them simply sit in her presence without speaking. She gave a name to this exercise, calling it "silent communication," and it became the mark of her unique apostolic style in the eyes of the public. Silent communication was also in keeping with the new ideal of maternal behavior that educators like Fénelon, a close follower of Guyon, were promoting as an innovative method of educating girls. It was a mother's responsibility to aid in the formation of her children simply by being present and remaining in the domestic sphere, by keeping her children close to her, by offering them love and by offering herself (a mother) as a model of filial and conjugal obedience.[19]

Describing her practice of unreflective preaching or "talking about God", during a particularly successful visit to Grenoble in 1685, she writes:

> ... depuis six heures du matin jusques à huit heures du soir, j'étais occupée à parler de Dieu. Il venait du monde de tous côtés, de loin et de près, des religieux, des prêtres, des hommes du monde, des filles, femmes et veuves, tous venaient les uns après les autres, et Dieu me donnait de quoi les contenter tous d'une manière admirable, sans que j'y pensasse ni que j'y fisse aucune attention. ... Ce fut là que je compris mieux la véritable maternité ... (374–7)

> (From six in the morning to eight at night I was speaking of God. People came from everywhere, from far and near, monks, priests, men of the world, girls, wives and widows, everyone came one after the other and God gave me what I needed to satisfy them all admirably, without my even thinking or paying attention. ... It was there that I better understood true maternity ...)

The act of writing is thus described as an extension of oral verbalizing. During this period in Grenoble she spoke all day and wrote all night, never reflecting, never consciously planning or knowing what she would be saying or writing (*Vie*, 400–405). It was during this period in Grenoble, Guyon tells us, that her manuscript copy of *Le Moyen Court* was brought to a printer. One of her many visitors, she writes, picked up the manuscript that happened to be lying on a table:

> Il me vint voir un conseiller du Parlement, qui est un modèle de sainteté. Ce bon serviteur de Dieu trouva sur ma table une méthode d'oraison que j'avais écrite il y avait longtemps. Il me la prit et l'ayant trouvée fort à son gré, il la donna à quelques personnes de ses amis à qui il la crut utile. Tous en voulaient des copies. Il résolut avec le bon frère de la faire imprimer: l'impression commencée, et les approbations données, il me prièrent d'y faire une préface. Je le fis; et c'est de cette sorte que le petit livret, que l'on a pris ensuite pour prétexte de m'emprisonner, fut imprimé. Ce Conseiller est un de mes intimes amis et un grand serviteur de Dieu. Ce pauvre petit livret n'a pas laissé d'être déjà imprimé cinq ou six fois malgré la persécution et Notre Seigneur y donne une fort grande bénédiction. Ces bons religieux en prirent quinze cents. (406)

> (A Counselor of Parliament came to see me, who is a model of sanctity. This good servant of God found on my table a method of prayer that I had written a long time ago. He took it from me and having found it to his liking, he gave it to some of his friends who he thought would find it useful. Everyone wanted copies. He resolved with the good brother to have it printed: once the printing was started and the required approvals were obtained, he asked me to make a preface for it. I did so; and that is how the little booklet, that soon after became the pretext to imprison me, was printed. The Counselor is one of my dear friends and a great servant of God. The poor little book has continued through five or six printings despite persecution, and Our Father gives it a great blessing. The good friars took five hundred copies of it.)

Stressing, on the one hand, the unconscious, unmediated nature of her communication with her followers, Madame Guyon at the same time carefully records the steps which led to her book being taken to the printer. It is precisely at the moment when she was perfecting her "silent communications" that her words are taken up, committed to print, and disseminated, as she records with a conscious pride she cannot suppress, in an impressive number of copies. The printed book is a form of disembodied conversation, silently conveying her words to readers while separating them from their female author-mediator. The monks who were the first to buy and distribute the book, Guyon notes, were subverting the efforts of other members of their order to dismiss the words of a "miserable" female (395).

Like these first readers, Guyon's later editors were to foster the notion that her printed texts offered a means of understanding her teachings without focusing on her personal identity as a woman. Even her *Life* is presented as a pedagogical text in a new style, a book that, despite its private, confessional declaration of intent, in fact is meant to show by example how readers might learn to speak of the inner life, how they can reflect on themselves, how they too can converse with God. In this respect Guyon's *Vie* functions like her *Moyen Court* as a kind of progressive manual of conduct for the soul.

This pedagogical purpose of Guyon's autobiography was enhanced by her first editors, and advertised on the title-page beginning with its second printing. To the original title of the 1720 edition (*La Vie de Madame J.M.B. de la Mothe-Guyon, écrite par elle-même*), the 1791 edition added: *qui contient toutes les expériences de LA VIE INTERIEURE, depuis ses commencemens jusqu'à la plus haute consommation, avec toutes les directions relatives*. The autobiography came to be promoted as a kind of textual substitute for a religious director, but one who directs in a new style, by simply testifying to a personal experience. Her readers, in turn, are invited to draw sustenance more than instruction from her message, like children taking good nourishment from their mother.

From body to book

After Guyon and La Combe were arrested, ostensibly for their affiliation with Quietism, Guyon's descriptions of her beliefs change noticeably in one respect: as she continues writing her autobiography she ceases to use the vocabulary of maternal intimacy to describe her relationship with her followers and she concerns herself principally with a more precise chronology of the events leading up to and including her final confrontation with Bossuet in 1694. When Bossuet asked to examine her writings she offered to show him everything, including her life story, which she describes as a private text:

> Pour lui marquer plus de confiance, et lui montrer jusqu'aux derniers replis de mon coeur, je lui fis remettre (ainsi que je l'ai dit) l'histoire de ma vie où mes dispositions les plus secrètes étaient marquées avec beaucoup de simplicité. Je lui demandai sur cela un secret de confession, et il en promit un inviolable. (551)

> (As a mark of my trust, and to show him the depths of my heart, I had my life story sent to him (as I have said), where my most secret dispositions were written with great simplicity. I asked that he treat this in confidence, as a confession, and he promised it would remain an inviolable secret.)

Six months later the ecclesiastical commission convened by Bossuet condemned Guyon's doctrine, and she was arrested and imprisoned in the Bastille, where she was to remain until 1703. For this public examination of her works Bossuet insisted on the inclusion of her *Life*, without which he was unsure of a condemnation. Guyon writes that she knew he was particularly interested in how the memoir could be used against her:

> ... j'avais lieu de croire qu'il ne songeait qu'à me condamner. Il avait dit que sans l'histoire de ma vie on ne le pourrait faire et qu'on y verrait un orgueil de diable. C'était pour cela qu'il la voulait faire voir à ces autres messieurs. (585)

> (I had reason to believe that he wanted only to condemn me. He had said that without the story of my life it would not be possible and that it showed a diabolical pride. This is why he wanted to show it to the other gentlemen.)

In 1687 Father La Combe was arrested and imprisoned on suspicion of heresy. During the next year Guyon initiated an intense correspondence with Fénelon, who she invited to assume the responsibilities of her director. One of the first points she inquired about in her letters to him was the continuation and circulation of her life story. She asks for instructions, but reminds Fénelon of the ostensible origin of the text in a director's command, a point that would presumably predispose her new director in favor of her continuing the project:

> ... je vous prie, Monsieur, de me dire, si je dois conserver ou brûler ce que l'on m'a fait écrire ou continuer? ... Si vous voulez bien m'honorer d'un petit mot de réponse, je vous prie qu'elle soit cachetée, et que l'on ne sache point ce que vous aurez décidé là-dessus. (*Fénelon et Madame Guyon*, 24)

> (... I beg you, Sir, to tell me if I must conserve or burn what I was made to write, or continue? ... If you would be so kind as to honor me with a brief word in reply, please take care that it is sealed and that no one knows what you have decided on the matter.)

In his response to her inquiry, Fénelon sidesteps the directorial role which she had offered him, but he also makes it clear that he wants her to not only save what she has written, but keep writing (25). Recent events had made the need for secrecy an urgent reality for both of them, but they worked together to rationalize Guyon's activities as a writer. It is Fénelon who indicates to Guyon, in these letters, how her own claim to spontaneous and unself-conscious writing could potentially be used as a defense against charges of heresy or even willful violations of religious proscriptions against female proselytizing. At the same time, he argues forcefully for her writing to disengage itself from the personal. "Write if God inspires you to," is his directive, "but strip your writing of any personal references that could get you or others in trouble":

> Pour les choses de votre vie qu'on vous a obligé d'écrire, je n'hésite pas à croire que vous ne devez pas les brûler. Elles ont été écrites simplement par obéissance ... Je raisonnerais autrement pour la suite. Vous ne devez écrire qu'autant que vous vous y sentez poussée. Non seulement vous devez suivre votre grâce, mais encore ceux qui vous donnent leur avis doivent l'observer et la suivre, ce me semble, en tout ... Pour les dispositions qui vous viennent soit à l'égard des autres personnes, soit à l'égard des dispositions extérieures, je crois que vous feriez bien de les écrire librement, courtement et avec les précautions nécessaires pour la sûreté du secret, ne marquant jamais aucun nom qu'on ne puisse lire, ni deviner, si vos papiers viennent à être lus ... (25–6)

> (For the things of your life that you were obliged to write, I don't hesitate to believe that you should not burn them. They were written simply out of obedience ... I would think otherwise about the continuation. You must write only as much as you feel yourself pushed to. Not only must you follow your grace, but also those who give you their advice must follow and observe it, it seems to me, in all things ... As for the dispositions that come to you either relating to other people or outside dispositions, you would do well to write them freely, quickly and with the necessary precautions for their security and secrecy, never putting

down any name that could be either read or guessed if your papers came to be read ...)

Fénelon thus provides Guyon with a new set of guidelines for how to be an author in her changing circumstances. By the end of 1688, when these letters were exchanged, Madame Guyon was already assuming a more defensive position before a public that was no longer limited to her followers. Following the publication of a pastoral letter that condemned Guyon's *Moyen Court* and denounced as heretical the methods of prayer she was promoting, the Archbishop of Paris had her confined for eight months in the Visitandine convent on the rue Saint-Antoine. During this period she was cut off from regular contacts with her children and community for the first time since she had left her husband's house. The purpose of continuing and revising her *Vie* at this point was to set the public record straight and claim a place for her own voice among the other accounts of her life that were being publicly circulated.

In matters of religion, the Guyon–Fénelon correspondence leaves the impression that she was the advisor more than the other way around. But when it came to deciding if and how to circulate her works, Guyon pressed for Fénelon's opinion. At times their correspondence is very precise on the point of who her public should be and which of her writings should be printed, as when he responds to a reading of her notion of "passive purification":

> Pour les purifications passives, je crois qu'il n'en faut pas écrire, c'est à dire n'en rien faire imprimer. La raison que j'en ai dite montre assez que je n'ai voulu parler que de l'impression par rapport au public; car j'ai dit qu'on scandalisait bien plus les âmes faibles qu'on n'édifiait le petit nombre des âmes éprouvées. (Fénelon, *Correspondance*, vol. II, 111)

> (As for passive purifications, I think that you shouldn't write about them, that is to say don't print anything. The reason that I gave you shows well enough that I only meant printing with respect to the public; for I said that weak souls were much more scandalized than the few strong souls were edified.)

Usually, as here, Fénelon recommends against printing, but Guyon, while not contradicting him, took care to assure that the writings that she sent him were preserved. Both of them routinely returned each other's letters, while Guyon also would ask Fénelon to make copies of her letters to him, or sometimes to keep something she had sent him until such time as he would be able to understand it:

> Oserais-je vous prier de garder ces lettres? parce qu'il viendra un temps où vous les comprendrez encore d'une autre sorte; et vous trouverez vos dispositions, quoique changées, conformes à ceci ... (*Madame Guyon et Fénelon*, 100)

> (Should I dare ask you to keep these letters? Because there will come a time when you will understand them in another way; and you will find your dispositions, although changed, conforming to this ...)

Guyon's letters to the Duc de Chevreuse, one of her most devoted followers, constitute a valuable daily record of her reactions to Bossuet as it became clear that he was moving toward a condemnation of her writings. In early 1693 Madame de Maintenon, alarmed by reports of Guyon's influence at Saint-Cyr and responding to pressures from courtiers allied against Fénelon, asked both Guyon and Fénelon to cease visiting her school for young aristocratic women. Drawing her allies more closely about her and responding to the threat of a public judgment against her teachings, Madame Guyon turned to loyal friends like Chevreuse in an attempt to influence Bossuet's reading of her works. Chevreuse was in charge of communicating Guyon's texts to Bossuet, and Guyon's barrage of often panicky messages gave him specific instructions as to how to present these writings, in what order to give them to Bossuet, and at what pace.[20] At first, she seems confident that Bossuet's reading will convince him of the orthodoxy of her thought, and asks only that her spokesmen stress that she would welcome the examination and has no fear of it.[21] But as Bossuet's stance toward her became more harsh, she takes a more strategic attitude in her letters, asking Chevreuse to read and "correct" her manuscripts before passing them on, and then frequently changing her mind about the order in which Bossuet should be sent her volumes of biblical interpretation.[22] As she becomes progressively uneasy with an examination based on her writings, she repeats her desire to meet in person with her judges. In person, she seems to feel, she has a chance of convincing them of her innocence, and a personal confrontation would also provide the opportunity to render more dramatic a kind of public martyrdom that was already beginning to appear inevitable.[23] Finally, in a letter to Chevreuse dated 1 November 1693, Guyon indicates that she is resigned to being unable to dissuade Bossuet from a willfully literal reading of her metaphoric language of the body:

> Je vois bien que M. de Meaux prend un côté du corporel et du sensible des choses purement spirituelles. ... Ne vous donnez plus, s'il vous plaît, la peine de m'écrire; il n'y a qu'à me condamner, brûler mes écrits ...

> (I see clearly that M. de Meaux sees a bodily and sensory side to things that are purely spiritual. ... Please don't trouble yourself any more with writing me; there is nothing to do but condemn me, burn my writings ...)

Re-embodying Guyon's voice

Bossuet's condemnation of Guyon is a case history in the thinking that led to a general imposition of limitations on female proselytizing by the Catholic church at the end of the seventeenth century. It has interested historians as a classic confrontation of two strains of Catholic thought in the seventeenth century – popular mysticism and a more rationalized form of Gallicanism that tended to view some of the cruder manifestations of religious ecstasy as a form of madness, if not worse.[24] When Guyon's works were finally condemned by Bossuet's examining committee, she was forbidden any further communication with her followers on religious matters, and specifically instructed to cease writing and publishing. In his *Relation sur le Quiétisme* Bossuet reports that in her letter of submission Guyon "acceptait le conseil de se retirer sans voir ni écrire à personne autrement que pour ses affaires ..." (1114) (accepted the advice to withdraw without seeing or writing to anyone except for her personal business). He makes it clear, moreover, that he had particularly objected to her claiming apostolic authority on the basis of her concept of spiritual mother-hood. Guyon's practice of religious direction as a form of mothering was distasteful to him:

> ... la Dame promettait d'obéir et de n'écrire à personne; ce que j'avais entre autres choses trouvé dans sa *Vie*, ce qui parait aussi dans son *Interprétation* imprimée sur le *Cantique*, que par un état et une destination apostolique, dont elle était revêtue et où les âmes d'un certain état sont élevées, non seulement *elle voyait clair dans le fond des âmes*, mais encore *qu'elle recevait une autorité miraculeuse sur les corps et sur les âmes de ceux que Notre-Seigneur lui avait donnés. Leur état intérieur semblait*, dit-elle, *être en ma main* (par l'écoulement qu'on a vu de cette grâce communiquée de sa plénitude): *sans qu'ils sussent comment ni pourquoi ils ne pouvait s'empêcher de m'appeler leur mère; et quand on avait goûté de cette direction, toute autre conduite était à charge*. (1108–9, emphasis in original)

> (The lady promised to obey and to write no one; among other things, what I had found in her *Life*, and what appears also in her printed *Interpretation* of the *Songs*, was that through an apostolic state and sense of destiny which she had assumed and to which souls in a certain state are elevated, not only did she "see clearly to the depth of souls," but also she "received a miraculous authority over the bodies and souls of those who had been given to her by Our Lord. Their interior state seemed," she says, "to be in my hands" (by the flowing of this grace from her plenitude, as we have seen): "without them knowing either how or why they could not help calling me their mother; and when one had tasted of this type of direction, all other guidance was a burden.")

Whereas the eventual outcome of Bossuet's battle with Fénelon and Guyon was to alienate French Catholic practice from private spirituality, prior to his encounter with Guyon, Bossuet had not been hostile to the principle tenet of the new style of devotion: that personal experience, not religious training, was the *sine qua non* for understanding mysticism. Guyon herself repeatedly claimed that her doctrine was no different from that of other mystics who had been canonized by the church, and she suggests that Bossuet was uneasy with mystical language in general. His conversations with Jeanne Guyon became the springboard for Bossuet to develop what one writer has called his "visceral anti-mysticism" into a more rationalized rejection of experience as a basis for religious authority.[25] In the text that launched his crusade against mysticism,

Relation sur le Quiétisme, Bossuet made only indirect reference to Fénelon's published defense and focused instead on Fénelon's personal connection with Guyon, using her autobiography as his principal textual reference.

Bossuet opened his attack with a critique of Guyon's notion of grace or divine blessing as expressed through the metaphor of lactation:

> Je trouvai dans la Vie de cette Dame que Dieu lui donnait une abondance de grâces dont elle crevait au pied de la lettre ... on venait recevoir la grâce dont elle était pleine ... C'était comme une nourrice qui 'crève de lait' ... Frappé d'une chose aussi étonnante, j'écrivis de Meaux à Paris à cette Dame que je lui défendais ... d'user de cette nouvelle communication de grâces, jusqu'à ce qu'elle eût été plus examinée. (1105)

> (I found in the Life of this lady that God gave her an abundance of blessings which were literally killing her ... one was supposed to come and receive the grace which filled her ... She was like a wet nurse who 'is bursting with milk' ... Struck by such an astonishing thing, I wrote from Meaux to this lady in Paris that I forbad her ... to use this new communication of blessings until she could be further examined.)

Proceeding through a series of lengthy quotes from the autobiography, each of them vividly illustrating Guyon's use of the imagery of pregnancy, motherhood, and breastfeeding to describe her attachment to her followers, Bossuet expresses his shock that a man of Fénelon's stature would have embraced such a vision of spiritual direction:

> Il y avait assez longtemps que j'entendais dire ... que M. l'abbé Fénelon était favorable à la nouvelle oraison, ... Inquiet pour lui, pour l'Eglise et pour les princes de France dont il était déjà Précepteur, ... je tâchais de découvrir ses sentiments dans l'espérance de le ramener à la vérité ... je vis Mme Guyon: on me donna tous ses livres, et non seulement les imprimés, mais encore les manuscrits, comme sa Vie qu'elle avait écrite ... (1103–4)

> (For a long time I had heard ... that the abbé de Fénelon was favorably disposed toward the new way of prayer ... Worried for him, for the Church and for the princes of France to whom he was already appointed Tutor, I tried to uncover his feelings in the hopes of bringing him back to the truth ... I saw Mme Guyon: I was given all her books, not only the printed ones but also the manuscripts such as her *Life* that she had written ...)

Outlining his objections to and repugnance for Guyon's unusual methods of proselytizing and her manner of describing them, Bossuet deflects his criticism away from Fénelon and addresses himself instead to establishing the heterodoxy of the woman who had managed to infantilize his colleague. He thus leaves the path clear for an eventual reconciliation with the powerful Fénelon. In this representation of Guyon first popularized by Bossuet, Guyon's maternal metaphor is inverted by her enemies and she becomes a bad mother-figure from whose clutches Fénelon, the young heirs to the French throne, and indeed all good Catholics needed to be rescued.

Ultimately Bossuet was to argue that the most threatening consequence of Guyon's doctrine was her effort to disclaim personal responsibility for it by asserting this form of involuntary communication. Indeed, Guyon's use of the idea of spiritual motherhood was her own best defense. Once assured of a community of followers who believed in her system of voiceless communication, she could claim that she was not asserting personal authority over her teachings, but only lending her bodily presence to facilitate other's conversations with God. She did not need to leave the domestic sphere to proselytize, she did not even need to speak; her "children" would come to her and be nourished by the fullness of her presence.

Bossuet and his colleagues devoted considerable effort to persuading Fénelon to denounce Guyon personally, not just her writings. Against the advice of friends who counseled a more aloof stand, Fénelon responded directly, focusing on Guyon's personal innocence, integrating his arguments for her doctrinal purity with the assertion that her private life was beyond reproach. If she in fact could be proven to have erred in matters of doctrine, he argued, she must not be held personally accountable, for her writings were simply verbal (and thus by definition imperfect) accounts of divine spiritual experiences. There could be no question of condemning her as an author. She was simply "une femme qui aide les âmes, en leur donnant des conseils fondés sur ses expériences ..."[26] (A woman who helps souls, by giving them advice based on her experiences.)

But even after Guyon passively agreed to sign a statement submitting herself to the rule against female preaching, Bossuet continued to insist that she assume personal responsibility for all of her writings, refusing to accept her response that she was simply a vehicle or mediator for divine grace (*Relation*, 1111). Guyon's mother imagery, and her practice of "silent communication" based on the paradigm of the maternal bond, rendered more dangerous a subversive strain in female spirituality that Bossuet had previously been able to accept.[27] Guyon held to the special status of her metaphor of spiritual maternity, which enabled her to lay claim to a uniquely feminine form of authority and at the same time refuse full parental responsibility for her writings. Bossuet understood that in order to obtain a condemnation of her thought he would have to reestablish its connection to a personal author. The most threatening consequence of Guyon's doctrine, he argued, was her effort to disclaim personal responsibility for it. Without a condemnation of Guyon the *person*, she could remain free to minister to her public, taking shelter behind her disclaimer of authorship of her writings.[28]

After her release from prison in 1703 Guyon lived for another fourteen years, officially consigned to the care of the son whom she had abandoned as a boy to follow her spiritual calling. But the spiritualist movements of the age had been dealt a death blow by the judgments pronounced against her at the Issy conferences in 1694 and by the papal judgment issued five years later against Fénelon's defense of mysticism.[29] Considered purely as an expression of her mystical doctrine, Guyon's account of her life has too often been treated, in the Catholic tradition at least, as a kind of vulgarized version of the discourse of more illustrious predecessors – a discourse emphasizing interiority over outward signs of religious practice, direct communion with God over the mediation of the church, and the annihilation of the self as a means to achieve this "pure love".[30] But what gave her version of evangelical mysticism its particular originality was her cultivation of the many ways in which she could claim a mother's power over her followers, and her elaboration of this metaphor as a way of explaining such notions as the non-referentiality of mystical language. For Bossuet, this made her doubly "errant", for to formulate her authority and her way of communicating religious experience as an extended experience of maternity was to make it inassimilable by a patriarchal institution such as the church. Her most egregious offense was her posture toward Fénelon (and his acceptance of it!), her claim that he was "closer and more attached to me than the children I have carried in my belly".[31]

Building a community of readers

After her confrontation with Bossuet, Guyon's idea of her public and her relation to it changed. The most explicit record of this is to be found in a recently discovered final chapter of her life story, that Guyon completed in 1709. Entitled *Récits de captivité* by Marie-Louise Gondal, who discovered the manuscript in 1989, this text recounts Guyon's experiences in prison, from 1695 to 1703.[32] In a prefatory statement which she entitles *"envoi"*, Guyon makes it clear that she had initially withheld this text from the manuscript of her autobiography. She alludes, moreover, to her own earlier explanation of her reasons for not circulating this part of her account, which she had given in one of the final chapters of her published *Vie*.[33] There she had declared that a spirit of charity and respect prevented her from detailing her persecutors' unjust treatment of her to the public. In her *"envoi"* she claims to have submitted to the insistence of an unnamed friend and the desires of a more circumscribed circle of followers who wanted a fuller account of her imprisonment. This final chapter of her life story, by comparison with the first which she knew would have readers unknown to her personally, is destined for a small public of *"amis les plus particuliers"*:

> J'ai cru devoir en supprimer le récit dans l'histoire de ma vie que l'on avait exigée de moi. J'en ai expliqué les raisons, et elles me feraient encore garder le silence, si je n'étais persuadée que ce qui m'en reste à vous dire ne sera uniquement que pour vous et un petit nombre de mes amis les plus particuliers, à qui je ne

puis refuser cette consolation, si c'en est une pour eux, mais qui voudront bien entrer dans les vues et les motifs qui me les font supprimer pour tous les autres. (*Récits*, 31)

(I thought it necessary to suppress this story in the account of my life that I had been ordered to write. I have explained my reasons, and they would still hold me to silence if I were not persuaded that what remains for me to tell you will be only for you and a small number of my closest friends, to whom I cannot refuse this consolation, if it is one for them, but they must agree with the views and the motives that push me to suppress them for everyone else.)

This statement belies her opening claim, in the autobiography, to be writing for the eyes of one reader alone, and shows that initial opening to be a pretext, a point of departure from which she deviated, as we have seen, even as she was composing it. The shifting ground that Guyon established in her autobiographical writing to describe her connection to her public points to the originality of her enterprise as well as to the evolution of her own notion of a reading public for her work. It also reflects the coexistence, in the late seventeenth century, of two different kinds of publics for the printed word – one a limited circle of readers such as the one that is implied for the *Récits de captivité*, the other a larger, more anonymous public – in Guyon's phrase, "*tous les autres*".[34] The latter is a public exposing the writer, especially the woman writer, to an increased risk of opposition or censorship. The former is more personal, based on a circumscribed notion of community as found in salon culture as well as in other ideas of religious community promulgated at this time.[35]

The public that was eventually to prove the most receptive to Madame Guyon's religious teachings was neither French nor even Catholic, but rather spiritualist Protestant sects in England, Scotland, Holland, and Germany.[36] It is interesting to observe that Guyon herself also actively cultivated this particular public at the end of her life, during the period when she was supposedly following Bossuet's directive and retiring from her evangelical activities. From 1703 to her death in 1717 she was in fact very busy orchestrating the dissemination of her works outside of France. Aided by her personal secretary and follower Andrew Ramsay, who helped her maintain epistolary connections with Pierre Poiret in Amsterdam and a group of devotees in Scotland and England, Madame Guyon supervised the translation and publication of most of her works during her last years at Blois, where she was living officially in the care of her son. Even her autobiography and personal letters were being prepared for publication by the late 1690s.[37] Like her *Vie*, many of Guyon's letters seem to address both a particular and a more general public. In a letter to Poiret placed by him at the end of the published correspondence, Guyon instructs her audience in a method of "passive" reading which would depersonalize her connection with her readers and facilitate an acceptance of the divine origin of her writing.

Si jamais ces écrits tombent entre les mains de quelqu'un devant ou après ma mort, je les prie de ne point examiner scrupuleusement; mais en tirer le fruit que Dieu prétend ... Si on lit quelque chose qu'on n'entend pas, qu'on travaille à mourir à soi-même, Dieu en donnera l'intelligence lorsqu'on sera plus avancé. (*Lettres Chrétiennes*, vol. V, 556–7)

(If these writings ever should fall into the hands of someone before or after my death, I ask that they not examine them scrupulously, but that they take from them the fruit that God wishes ... If something one reads is not understood, then one should work to die unto oneself, and God will provide an understanding of it when one is more advanced.)

Like the notion of silent communication, this way of reading is very similar to the practice of *lecture méditée* that Guyon prescribes in her book *A Short and Easy Method of Prayer*. Reading is described as form of ingestion and as a practice in which the textual matter is less important than the experience of intimacy with God to which an exposure to it can lead:

La lecture méditée n'est autre que de prendre quelques vérités fortes pour la spéculative et pour la pratique préférant la dernière à la première, et de lire de cette sorte. ... lire deux ou trois lignes, les digérer et goûter, tâchant d'en prendre le suc et de se tenir arrêté à l'endroit que l'on lit, tant que l'on y trouve du goût, et ne passant point outre que cet endroit ne soit rendu insipide. (64)

(Meditated reading is simply taking some strong truths for speculation and practice, preferring the latter to the former, and to read in this way. ... read two or three lines, digest and savor them, striving to draw out the juices and stick to the spot one is reading as long as one can taste it, then pass on only when this particular spot has lost its flavor.)

The novelty of the practice of silent reading is graphically evoked here. Readers are both instructed in the habit and pushed toward taking their own pleasure from the text rather than reaching for directions or explications provided by experts. The author herself is effaced from this description, leaving room for the reader to ingest the nourishment that is being offered, like an infant draining one breast before turning to the other.

Letters written by Guyon and her followers in her last years at Blois show the entourage cultivating the habit of passive reading while at the same time insuring that Guyon's writings would be preserved, circulated, printed, and eventually properly explicated. A fascinating circuit of epistolary contacts record the care with which the community was orchestrating the dissemination of many of her writings well before they went into print. Letters exchanged between Blois, Aberdeen, London, and Amsterdam clarify points of her already published works and discuss plans for printing others. These instructions from Ramsay to Lord Deskford in 1714 are typical: "Je vous prie de garder toujours une copie des lettres que je vous écris de la part de Notre Mère. Il faut en faire faire quelque jour un recueil et les envoyer à Doctor Keith afin qu'il les envoie avec les autres écrits aux amis à M. Poiret" (Henderson, 88). (Please always keep a copy of the letters I write you on behalf of Our Mother. One day a collection will have to be made of them to send to Doctor Keith so that he can send them with her other writings to M. Poiret's friends.) It is clear, too, from these letters that the autobiography was circulating in manuscript form outside of France during Guyon's lifetime, and with her permission was scheduled to be printed (143–4).

Madame Guyon's public, then, by the end of her life was both intimate and far-flung; through letters and the testimonials of those who continued to visit her she managed to sustain a community of followers that reached far beyond the territory of France. If it is indeed true, as Jacques Le Brun has remarked, that the papal condemnation of Fénelon's *Explication des Maximes des Saints* effectively suppressed "presque toute expression publique des tendances mystiques" ("Quiétisme", p. 2838) (almost all public expression of mystical tendencies), then what Madame Guyon and her followers managed to do during her years of exile at Blois was to create another forum for such public expression. Bossuet's *Relation sur le Quiétisme* had succeeded, by its relentless attack on Guyon's bodily metaphors for spiritual life, in turning a certain community of readers away from her doctrine.[38] Guyon and her followers responded by insisting on her own passivity as an author, on the necessity of reading her writings as unmediated spiritual nourishment. Guyon's pedagogical approach, she would insist, was simply to strive, imperfectly, to communicate her personal experience. At the same time she presented this experience to a public not because it was exemplary but because it testified to a "way", a process which her readers could imitate, adapt, "ingest", or otherwise absorb in their own spiritual quest. It would fall to the editors of Guyon's printed work to pursue the task of presenting their spiritual "mother" as a writer to be followed, but who would not lead. As an editor who was also her friend and disciple, Pierre Poiret introduced anecdotes drawn from his personal contacts with Guyon to enhance his representation of her voice while also justifying its disembodied authority. At the end of one collection of her letters he appended the letter she had addressed to him anticipating the publication of her writing and prescribing the reading method of passive reception.[39]

Michel de Certeau has written suggestively of the discovery of the female voice in seventeenth-century spiritualist movements. "Learned clerics", he writes, "became exegetes of female bodies, speaking bodies ... these magi came to the 'little ones' to listen to something that still spoke."[40] To some extent, Madame Guyon placed herself in the position of a speaking body whose natural, unreflective, spoken emissions were meant to be interpreted after the fact by more qualified listeners than herself. But at the same time, in extending her words to the world via letters, manuscripts, and the printed word, she wanted to become the principal interpreter of her own voice, to be both the oracle and the magus, the innocent child and the spiritual guide. A slippery, contradictory, even, perhaps, as some have suggested, a hypocritical form of self presentation.[41] But in her efforts to define her particular relationship to a public, Guyon managed to assure herself and the mystical literature that had nourished her a continued readership beyond the reaches of impressive mechanisms of censorship within her own country.

Notes

1. In fact, none of the mystics accused of Quietism ever declared their affiliation with it. It is a doctrine that seems to have been defined only by the texts condemning it, beginning with the papal bull of 1687 which provided the antiquietists with what one historian has called a "reading grid" for identifying and repressing the fascination with mysticism perceived as a growing threat to church doctrine. For a summary see Jacques Le Brun, "Quiétisme", in *Dictionnaire de la Spiritualité ascétique et mystique*, ed. M. Viller et al. (Paris: Beauchesne, 1985), pp. 2805–10. Marie-Louise Gondal's edition of Guyon's *Moyen Court* also provides a good introduction to her teachings.
2. On the Christian tradition of spiritual couples and its implications for women's freedom in the early modern period see Wendy Wright, *Bond of Perfection: Jeanne de Chantal and François de Sales* (New York: Paulist Press, 1985).
3. The classic study of this episode is Louis Cognet's *Crépuscule des Mystiques: Le conflit Fénelon–Bossuet* (Tournai: Desclée, 1958).
4. This religious movement advocated worship of the infant Jesus and encouraged followers to return to childlike ways of perception and communication. The best study is Yvan Loskoutoff, *La Sainte et la fée: Dévotion à l'enfant Jésus et mode des contes merveilleux à la fin du règne de Louis XIV* (Geneva: Droz, 1987).
5. *Moyen court et très facile de faire oraison, que tous peuvent pratiquer très aisément et arriver par là dans peu de temps à une haute perfection*, in Guyon, *Le "Moyen Court" et autres récits*, ed. Marie-Louise Gondal (Grenoble: Jérome Millon, 1995), p. 86. On the radical nature of Guyon's insistence on simplicity, see Gondal's comments in her introduction. Loskoutoff also discusses the particular appeal that Guyon had for women, and the originality of her speaking as a mother, in *La Sainte et la fée*, pp. 85–8; 97–9. All translations into English are my own.
6. See Certeau, "La Pensée religieuse", in Pierre Abraham and Roland Derné (eds), *Histoire littéraire de la France* (Paris, 1975), vol. III, pp. 161–2.
7. On the typical grounding of mystical discourse in the principle of marginality, as well as the rejection of writing, see Certeau, "La Pensée religieuse."
8. Guyon's autobiographical writings consist of (1) her *Vie*, (2) an addendum only recently discovered in manuscript treating the years of her imprisonment, and (3) her extensive letter correspondences. *La Vie de Madame J. M. B. de la Mothe-Guyon, écrite par elle-même* was first published in Amsterdam in 1720 by Guyon's editor and disciple Pierre Poiret. Page references to Guyon's *Vie* will be to the modern edition (Paris: Dervy-Livres, 1983), unless otherwise noted. Guyon's addendum was given the title *Récits de captivité* by Marie-Louise Gondal, who discovered and published the manuscript in 1992. Many of Guyon's letters have been printed, in a scattered fashion, from early editions of her own works to modern published correspondences of Fénelon and Bossuet, as I will note below. There is no integral edition of her letters, and many remain unpublished.

9.   "Christian motherhood was generally seen as the means to convert the world", *The Dévotes: Women and Church in Seventeenth-Century France* (Montreal: McGill-Queens University Press, 1990), p. 157. For a summary of the contributions of the Ursulines to methods of educating women, see pp. 142–66.

10. See Marie-Florine Bruneau, "Le Projet autobiographique: Guyon à l'orée de la modernité", in *Papers on French Seventeenth-Century Literature*, **10** (1983), p. 64. Donald Weinstein and Rudolph M. Bell's survey of the hagiographic literature of the sixteenth and seventeenth centuries shows also that in general "childhood loses its interest for hagiographers" during this period, in *Saints and Society: Two Worlds of Western Christendom, 1000–1700* (Chicago: University of Chicago Press, 1982), p. 24.

11. For a history of seventeenth-century changes in attitudes toward children and their upbringing, which was marked by an increasing emphasis on the importance of nurture and mothering in early childhood, see Elizabeth Wirth Marvick, "Nature Versus Nurture: Patterns and Trends in Seventeenth-Century French Child-Rearing", in *The History of Childhood*, ed. Lloyd de Mause (New York: Harper & Row, 1974), pp. 259–302.

12. On the generational changes in standards of female piety during the second half of the seventeenth century, see Rapley, pp. 3–9, and Linda Timmermans, *L'Accès des femmes à la culture en France, 1598–1715* (Paris: Champion, 1993), pp. 501–621.

13. On Chantal's ideas concerning spiritual friendship see Wendy M. Wright, *Bond of Perfection*, cited above. To describe her relationship with La Combe, Guyon adopted a vocabulary more closely resembling the "mother mysticism" analysed by Rosemary Hale in "Imitatio Mariae: Motherhood Motifs in Devotional Memoirs", *Mystics Quarterly*, **16** (1990), 193–203.

14. Clarissa Atkinson has examined the impact of new standards of maternal behavior – both secular and Christian – on notions of female spirituality, as illustrated in the relationship between François de Sales and Jeanne de Chantal. Sales placed great emphasis on the obligations of wives to their children and husband, and exhorted Chantal to exhibit more affection for her own children – whom she had abandoned to follow him – when they visited her. See Atkinson, pp. 224–30.

15. See Atkinson pp. 233–43.

16. Linda Lierheimer has examined the metaphor of maternal ministry as invoked by the teaching orders in the seventeenth century in "Female Eloquence and Maternal Ministry: The Apostolate of Ursuline Nuns in Seventeenth-Century France" (Princeton: PhD dissertation, 1994), pp. 381–436.

17. See his "Madeleine, ou le corps de Jeanne: Le corps mystique dans l'auto-biographie de Jeanne Guyon", in *La Folie et le corps* (Paris: Presses de l'ENS, 1985), pp. 258–9. Caroline Bynum analyzes the place of maternal imagery in what she terms "the feminization of religious imagery" in twelfth- and thirteenth-century texts, in *Jesus as Mother* (Berkeley: University of California Press, 1982), pp. 125–70. Marie-Louise Gondal comments on Guyon's appeal to women readers in *Madame Guyon: Un nouveau visage* (Paris: Beauchesne, 1989), pp. 38–40, 72–5. In comparing Guyon's version of Quietism to that of Molinos, Leszek Kolakowski has noted that Guyon does not invoke the absolute authority of the *directeur de conscience*, which Molinos had stressed was crucial to the spiritual development of the individual. Molinos figures himself as the director, a function which Guyon, as a woman, could not officially assume. See *Chrétiens sans église: La conscience religieuse et le lien confessionnel au 17e siècle* (Paris: Gallimard, 1969), p. 543.

18. See Timmermans, pp. 539–67, for documentation of this literature.
19. In *De l'Education des filles*, Fénelon argued against convent schooling for girls and promoted instead the role of mothers in the early education of children. See for example ch. XI, "Instruction des femmes sur leurs devoirs".
20. Guyon's letters to Chevreuse are in the Saint-Sulpice archives in Paris. Chevreuse originally preserved the letters and noted their dates in a careful, tidy hand that contrasts with Guyon's hasty scrawl (in some cases he gave the letters two possible dates). A number of these letters were published in the journal *Revue Fénelon*, **II**, 3–4 (December–March 1912), pp. 194–217. This published selection, however, was based on a manuscript copy of the letters and is not always accurate. I have quoted from the autograph letters, modernizing the spelling.
21. "Je crois que vous pouvez vous ouvrir à M. de Meaux sur ce que vous croyez de moi ... Ne serait-il point bon de dire à M. de Meaux comme il est vrai que c'est moi qui ai souhaité qu'il eût la liberté de me voir. Je n'ai pas envie de le lui dire" (20 août 1693). (I think that you can be open with M. de Meaux about what you think of me ... Would it not be good to say to M. de Meaux how it is true that it is I who wished that he would be free to see me. I don't feel like telling him that.)
22. "Donnez à M. de Meaux ce qu'il voudra des écrits: Les Juges, Job, l'Evangile de St. Mathieu, tous l'un après l'autre ..." (22 septembre 1693) ("Give M. de Meaux what he would like from the writings: Judges, Job, The Gospel of St. Matthew, all one after another ..."); "Je vous prie instamment d'envoyer à M. de Meaux dans un même paquet les Juges, Job, et les Prophètes. Mais n'envoyez pas sitôt l'Apocalypse. Faites-lui voir auparavant ceux-là et l'évangile de Matthieu. Cela est nécessaire mais faites-le s'il vous plaît de manière que cela paraisse tout naturel ..." (20 octobre 1693) ("I earnestly beg you to send M. de Meaux Judges, Job, and the Prophets in one package. But don't send the Apocalypse just yet. First have him see those and the Gospel of Matthew. This is necessary, but please do it in a way that seems perfectly natural ..."); "Vous pouvez donner l'Apocalypse à M. de Meaux si vous le jugez à propos après l'avoir lue" (28 octobre 1693) ("You may give the Apocalypse to M. de Meaux if you think it wise, after having read it"); "Je crois qu'il ne faut pas montrer à M. de Meaux l'Apocalypse. Il n'y a qu'à la brûler avec le reste des écrits ... Je vous prie de ne lui donner plus les torrents, cela ne sert qu'à le peiner davantage et ne produirait pas un bon effet" (30 ou 31 octobre 1693) ("I think M. de Meaux must not be shown the Apocalypse. It must simply be burned with the rest of the writings ... I beg of you do not give him the torrents, that would only serve to strain him further and would not produce a good effect").
23. "Je voudrais, s'il m'était permis, assembler tous les docteurs et parler devant eux tous; il me semble que je les convaincrais tous pour le moment présent, mais la politique l'emporte sur tous" (15 octobre 1693). (I would like, if I were permitted, to assemble all the doctors and speak before all of them; it seems to me that I would convince them all for the present moment, but politics holds sway over all.)
24. Certeau describes this confrontation as follows: "Gallicanism, or support of the administrative autonomy of the French Catholic Church, and Quietism faced each other, as if the new 'reason' which placed ecclesiastical action within the framework of national politics and positivity had for its contrary and correspondent a spirituality of abandon and passivity, as much more foreign to institutional boundaries (religious ones included) as it was more 'interior'." *The Writing of History*, trans. Tom Conley (New York: Columbia University Press, 1988), p. 133.
25. Françoise Mallet-Joris uses this expression in her biography *Jeanne Guyon* (Paris: Flammarion, 1978), 526. Guyon described her discomfort in conversations with

Bossuet: "Ce que j'aurais souhaité de Monsieur de Meaux était qu'il ne jugeât pas de moi par sa raison, mais par son coeur. ... Les difficultés qu'il me faisait ne venaient (comme je crois) que du peu de connaissance qu'il avait des auteurs mystiques qu'il avouait n'avoir jamais lus, et du peu d'expérience qu'il avait des voies intérieures." (560) (I would have wished that M. de Meaux not judge me with his reason, but with his heart. ... The difficulties he gave me came, I believe, from the little knowledge that he had of mystical authors which he admitted never having read, and from the little experience he had of inner ways.) Jacques Le Brun has argued that Bossuet's hostile attitude toward mysticism dates precisely from the quarrel over Quietism, which began with his interrogation of Madame Guyon. See Le brun, "Expérience religieuse et expérience littéraire", in *la Pensée Religieuse dans la littérature et la civilisation du XVIIe siècle en France* (Paris: Biblio 17, 1984), p. 132.

26.   Letter from Fénelon to Madame de Maintenon, 7 March 1696, in Fénelon, *Correspondance*, ed. Orcibal (Paris: Klincksieck, 1972), vol. IV, 60. He elaborates: "Dans l'état le plus libre et le plus naturel, elle m'a expliqué toutes ses expériences et tous ses sentiments. Il n'est pas question des termes, que je ne défends point, et qui importent peu dans une femme, pourvu que le sens soit catholique. C'est ce qui m'a toujours paru." (In a most free and natural state, she explained to me all of her experiences and all of her feelings. It is not a question of the terms, which I do not defend, and which matter little in a woman, as long as the sense is catholic. That is what it always seemed to me.)

27.   Teresa of Avila, for example, whose writings Bossuet admired, proposes her special feminine capacity for intimacy and love (all the while conceding women's weakness and intellectual inferiority) as a source of authority, thus justifying her own teaching mission and circumventing the Pauline proscription. See Carole Slade, "Saint Teresa's *Meditaciones sobre los cantares*: The Hermeneutics of Humility and Enjoyment", *Religion and Literature*, **18** (1986), 40; and Alison Weber, *Teresa of Avila and the Rhetoric of Femininity* (Princeton: Princeton University Press, 1990), pp. 35–41. As I discuss in Chapter 1 above, there is a similar rhetorical strain in the writings of Marie de l'Incarnation (whom Bossuet admiringly called "the French St. Teresa"). The extensive literature on the conflict between Bossuet and Fénelon over Guyon and the mystical tradition usually takes the position that Guyon's thought was not markedly different from that of many earlier mystics. Scholars who have dealt closely with her autobiography and letters, though, have correctly noted their subversive claims. See, for example, Loskoutoff (85–8; 112–15), and Bruneau, "Le Projet autobiographique." Bruneau's later book discusses the question of Guyon's originality and the threat to the Church posed by her "democratization of mystical practices," *Women Mystics Confront the Modern World: Marie de l'Incarnation (1599–1672) and Madame Guyon (1648–1717)*, (Albany: State University of New York Press, 1998), pp. 135–66.

28.   Fénelon was one of a few ecclesiastical figures who had argued that women could be religious directors. Bossuet's victory in the debate over Quietism also marked an end to the possibility of women assuming this sort of role within the church. See Timmermans, 555–67.

29.   Fénelon's *Maximes des saints* was condemned in a papal brief of 1699. After this date, according to Le Brun, "all public expression of mystical tendencies was practically impossible in France" ("Quiétisme", 2838–9).

30.   For an example of a reading in this tradition see George Balsama, "Madame

Guyon, Heterodox", *Church History*, September 1973, 350–65. In *La Fable mystique*, Certeau situates Guyon at the end of a long tradition of mystics searching for a "pure", unmediated experience of communication (Paris: Gallimard, 1982), pp. 216–42.

31. ("plus proche et plus pressant que les enfants que j'ai portés dans mes entrailles.") Quoted in M. Masson, *Fénelon et Madame Guyon, documents nouveaux et inédits* (Paris: Hachette, 1907), p. 6. When she realized the use to which Bossuet was putting her autobiography, Guyon wrote her friend the Duke of Chevreuse asking him to tear out the pages describing her connection to Fénelon. This was done, but too late – Bossuet quoted liberally from this section in his *Relation sur le quiétisme*.

32. Guyon, *Récits de captivité*, ed. Gondal (Grenoble: Jérôme Millon, 1992).

33. Part III, ch. 20.

34. For a discussion of the different "publics" for the seventeenth-century woman writer, see Erica Harth, "The Salon Woman Goes Public, ... Or Does She?", in Elizabeth C. Goldsmith and Dena Goodman (eds), *Going Public: Women and Publishing in Early Modern France* (Ithaca: Cornell University Press, 1995), pp. 179–93.

35. The abbé de Bellegarde, for example, sponsored a notion of Christian community based on the ethic of sociability and *politesse*. See Daniel Gordon's discussion of Bellegarde in *Citizens Without Sovereignty: Equality and Sociability in French Thought, 1670–1789* (Princeton: Princeton University Press, 1994), pp. 122–6. Guyon's own written rules of interaction for her "*Confrérie du pur amour*" also are based on a blend of courtly and ecclesiastical codes of conduct. On this see Loskoutoff, 105–15.

36. See Le Brun, "Quiétisme", pp. 2840–42, and J. Orcibal, "L'Influence spirituelle de Fénelon dans les pays anglo-saxons du XVIIe siècle", *XVIIe siècle*, 12–14 (1951), pp. 276–87.

37. In "L'Autobiographie de Madame Guyon, (1648–1715): La découverte et l'apport de deux nouveaux manuscrits", Gondal presents evidence that Guyon may even have been preparing two different versions of the *Vie*, one for her friends and another for a larger public (*XVIIe siècle*, 164 (1989), p. 311). She points out, moreover, that the extant manuscript copies of the autobiography suggest that Guyon was more attentive to rewriting this text than any of her other works, and the process of revision did not cease until her death (320–21).

38. On the historical novelty of this strategy and its consequences see the remarks by Louis Cognet in *De la Dévotion moderne à la spiritualité française* (Paris: Fayard, 1958), pp. 112–13. He argues that Bossuet's insistence on linking Guyon's spiritual vocabulary to an assessment of her character and personal morals initiated a new way of attacking mysticism, and contributed to the subsequent impoverishment of mystical thought.

39. *Lettres chrétiennes et spirituelles* (London: n.p., 1768), vol. V, pp. 556–57. See extract on page 91 above ("Si jamais ces écrits tombent ...").

40. *The Mystic Fable*, trans. Michael B. Smith (Chicago: University of Chicago Press, 1992), p. 26.

41. See Kolakowski, p. 521; or Karl Juachim Weintraub, *The Value of the Individual: Self and Circumstance in Autobiography* (Chicago: University of Chicago Press, 1978), pp. 224–5.

CHAPTER FOUR

Scripting Errant Lives: The Memoirs of Hortense and Marie Mancini

Et de petits esprits vous nomment vagabonde
Quand vous allez régner en tous les lieux du monde.

Saint-Evremond

In many respects, there would seem to be little common ground for discussing the memoirs of Hortense and Marie Mancini with the spiritual outpourings of the three writers we have been studying. When Hortense and Marie Mancini are given a place in the history books it is under the category of Royal Mistress, and the celebrity they gained in their own lifetime came from their flamboyant neglect of the prescribed norms of virtuous conduct. But all of the women we are studying here undertook, for different reasons, the unusual step of presenting their lives to a public in the form of a written autobiography. With the single exception of the memoirs of Marguerite de Valois, published in the sixteenth century, the memoirs of Hortense and Marie Mancini, published in 1675 and 1677, are the first instances in France of women putting their life stories into print.[1] Their editors were male acquaintances who collaborated with them to circulate their writing; we might call them their 'literary' rather than 'spiritual' directors. All of these women lived for a time in convents. The space of the convent represented for all of them a paradoxical combination of refuge and intolerable restraint. All of them moved toward authorship first through letter writing, in an age when the letter was the single written form which women were encouraged to cultivate and at which they were expected to "naturally" excel. All of them traveled, too, and their voyages – both spiritual and physical – are invoked in their memoirs as compelling metaphors for both self-discovery and the entry into the world of writing, carrying particular meaning for women. Jeanne Guyon and Marie de l'Incarnation, like many of the women who influenced the development of Counter-Reformation devotional practices, launched their careers as writers and mystics only after being "freed" from their families by widowhood. Marie de Chantal, like her granddaughter in the secular sphere Marie de Sévigné, rediscovered and refashioned herself through writing after being widowed.

Early modern women who wrote more worldly accounts of their lives almost always did so only after similar breaks with their husbands, either through

98

Fig. 4.1   Hortense Mancini

Fig. 4.2   Marie Mancini Colonna

widowhood (La Guette) or, more frequently, separation (d'Aulnoy, Courcelles, Du Noyer, and both Mancinis).[2] By taking the bold step of being the first to commit their memoirs to print, Hortense and Marie Mancini were asserting not only their own right to defend their personal reputations, but also they were simply adding the printed words of women to the variety of discursive forms in which a public debate about marriage was being conducted. The life narratives written by Hortense and Marie Mancini were conceived and published as part of a complicated strategic conversation about the freedom of women to choose to live apart from their husbands, and about their ability to move freely in a cultural environment that was beginning to make anonymous travel possible for women. In the case of Marie Mancini, the extant archival material relating to her life is particularly rich. Thus we can trace how her private letter correspondence as well as her autobiography engaged in contemporary debates about marriage as a contract or a way of life, a legal obligation or a means to happiness. Her letters record, moreover, her own reflections and those of her correspondents on the project of committing her life narrative to print.

The judicious and judicial uses of memoirs

The two nieces of Cardinal Mazarin published their memoirs for very specific reasons, which both of them state in the first paragraph of their narratives. Printing their lives was a way of defending their reputation, by adding their voices to the clamor of accounts that were already being told, written, circulated, and published by others. Hortense's memoirs were published in 1675, just after she decided to leave France in order to escape her husband's efforts to force her to return to conjugal life. Marie published her own story two years later, while hiding in Madrid from her estranged husband, and after reading another printed memoir purporting to be her own. Both sisters recount awakening to the fact that the patronage ties that they had hoped would sustain them would not be enough to support their ambition to live independently. Their books represent an attempt to forge new links with a public – the public of their contemporaries, whose response will influence their immediate fates, as well as a more distant, unfamiliar public that will judge them for posterity. In Hortense's case, writing her story was initially an exercise in lobbying, in absentia, at the court and in Paris. Marie's memoirs were also used as part of an official dossier she submitted on her own behalf at the Spanish court in 1677. Both writers inserted their life stories into the public realm at moments when the viability of their existence as independent women was being determined by judicial and political authorities. These memoirs, and the manner in which they were first circulated, reflect a certain optimism about the future for wayward married women who were making the radical choice of separation.

The 1670s were important years for the evolution of marriage legislation in Europe, as well as for the history of women's participation in the literary sphere. Joan DeJean has written about the preoccupation with the possibility of divorce in the works of Madame de Lafayette and other novelists of the 1670s. As she points out, Colbert moved in the early part of the decade to claim for the crown the power to adjudicate cases involving marriage contracts. Optimism about the future for women who separated from their husbands or brought cases against them was prevalent in this period of relatively open discussion and fluidity in judicial protocol. This would change by the 1690s, when it had become more apparent that divorce would not be a viable choice for women under the absolute monarchy, and when Hortense's case was again publicly aired, this time contrary to her wishes.[3]

There are probably no women from the reign of Louis XIV whose private lives were more relentlessly on public view than were those of Cardinal Mazarin's nieces. Hortense Mancini became her uncle's principal heiress in 1660, when, at the age of 15, she agreed to the marriage he had arranged for her to the fanatically devout Armand de la Meilleraye. Although most observers viewed the choice as ridiculous (Madame de Sévigné and her friends, for example, would later amuse themselves by describing the spectacle of Cardinal Mazarin playing Orgon to Meilleraye's Tartuffe), initially Mazarin must have believed in Meilleraye's integrity, for he inserted in the marriage contract the unusual stipulation that both Hortense and her husband would assume the family name Mazarin. The new Duc de Mazarin was further given sole control of his wife's dowry, a significant share of the cardinal's large fortune. For the next 30 years the public was treated to accounts of this disastrous union through letters, gazette notices, published court proceedings, real and false memoirs, and character portraits.

Hortense ran away from her husband in 1668 to live for a time in Rome with her sister Marie. Marie Mancini's own exposure to publicity had begun with her affair with the young Louis XIV in 1660, just prior to his marriage to the Spanish Infanta, and continued after she left Rome to embark on a series of journeys with Hortense, in search of provincial or foreign courts where they would be permitted to live apart from their husbands. Hortense settled at the court of the duke of Savoy in 1672, then moved to London in 1675 where for 24 years she was prominently engaged in court society and politics. Marie's itinerant life-style ended only with the death of her husband, Lorenzo Colonna, in 1689.

Just how outrageous their behavior was may be gauged in part by the commentary it received, but also by the two husbands' persistent efforts to force their wives to return. Armand de Mazarin pursued every possible legal avenue, appealing to family and king and finally, more than 20 years after Hortense's departure, to the Parlement of Paris in a highly publicized case.

Colonna was not so scrupulous. He had his wife followed and on one occasion kidnapped and imprisoned by his private agents. Armand showed a similar, if more restrained, determination: he not only retained Hortense's dowry, but also threatened to restrict her freedom of movement by having her confined to a convent or prison if she refused to return to him.[4]

Following Hortense and Marie's "adventures", as the events of their lives came to be called, was a favorite pastime for those who stayed at court or who maintained contact with it through letters. Moreover, in their own published memoirs the sisters discuss the publicity they had generated and comment on its consequences. In deciding to assume themselves the task of committing their lives to print, they took a step that, for women, was unprecedented. It is not surprising, then, that the Mancinis begin their memoirs defensively. Hortense indicates in her opening sentence that she knew she was playing a dangerous game, but, she asserts, it is one that has been thrust upon her by circumstances:

> ... si les choses que j'ai à vous raconter vous semblent beaucoup tenir du roman, accusez-en ma mauvaise destinée, plutôt que mon inclination. Je sais que la gloire d'une femme consiste à ne faire point parler d'elle; et ceux qui me connaissent savent assez que toutes les choses d'éclat ne me plaisent point: mais on ne choisit pas toujours le genre de vie qu'on voudrait mener, et il y a de la fatalité dans les choses mêmes qui semblent dépendre le plus de la conduite.[5]

> (If the things I am about to tell you seem to come out of a novel, blame my destiny rather than my inclination ... I know that a woman's good name [*gloire*] depends on her not being talked about; and those who know me also know that display pleases me not at all. But one does not always choose the kind of life one would like to lead, and fate is to be found even in those things that seem to most depend on conduct.)

By invoking destiny and fate, Hortense suggests that publishing her story is the inevitable next step in the sequence of events that has caught her up. Furthermore, she stipulates that she is presenting her story to comply with the request of an unnamed benefactor who has indicated he expects her to defend herself against gossip or *médisance*. That she is telling her own, personal story, though, she leaves no doubt, and she does not make the conventional claim of a memoir writer that she is presenting her life simply to contribute to the historical record.[6]

René Démoris has remarked that one of the most innovative features of Hortense Mancini's memoirs is that they read more like a novel than a historical account.[7] Indeed, her story, as well as her manner of telling it, bears comparison with a work of fiction published in 1672 by Hortense's friend Marie-Catherine Desjardins, also known as Madame de Villedieu.[8] The heroine of her novel *Mémoires de la vie de Henriette-Sylvie de Molière* narrates a picaresque tale of her adventures alternately on the road and behind the walls of convents and castles. She makes regular forays out into the world to hear what others are saying about her, and attempts to correct her public image whenever she can. Madame de Villedieu knew the difficulty of this task only too well from her own life, as well as from observing the experience of others, particularly her friend the Duchess of Mazarin. Villedieu had dedicated her first published work to the Duchess, and she wrote the fictional memoir (of a woman whose initials were also H.M.) during the years immediately following Hortense's flight from her fanatical husband.

Villedieu's novel was published in six parts between 1671 and 1674. In 1675 Hortense Mancini published her own life story. If Villedieu had modeled her fictional heroine on Hortense's life, Hortense in turn seems to be aware of the novelistic cast to her own life. The plot devices – disguise, repeated flight, male protection – that get Villedieu's heroine out of trouble, however, don't work in Hortense's real story, which is infused with the rhetoric of testimony or legal deposition. She recounts how she and her sister traveled all over Europe looking for a court that would allow them to remain and live protected from their husbands. But, unlike a heroine of fairy tale or novel, they found no doors open to them, and inevitably resumed their clandestine travels, often in male disguises which, Hortense pointedly notes, never fooled anyone.

The genesis and even the authorship of Hortense's memoirs has been debated over the centuries. It is clear that the text was written while Hortense was residing in Chambéry, under the protection of the Duke of Savoy. From 1664 to the end of 1665, the Savoyard novelist and "man of letters" César de Saint-Réal was also at the Chambéry court. Contemporary accounts document their friendship and Saint-Réal's infatuation with Hortense, and it has generally been thought that Saint-Réal had a hand in the composition and publishing of Hortense's story.[9] Indeed, from 1722 through the nineteenth century her autobiography was alternately published as part of the complete works of Saint-Réal, or with the works of Saint-Evremond, who frequented her salon in England. Neither of these writers ever claimed to have either authored or edited the work. There is in fact no contemporary documentation to confirm that the two collaborated on it. This is particularly significant given the fact that Hortense's activities and social contacts in Chambéry were meticulously recorded, by the keeper of the Chambéry castle, who sent daily letters reporting her movements to Duke Emmanuel in Torino. In all of these reports Saint-Réal is mentioned only once.[10] The English translation of Hortense's memoirs, published in 1676 immediately after her arrival in London, is prefaced by a letter, bearing the signature "P. Porter", bringing readers up to date concerning the reasons for Hortense's departure from Chambéry and her reception at the court of Charles II.[11] In 1677 an Italian translation appeared, prefaced by yet another letter responding to the English one, and with the author identified only as "a gentleman in the entourage of the Duchess Mazarin".[12]

While nothing about these editions can indicate with any certainty that

Saint-Réal participated in the writing of the memoirs, what they do establish is a manner of presenting her life story to the public stressing her contacts with a circle of male "protectors" and admirers. Appended to all three editions is an anonymous portrait of Hortense describing the seductive appeal of her speech and conversation, and her ability to sustain a mobile salon as she moved from one social space to another across great distances.[13] Presenting themselves as advocates of Hortense Mazarin as well as insiders with accurate information about the character and motivations of a woman who was the subject of intense public scrutiny, the authors of the portrait and liminal letters serve as editorial escorts, directing the reader as to how to interpret Hortense's personal voice.

It seems most likely that Saint-Réal's role in the publication of Hortense's memoirs was that of an editor or secretary in a position to assist her in the preparation of a manuscript, a fairly conventional role for an *homme de lettres* of the period to play for any aristocratic writer whose formal education might well have been inadequate. We can establish that he assisted her in the original distribution of the manuscript in December 1675, by acting as her advocate in Paris and at Louis XIV's court, and using the newly written memoirs to support her position. In the meantime Hortense had been forced to leave Chambéry after the death of her protector Charles-Emmanuel de Savoie. She arrived in London in January 1676, where Saint-Réal soon joined her.

At the time of their first circulation, then, Hortense Mancini used her memoirs as a legal *mémoire*, to advocate for herself in her conflict with the Duc de Mazarin. One meaning of the word *mémoire* is a judicial memoir, a narrative presented to a judge or lawyer by the concerned party in a legal case.[14] Hortense's narrative blends the rhetorical style of a novel with that of a legal deposition, itemizing grievances and countering accusations that had been made against her.[15] She details a series of earlier attempts she had made to obtain a favorable hearing before two different courts and the king. Clearly, she thought she had a chance to win authorization to live separately and recover her dowry. After her two appeals failed, she recapitulated her defense in her printed memoirs.

In the opening pages of her story, Hortense offers a candid description of her indulged youth at the French court, as the favored niece of Jules Mazarin. She is explicit on the subject of her debt to him – she owes him her "fortune", in both senses of the word. It was he who, though exasperated with her lack of discipline and religious devotion, chose her as the vehicle by which he would assure the continuity of his family name. She describes her betrothal and marriage as the result of crude market negotiations, with her future husband offering the biggest bribe to Cardinal Mazarin's confidant:

> Le désir d'éterniser son nom l'emporta sur l'indignation qu'il avait conçue contre moi. Il s'en ouvrit à l'évêque de Fréjus, et lui demanda son avis sur plusieurs partis qu'il avait dans l'esprit. L'évêque, gagné par M. Mazarin [Armand]

moyennant une promesse de cinquante mille écus, n'oublia rien pour les mériter. … Aussitôt que le mariage fut conclu, il [Cardinal Mazarin] m'envoya un grand cabinet, où entre autres nippes, il y avait dix mille pistoles en or. (39)

(The desire to eternalize his name overcame the indignation that he had formed against me. He confided to the bishop of Fréjus about it, and asked him his opinion of several matches that he had in mind. The bishop, won over by M. Mazarin [Armand], based on a promise of fifty thousand écus, spared no effort to earn them. … As soon as the marriage was concluded, he [Cardinal Mazarin] sent me a large cabinet, containing, among other baubles, ten thousand gold pistoles.)

Hortense's husband, the new M. Mazarin, inherited her uncle's *"rigueur"* along with his wealth. In her detailing of the trials of this unwanted marriage, Hortense stresses Armand's hatred of the social circles she frequented in Paris, and his insistence that she perpetually travel with him to his provincial properties. She was ashamed to admit to friends, she writes, the extent of his paranoia:

Qu'eussent-ils dit, s'ils eussent su que je ne pouvais parler à un domestique, qu'il ne fût chassé le lendemain, … si je demandais mon carrosse et qu'il ne jugeât pas à propos de me laisser sortir, il défendait en riant qu'on y mît les chevaux, et plaisantait avec moi sur cette défense, jusqu'à ce que l'heure d'aller où je voulais aller fût passée? Il aurait voulu que je n'eusse vu que lui seul dans le monde; surtout il ne pouvait souffrir que je visse ses parents ni les miens … (43).

(What would they have said, if they had known that I couldn't speak to a servant, without him being fired the next day, … that if I asked for my carriage and he did not deem it proper to let me go out, he would, laughing, forbid the harnessing of horses to it, and he would tease me about his order until the hour had passed in which I had intended to go out? … He would have wanted himself to be the only person in the world that I could see; above all he could not stand for me to see either his family or my own …)

After itemizing at length the abuse she has suffered, though she knew such details would not be enough to grant her a legal *séparation de biens*, Hortense makes the claim that she says is the most crucial one, namely that her deranged husband was dissipating the fortune that Cardinal Mazarin had bequeathed him, thus destroying her children's inheritance.[16] That her own right to her dowry was inalienable was uncertain, but her son's right to his inheritance was more likely to be supported by law.[17] This, then, is the angle she stresses.

The sequence of events that Hortense next lays out for her readers constitutes in itself a fascinating study of the instability of marriage legislation in the 1660s and 1670s, particularly in the standards governing marital separations. Before she finally decided to flee, Hortense had obtained a favorable hearing from one lower court which had granted her request to live apart from her husband, to obtain records of his financial affairs, and to receive financial support from him while these records were being examined (*Mémoires*, 56–7). Armand de Mazarin meanwhile obtained a hearing from a higher court, which in turn was interrupted when the king himself decided to intervene with a directive permitting Mazarin to continue to reside with his wife in the Palais Mazarin, but in a separate apartment. The issue of the *séparation de biens* was redirected for judgment by the king's ministers (*Mémoires*, 57). When Mazarin decided that he did not in fact wish to observe the separate living arrangement, Hortense agreed to an annulment of the king's directive, provided that the case be resubmitted to the judges of the *grande chambre*. Finally, when Hortense learned that the judges were preparing to decide against her and require that she resume conjugal life with Mazarin, she abandoned her legal efforts and fled.[18]

Looking back on her dramatic escape seven years later, Hortense describes it as a move from the judicial realm into an implausible, new world. With her departure she abandoned the waiting strategy she had been counseled to follow by her legal advisors and friends. For this new role she could hope to find sympathetic models only in fiction. Observers stressed the extraordinary nature of her move, while expressing some excitement at its romanesque qualities. Madame de Grignan, who greeted the refugees upon their arrival in Marseilles, seemed to enjoy playing a role in this unprecedented plot. She remarked that Hortense and Marie "voyageaient en vraies héroines de roman, avec force pierreries, et point de linge blanc" (*Mémoires*, 86) (... were travelling as true heroines of a novel, with plenty of jewels and no clean clothes). But while Hortense is aware of the unprecedented, and thus "*invraisemblable*" nature of her predicament, she is interested in calling attention to plausible happy endings, legally sustainable solutions to her case that would offer hope to other women and vindicate her own claims. Her memoirs close on a hopeful, if humble, note, alluding to her benefactor and suggesting that his protection may provide her with a safe haven in Chambéry, "où j'ai enfin trouvé le repos que je cherchais ..." (87) (where I finally found the repose that I was seeking).

Rewriting Hortense's life

Soon after Hortense Mazarin's memoirs appeared in print, her husband announced his intentions to publish his own version of events in response. Although he desisted in his plans for his own publication, his pursuit of Hortense via both legal and diplomatic channels continued unabated until finally, in 1689, he decided to bring a legal suit against her to force her to return to France and resume conjugal life, after more than twenty years of separation. He engaged the eloquent lawyer Claude Erard to represent him in his suit, and then authorized the publication of Erard's court briefs. Erard was already known for his successes in prosecuting wayward aristocratic women, and the texts of his arguments received a wide readership.[19] This was the final public forum for Hortense Mazarin's life story. Her husband was determined to make

PLAIDOYEZ

TOUCHANT LA DEMANDE

FAITE PAR MONSIEUR

LE DUC DE MAZARIN

pour obliger Madame la Ducheſſe de
Mazarin ſon Epouſe de revenir avec
luy, aprés une longue abſence, & de
quitter l'Angleterre où elle eſt preſente-
ment.

*Avec l'Arreſt intervenu le 29. Decembre 1689.
ſur ces Plaidoyez.*

A TOULOUSE,
De l'Imprimerie de J. J. BOUDE, Imprimeur du Roy, de Monſeigneur
le Duc de Noailles, des Eſtats de la Province de Languedoc, de la Cour,
de l'Univerſité, du Clergé, des Eſtats de Foix & des Monnoyes.

Avec Permiſſion.

Fig. 4.3   Title-page of pamphlet reproducing arguments presented in Mazarin's suit to force his wife's return

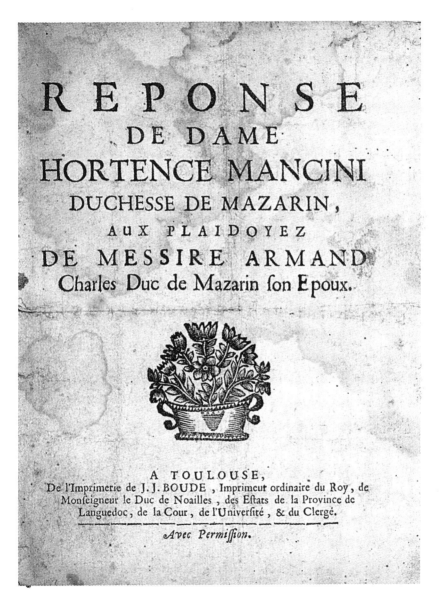

Fig. 4.4   Title-page of pamphlet presenting Hortense Mancini's response to her husband

it impossible for her to inherit their wealth (including her dowry) after his death. In order to accomplish this disinheritance, Mazarin had either to prove that his wife had committed adultery or that she had no grounds to divorce him.[20]

Hortense had never accused her husband of extreme physical cruelty, which would have been grounds for a divorce. In her memoirs she asserts only that she had wanted to protect her children's estate from being totally dissipated by her husband. But Erard used the case to articulate a broad definition of a husband's authority over his wife. He argued that Hortense had violated her obligations to her husband in two respects: first, by traveling alone to many different countries and courts (here he also insinuated that she was disloyal to France and the Catholic church), and second, by establishing a residence and style of life in England in which she consorted with men to whom she was not related.

In England, the flight of James II in 1688 had made Hortense vulnerable, for it meant the loss of the pension and the protection that he and Charles II before him had accorded her. For ten years she had presided over a "French" salon in London frequented by illustrious expatriates as well as leading British political and intellectual figures. She had maintained a delicate web of social ties with both a French and an English public (while also, it seems, becoming a mistress of Charles II). Her salon in St James's Palace had become a prestigious meeting ground for the elite society of two nations which at the time were on very bad terms. Her most vocal ally in this French circle, Saint-Evremond, was inspired by Hortense's predicament to write his most impassioned satirical attacks on the institution of marriage. Mary Astell, the English philosopher and champion of women's emancipation, in 1700 published a pamphlet entitled "Some Reflections upon Marriage, Occasioned by the Duke and Duchess of Mazarine's case, which is also considered".

Correspondence between the French court and the ambassador to England in the late 1670s and early 1680s records the latter's efforts to engage Hortense as a spy for France. Ruvigny, the ambassador to England at the time of Hortense's arrival, suggested, unsuccessfully, that Colbert obtain a pension for her. The French ambassador to England wrote letters to Colbert, warning that she might well become the mistress of Charles II, that her animosity for the French government was dangerous, and that she should be granted whatever terms she demanded to return to France. In a letter to Louis XIV he wrote:

[The King of England] assured us that he will not be won over. But she is beautiful. ... All those closest to him talk only of her merits. It will be very difficult for him to resist temptation much longer, and moreover it will be very dangerous to have to fight the minister and the mistress at the same time. ... The best thing would be for her to cross the sea again. It matters little to Your Majesty that she not sleep with M. Mazarin, and that she be given fifty thousand francs, but it matters a great deal to you that in the meantime England not join your enemies.[21]

In the brief presented to the court in Paris on behalf of Armand de Mazarin, Erard described Hortense's famous salon as a "public academy of gambling".[22] Although this highly visible life led apart from her husband did not prove her an adulteress, said Erard, it generated the suspicion that she was one, and this appearance of infidelity in itself constituted a derogation of her right to her dowry:

> La raison pour laquelle on impose à la femme cette peine pour ces continuels repas parmi les hommes qui ne lui sont point parens, et toutes ces courses nocturnes, de même que dans le cas d'adultère, est que si les dérèglements ne font pas contre elle une preuve entière de débauche, ils emportent au moins un violent soupçon, et qu'il ne suffit pas pour l'intérêt du mari que la femme soit exempt de crime: il faut encore qu'elle ne donne pas sujet de la *croire* criminelle.[23]

> (The reason that we wish to impose on the woman this punishment for the continual meals with men who are not her relatives, for all those nocturnal travels, just as we would in the case of adultery, is that while these disorderly behaviors [*dérèglements*] do not establish proof positive of debauchery, they nonetheless provoke a strong suspicion of it. In the husband's interest, it is not enough that his wife be exempt of the crime: it is further necessary that she not give reason to *believe* her a criminal.)

Erard seems to be responding here to the written portrait drawn by Hortense's most outspoken admirer, Saint-Evremond, who in 1684 had published an assessment of her life in the form of a funeral oration (which she had asked him to write, he said, so that she could imagine how people would talk about her after her death). In it he describes her as the consummate *salonnière*, able to create and preside over the same social space wherever she happens to be. Saint-Evremond made of her itinerant life-style a philosophical virtue. By creating a world for herself that was essentially movable, he wrote, she had exercised her right to freedom and showed others the kind of society that such freedom generates.[24]

Supportive views of Hortense's position in London were also expressed in contemporary letters by observers on the other side of the English Channel. Mazarin's acquaintances tried to persuade him to provide his wife with the means to leave London and live on her own, in France. Madame de Sévigné records one such effort and her own revulsion upon setting eyes on the deranged man, noting that while Hortense's choice to remain in England was politically and personally risky, her husband's irrational behavior justified her refusal to return to him.[25]

While Hortense's defenders suggested that simply laying eyes on the disturbed husband was enough to persuade anyone of her right to divorce, the judges who ultimately ruled in favor of Armand de Mazarin based their decision on textual arguments alone. As was the custom, testimony and arguments on both sides were not presented orally, but were submitted for judicial review as written dossiers. The pamphlet publishing the arguments of Hortense's lawyer in the 1689 trial shows that her memoirs were in fact introduced as part of this written testimony, evidence against her, and contrary to her wishes.[26] In 1689, 14 years after her memoirs were first printed, Hortense no longer considered it advantageous to her case to have them circulated.

Nadine Berenguier's work on published court cases from the early 1700s shows how quickly the business of a woman's written personal testimony, in cases brought against husbands or fathers, came to be viewed as invariably counter-productive. Their lawyers learned to develop rhetorical strategies that stressed each woman's exceptionality, thus fending off any suspicion that their clients were claiming solidarity with other women or making any arguments for women's emancipation in general. In Hortense's case, Mazarin's lawyer Erard apparently held the autobiography in reserve for his counter-attack after her own lawyer Sachot had submitted his narrative of Hortense's motives for wanting a separation from her husband. It is clear that Erard felt cocky about the strength of his position; he mocks Sachot's lack of preparedness, and in particular his failure to produce new *mémoires* in the form of written statements from Hortense. This, together with Hortense's absence, was enough to put Sachot at a disadvantage. Erard uses the story that Hortense had published fourteen years earlier to contradict her lawyer's statements: "Vous deviez vous accorder avec les Mémoires publics de Madame de Mazarin, puisque vous avouez que vous n'en avez point eu d'elle de particuliers, ..." (p. 36). (You should have held to what is said in the public Memoirs of Madame de Mazarin, since you admit that you have no other private ones from her ...).

Erard cites long passages from the printed memoirs in his brief, taking obvious glee in quoting Hortense's voice from those moments when she is being the least dignified or respectful of authority. He dismisses Sachot's presentation of some of Hortense's letters as evidence of her desperate financial situation, arguing that they were specially written for the court occasion, for they were not written in the same style as Hortense's published book:

> ... le stile même dont ces Lettres sont écrites, et que vous voulez faire trouver si naturel, est encore une preuve qu'elles ont été écrites de commande. Quand Mme Mazarin écrit naturellement et que c'est son coeur qui parle, elle écrit incomparablement mieux que ces Lettres ne le font ... (48).

> (... even the style in which these letters are written, and which you want to see as so natural, is one more proof that they were written to order. When Mme Mazarin writes naturally, speaking from the heart, she writes incomparably better than these letters do ...)

Erard's opening argument and his counter-argument to Hortense's defense were published together in pamphlet format in 1690, immediately after the trial and the decision that was handed down in favor of the duc de Mazarin. Sachot's defense of Hortense was not printed until much later, after Saint-Evremond had published, in 1696, his belated *Factum pour Madame la Duchesse Mazarin contre Monsieur le Duc Mazarin son Mari*. When it came to responding to the citations Erard had lifted from Hortense's autobiography, her lawyer argued that these memoirs represented a particular perspective from a particular moment in time, relying on information that their author had been able to correct or supplement since the first publication of the text:

> On ne répond point à quelques endroits que le Playdoyé a tirez d'un livre intitulé *Les Mémoires de Madame Mazarin*, ... parce que cet ouvrage est mêlé de ce qu'elle scavoit & de ce qu'elle avoit oublié, & qu'elle a souvent cru de bonne foy les avis dont on luy faisoit confidence, & qui n'estoient que trahison. (43)

> (We will not respond to those citations made from the book entitled *The Memoirs of Madame Mazarin*, ... because this work is a blend of what she knew and what she had forgotten; and she often believed on good faith the statements that were confided to her and that were in fact betrayals.)

Sachot argues that the book should not be viewed as having a special claim to immutable truth, but rather that it represented her remembrance and feelings at a specific time, as well as the testimony of others, some of which Hortense had since learned was false. Hortense's unwillingness to provide her spokesperson with more written testimonials further suggests that she had learned to be wary of how her written words might be appropriated. Sachot attacks the duc de Mazarin for not exhibiting a similar reluctance to further the publication of their marital disaster, while Armand de Mazarin argued that Hortense's vagabond life was in itself a form of scandalous publication:

> il [Mazarin] reproche à Madame sa femme qu'elle a promené leur honte en divers climats, & il la répand partout d'une manière qui ne doit estre borné ni par le temps ni par les lieux; Qu'a-t-il prétendu dans l'impression d'un ouvrage si scandaleux, ...? (44)

> (He reproaches his wife with having paraded their shame through various climates, and yet he spreads it everywhere in a way that will never be limited by either time or place; What was he attempting by printing such a scandalous work ...?)

The court, of course, had already been persuaded by the rhetorical force of Erard's arguments, in particular his appeal to the integrity of marriage as an institution. Hortense's story, he claimed, was not simply one particular life, but a case with generalizable, public significance, that would influence the morals of the French:

> C'est ici une affaire toute publique où vous devez, messieurs, considérer l'intérêt de la discipline autant et plus que celui des parties: vous avez à décider non pas simplement entre Monsieur et Madame de Mazarin de leurs intérests particuliers, mais entre l'honnesteté publique d'un côté, et l'inclination de Madame de Mazarin de l'autre; c'est à vous de voir si vous voulez sacrifier la première aux vaines délicatesses de la dernière, ou pour mieux dire à ses erreurs et à ses

caprices. Votre arrest est attendu dans le public comme un exemple mémorable qui maintiendra la discipline et les droits du mariage, ou qui autorisera le relâchement et la licence; qui rompra les barrières et qui ouvrira le champ à une infinité de femmes mondaines et emportées, ou qui les retiendra dans leur devoir. (55)

(This is a very public matter, Sirs, in which you must consider the interests of order as much and indeed more than that of the parties: you must decide not only between Monsieur and Madame de Mazarin on their particular interests, but between public honesty on the one hand, and the desires of Madame de Mazarin on the other; it is up to you to see if you wish to sacrifice the first to the vain tastes of the second, or rather to her errors and whims. The public awaits your decision as a memorable example that will maintain discipline and the rights of marriage, or one which will authorize laxity and permissiveness; one which will break down the barriers and open the field to an infinite number of worldly and excessive women, or one which will hold them to their duty.)

In his own published counter-argument to Erard, Saint-Evremond seemed to realize that Erard's position against Hortense was also an attack against salon society. Like Sachot, he stresses Hortense's reluctance to republish herself in any way, and he does not even mention her printed memoirs. He begins his statement by reminding his readers that it was Hortense's *husband* who had decided to go public with their private affairs and he satirizes Erard's notion of mixed society. He agrees with Erard that Hortense's predicament is emblematic of a larger social problem, but for him the problem is the tyranny of husbands. He uses the case to propose his own egalitarian definition of marriage, wherein the first duty of each party is to her or his self-preservation. Saint-Evremond's defense of Hortense took its place within his other published treatises arguing for egalitarian social reforms, in marriage practices as well as more broadly defined rights of citizens. Hortense Mazarin's case became an exemplary illustration of "natural" law which granted women the right to leave a tyrannical (or insane) husband.[27]

Thus once again in her lifetime Hortense's life was published, but now it was clearly situated, to her own private detriment, within a larger public debate about women's autonomy in the public sphere. When she refused to comply with the court's order that she return to France and to her husband's house, she permanently lost her claim to her dowry and spent the next ten years until her death in 1699 trying to keep her creditors at bay. Even after her death her husband pursued her, fighting another bizarre legal battle, this time with her creditors over her cadaver. Although he had refused to pay for passage to France while she was alive, he did pay to get her body back, and then proceeded to travel with it for a year to all of his properties in France before finally permitting his wife to be buried next to her famous uncle. With this final strange voyage Mazarin seemed to be ensuring that he would have the last word on the issue that had so vexed both of them – that of Hortense's right to move about freely or, alternatively, to choose to remain in Paris rather than be forced to accompany her husband on his tours of his provincial properties.

Marie Mancini's strategic publications

In 1676, one year after the appearance of Hortense's memoirs in print, an apocryphal autobiography of Marie was published under the same fictitious imprint as Hortense's real memoirs.[28] Marie was in Madrid, and when she read this scandalous printed account of her life that claimed to be her own, she recognized immediately that it would be a major setback in her battle for personal freedom. The fictitious memoirs described both sisters as pathetically unable to avert the disastrous consequences of public self-exposure. For Marie, they posed another challenge to her efforts to retain control of her reputation in the face of gossip or *médisance*.

The unknown author of this memoir attributes to Marie a motive for publishing which simultaneously accentuates her haughtiness and her vulnerability: she is presented as a noble lady confiding the truth to satisfy the "curiosity" of an exclusive group of readers who "have sympathy for the disaster of an unhappy lady such as I" (9). The printer's preface further makes it clear that he is publishing this text as a kind of sequel to Hortense's memoirs, which at the same time will show the public how to read that earlier text. What Hortense left out or lied about is supposedly corrected, but in such a way as to undermine the narrator's claim to dignity and honor. Hortense had cast herself as a novelistic heroine overwhelmed by the *médisants* and by material reality. Marie's impersonator goes on to accomplish exactly what he states he will not do at the outset: portray the "real" life of the sisters as exactly what it was claimed to be by their detractors, and thus showing the *médisants* to be right after all.[29]

When a copy of this memoir reached Marie in Madrid, she immediately decided to publish her own story. Marie's autobiography first appeared in 1677 under the unambiguous title *La Vérité dans son jour, ou les véritables mémoires de M. Mancini, Connétable Colonne*.[30] Like her sister, Marie declares in her opening paragraphs that she is writing to protect her reputation. But unlike the other memoir writers, she does not claim to be responding to pressure from a gentleman wishing to clear her name, nor does she say she is writing for a circumscribed audience of friends and peers. Neither, extraordinarily, does she make the conventional gesture of asking for protection for herself or her book. The preliminary pages of the text consist of poems and epigrams dedicated to the author and praising her skills as a writer. Marie begins her own prefatory remarks with an attack on writers who exploit public figures by printing gossipy stories about them:

... en France, ... ces sortes de libelles que la malice produit contre la réputation de notre sexe, avec un cours et un applaudissement qu'ils ne méritent point, passent pour des galanteries de cour ... [Quand] on m'écrivit de France qu'il courait une histoire de ma vie, qu'on supposait avoir été écrite par moi-même ... cette nouvelle m'inspira d'abord quelque curiosité de voir ce livre; et par la lecture que j'en fis, l'indignation que j'eus d'abord d'une pareille nouveauté se changea en un très grand mépris que méritait un tel auteur. Je ne dirai point pour ceux qui me connaissent que dans cette prétendue histoire il n'y a point d'incident qui ne soit supposé, qui ne soit aussi contraire à mon humeur qu'à la vérité ... Mais comme tous ceux qui ne me connaissent pas, pourraient se laisser prévenir à de pareilles impressions, j'ai cru qu'il était de mon devoir d'aller au-devant de ce qui pourrait faire tort à ma réputation, en donnant moi-même une relation sincère et véritable de tout ce qui m'est arrivé depuis mes jeunes années, à qui les pressantes instances de plusieurs personnes de qualité, qui sont intéressées à ce qui me touche, m'ont engagée. (*Vérité*, 33)

([In France], libels which have as their object to spread calumny and blacken the reputation of those of my sex, sell very well, and go under the name of "gallant pieces." ... [When] I received word from France that a book about my life was circulating, and under my name, I was very curious to see it. Since I have read it my initial annoyance and indignation has changed to the utmost scorn for the author. I do not need to tell those who know me that there is not one adventure in it that is not fabricated and as completely contrary to my character as it is to the truth ... But as there are people who, because they do not know me, might be likely to believe these allegations [*impressions*], I decided that I must anticipate the wrong that they could do me by myself giving to the public a sincere and true account of all that has befallen me since my tender years. I was further encouraged to do this by the pressing insistence of various people who are interested, out of duty or friendship, in all that relates to me.)

In contrast to both her sister and her impersonator, Marie makes no apologies for going into print. Her stated ambition is not only to clear her name with other "persons of quality", but also to reach a wider public of readers extending beyond her own social milieu, a public that she sees snapping up subversive and titillating accounts of the private lives of court figures.[31] Moreover, in telling her life story Marie repeatedly contrasts her narrative with the false memoirs and, more obliquely, with Hortense's account. Whereas Hortense presents both herself and her text as vulnerable, Marie sees herself as resistant to her misfortunes. And whereas Hortense had foregrounded the failures in her life's plot, portraying herself as overwhelmed by events, Marie foregrounds her own resilient character and shows how her experiences have shaped and strengthened it. The central event in both women's stories is their flight from their husbands, but in contrast to Hortense, Marie declares herself unrepentant as well as immune to the damaging consequences of her actions.

The apocryphal *Mémoires de M.L.P.M.M.C.* had closed on the picture of Marie plotting, like a prisoner in a dungeon, to flee the convent by digging a hole through the wall of her cell:

Je songe à tous moments comment je pourrai me sauver de ce couvent; les murailles en sont épaisses, et la situation très difficile: cependant j'ai dessein de suivre l'exemple du comte de Lauzun, qui a creusé à Pignerol deux ans entiers pour se sauver, ... Si je peux venir à bout de ce dessein, comme j'espère, vous saurez ce que je deviendrai. (208)

(I am perpetually thinking of how I could escape from this convent; the walls are thick, and the location very difficult. Still, I intend to follow the example of the count of Lauzun, who dug for two whole years at Pignerol in order to escape ... If I can realize this plan, as I hope to, you will know what becomes of me.)

This representation of herself seems to have particularly angered Marie. In her own account she takes pains to describe precisely how she had made her exits from within the convent walls, and to assert that her sojourns there were freely chosen. In fact, she suggests that her departure was precipitated by reading her impersonator's account – she left to show his script of her life to be false:

[J'ai pris] la resolution de sortir du couvent, pour faire voir que les soins à me garder ne m'y tiendraient enfermée qu'autant et si longtemps que je voudrais, et un jour que D. Ferdinand était sorti avec tous mes gens, je fis ouvrir en un instant et par mes filles, ces "fortes", ces "épaisses" et ces "hautes" murailles que l'auteur de mon histoire dit avoir été l'unique obstacle à ma fuite. (*Vérité*, 87)

(I resolved to leave the convent to show that efforts to keep me locked up there would work only so as long as I wanted them to, and one day when Don Ferdinand had gone out with my servants I had my maids open in an instant those "strong", those "heavy", and those "high" walls that the author of my story says were the only obstacle to my escape.)

Here as elsewhere in her text Marie mocks the melodrama of the apocryphal autobiography, and in her own version she makes no coy asides to the reader ("I don't know if I should tell you") of the sort that characterize the earlier narrative. Both the title of her book and the prefatory poems that were included in its first edition play on the idea that she is bringing her story into the open, out of the shadows of error and into the light of truth. She makes liberal use of proper names, direct quotations, and discussions of herself as a real, physical being.

Like Hortense's escape from the Duc de Mazarin, Marie's flight from her husband in 1673 had quickly engaged public attention, but in Marie's case the political ramifications were much more complicated. The Colonna family was the highest-ranking aristocratic family in Rome, with close ties to the Vatican as well as to the courts of France and Spain. Lorenzo Onofrio Colonna was quick to enlist diplomats at the highest levels in the project of forcing his wife's return, or at the least making it difficult for her to find protection at foreign courts. Letters in the Colonna family archives record incessant conversations and negotiations precipitated by Marie's audacious move, which surprised even her closest friends. Members of the Mancini family, including Hortense and her brother Phillipe de Nevers, who had both joined Marie in her flight, were quick to disassociate themselves from her decision and wrote letters to Colonna assuring him of their loyalty and promising to press for Marie's return. The particularly obsequious letters from the Duc de Mazarin, whose dismal status of abandoned husband Lorenzo Onofrio now shared, suggest that Mazarin, like other onlookers, viewed the situation as an opportunity to curry favor, a chance to cultivate potentially fruitful ties with the house of Colonna.[32] Marie, too, wrote letters to her husband every few days, messages at first attempting to negotiate an understanding that would permit her to live independently and in France, with the authorization of the king. She was quickly, and bitterly, disappointed, as she testifies in her autobiography and as the extant letters from Louis XIV and his envoys document. But her correspondence with her husband persisted, until Colonna's death in 1689. Although her letters home amount to a chronology of personal defeats, she never stopped repeating in them her refusal to return to Rome. Echoing throughout this correspondence as well as in her letters to friends in Rome is her acute awareness of the reports about her being circulated by others, in letters, conversations, or gazettes. She was painfully aware of the limited control that she had over the gossip that was reaching her husband and the public, but with a determination that amazed her contemporaries and continues to mystify historians, she responded to the attacks by accelerating rather than slowing her own fugitive itinerary and by exploiting all possible means of vocal and scribal self-defense.

In the first letter she wrote to Colonna after leaving him, Marie put her proposal very forthrightly, and it is a demand that she would continue to make, albeit more defensively, over the years: she wants to be permitted to live alone. Her first letter to him even puts it hopefully; "Have no doubt", she writes,

> I will always be happy to accept any kindness you choose to show me. Always, from wherever I am, you will hear good accounts of my conduct and my person, and I will prove to you that my resolution was not capricious, but rather by this act I have tried to satisfy my soul and live calmly [*quieta*] for the rest of my days.[33]

Very quickly, though, she would be confronted with the full impact of Colonna's impressive political clout and she would be forced to acknowledge the impossibility, or at least implausibility, of her ambition. Her requests become more specific, incremental. In letters to her friend Hortense Stella, in Rome, she confesses her dismay with the tone of Colonna's letters:

> Monsieur le Connétable n'a pas lieu de se plaindre ni de moi ni de ma conduite. Il m'a écrit une lettre si froide et si soutenue par mon frère que je n'ay pas eu le courage d'y répondre; je suis cependant dans un couvent comme Madame Mazarin luy avait mandé ou je demeureray plus longtemps qu'il ne croit ... (undated)

> (Monsieur le Connétable has no cause to complain of either me or my conduct. He has written me a letter so cold and so influenced by my brother that I have not had

the courage to answer it; meanwhile I am in a convent, as Madame Mazarin had written him, and where I will remain longer than he thinks ...)

Her messages to her husband reiterate, always, her appreciation for his continued tolerance, her assurances that she is conducting herself well, that she receives almost no visitors, that she is not shaming him, and her hope that she might be permitted a visit from her son. After three years of this, though, her deferential pleas become punctuated by outbursts of anger, as in this letter written shortly after her arrival in Madrid:

I wasn't expecting any other response than the one you gave me because I am already accustomed to your cruel jokes, nor will I make any more demands concerning Flanders, although the only reason you deny my request is that you go against whatever I desire ... (7 August 1675)

In 1676 Marie was in Madrid, where for two years she had been alternately residing in a convent and in the home of a member of the Colonna family, while pursuing epistolary negotiations with Lorenzo in the hopes of being permitted to establish an independent household at the Spanish court. Her letters from this period record her tenacious effort to remain optimistic in the face of public disapproval and her husband's hostility to any accommodation that would allow her freedom of movement. From a few letters that she wrote between March and September of 1677, we can trace her reaction. Outraged as she was to see her name assigned to a printed work she did not write, it is clear that to her the appearance of this book was part of a continuum of verbal assaults on her reputation that until now had circulated in the form of conversations, letters, pamphlets and gazettes. The few months separating the printing of the false memoirs and her own book would be the single most crucial period since her departure from Rome for determining Marie's fate. Her correspondence from this period confirms that she and her husband both moved to exert pressure on the Spanish court to achieve their own ends, capitalizing on political turmoil in Madrid. In January the exiled Don Juan of Austria seized control of the Spanish council of State and became prime minister to the young king Carlos II, then just 16 years old. Upon learning of the decline in influence of the queen mother, who had not been favorable to her own interests, Marie left the convent of San Domingo and began petitioning for her freedom. For the first time Marie Colonna's fate became an official agenda item for discussion by the state council. From her letters we now know that it was precisely at this time that she took her memoirs to the printer. She reports this in a letter to Colonna dated 4 March 1677:

I have been obliged (to counter the ridiculous and impertinent story that is circulating under my name) to give to the printer a true relation of my life. I am sending you the first pages of it. As far as the king is concerned, I could not have explained myself in less detail, because we are dealing with such public events that it would be worse to keep silent about it. Also, everyone knows already of

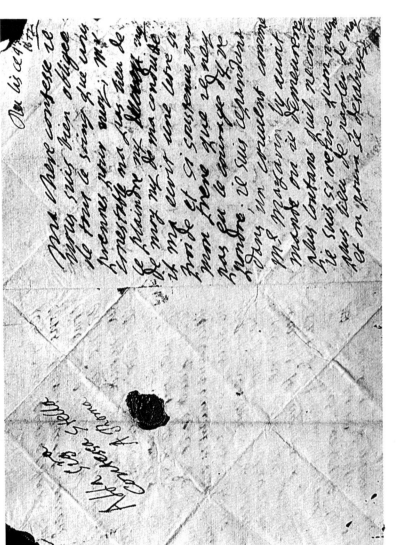

Fig 4.5 Letter by Marie Mancini Colonna to her friend Hortense Stella, 9 Spetember 1672

120

Fig 4.5 concluded

the good intentions that his majesty held toward me, so if they do not see it, they will gossip about what was a decent courtship. If my uncle had not stopped it, he [Mazarin] would not have had the good fortune to join our house [Colonna's], although our own tensions have been an obstacle [to this unity] these past years.[34]

There is a slight dig in these last sentences, as she simultaneously reassures her husband that she has written only what the public already knows of her liaison with Louis XIV, and reminds him – even while flattering him with the idea that Mazarin had been "fortunate" to achieve an alliance with the house of Colonna – that Mazarin's ambition to arrange this marriage for his niece came only after his failure to orchestrate a royal one for her.

Two weeks later, Marie angrily let Lorenzo know that she has learned he has been secretly petitioning the Spanish court to have her shut up in a castle:

> You have not told me anything in your last letter, but nothing has been hidden from me about the secret attempts you have made against my freedom, writing to the king to have his majesty shut me up in a castle, and writing to the ministers to carry out this request … by restraining me thus, using such extreme means, you intend to suppress a will that would surrender, were I treated differently. I am alerting you now that a memorandum has been written concerning me in the council of state, and I am waiting to hear from you regarding their consultation. (17 March 1677)

On 29 April she writes Colonna again, reminding him of her own participation, and that of the Spanish king, in her husband's authority regarding her place and manner of living:

> I am still in don Fernando's house, where I am living, and as is my duty, I write to you. I do not go out, except to take fresh air and exercise. If you and his majesty are not satisfied with this, I will go back to the convent, on the condition that I am allowed out two or three times a week. I cannot stand reclusion otherwise. … The book is finished and even if everybody had seen it before it is printed, no one could find an excuse to say anything against it. Neither the king [Louis XIV] nor anyone else could object, as everyone knows about his gallantry, and as I note in my book, I do not go into it out of modesty. (29 April 1677)

She thus holds her powers of publication out tantalizingly, over the heads of king and husband, those who legally hold the most authority over her. Both Louis XIV and the Spanish royal family might appreciate, she seems to think, her decision not to publicize Louis' original marriage promise to her. By the time she wrote this letter – at the end of April – Marie knew that the initial decision of the Spanish king's council had been favorable to her. Indeed, in May the council published their order authorizing her "to choose for herself a decent residence in a healthy site, where the air is good", but stipulating that this recommendation was "pending the approval of the Connétable".[35] Marie did not wait for Colonna's approval and moved immediately to a house she had managed to purchase, outside of Madrid.

This victory was not long-lived. In short, Colonna had more strings to pull, and his efforts resulted in his wife being returned once again to the convent of San Domingo, and finally back to the care of his relative Don Fernando. Marie's letters last mention her book a few months later, in a terse response to Colonna's apparent approval of it:

> I am pleased that the book has been to your liking. It is much better in Spanish. ... Don Fernando is driving me crazy ... he displays more power and authority over everyone without exception, even me ... I know very well that all these complaints will make you like him more. You should also know that all of this will not be enough for you to obtain what you want from me, since trust cannot be the daughter of distrust. This is what I must tell you, and God knows I wish I had more pleasant things to say. (13 September 1677)

Responding to his approval of the book, she also manages to remind him that it was never under his control, and that the version he read has already been transformed, translated and is circulating to a new population of readers.

Marie's letters to her husband written after 1677, following the failure of her most concerted attempts to negotiate on her own behalf, betray a new bitterness and a more thinly disguised anger. Forced to concede her own helplessness to some extent, she persisted nonetheless, with a stubbornness that continues to astonish her biographers, in her attempts to establish her independence and freedom of movement. In her letters to Colonna she continued to argue over, if not the legitimacy of his demands, then his way of making them. She challenged her husband's manner of exerting his authority over her, rather than asking him to relinquish it altogether. She declares that she might be convinced to return to him were it not for his abuse (there are veiled allusions to his previous violent behavior while she had still been in Rome, but more openly, she asserts that her will cannot be broken by the methods of persuasion he is launching against her). Their epistolary exchanges weave their own private dialogue within the public debates, not only about a husband's authority but about his style of imposing it.[36]

Already in the letters concerning the publication of her memoirs Marie shows that she knows perfectly well that her "*vérité*" will take its place within a web of ongoing public conversations about her. She insists, though, on participating in these conversations and on her right to assert that her version of her life is the true one. As she continues to reflect on her position in subsequent letters to her husband, she is also responding to what she knows of how her life is being debated as an illustration of the extent of a woman's rights within marriage, and of the range of a husband's authority over a wayward wife. As he alternately has his wife imprisoned then freed, cloistered then allowed to purchase and live in her own house; as he attends to her detailed requests for perfume, lace, body powders, portraits and exotic food stuffs, while refusing her money or any contact with her children, Lorenzo Colonna seems to be

intentionally sustaining a situation that allows him to test his powers in the
domestic and political spheres he occupies.

Copies in French and Spanish of *La Vérité dans son jour* were sent to
Lorenzo Colonna in Rome in 1677, but today there is no other evidence of the
book's circulation outside of Spain.[37] Rather, an altered version, edited by the
novelist Sébastien Brémond, appeared in France a few months later, under
the title *Apologie, ou les véritables mémoires de Madame la Connétable de
Colonna Maria Mancini, écrits par elle-même*.[38] Brémond agreed with the
author of one of the poems prefacing Marie's original version, who tells us that
she had been advised to change the title:

> Sur l'histoire de M. la Connétable Colonne intitulée,
> la vérité dans son jour.
> Le titre convient à l'histoire
> Mais si l'on m'avait voulu croire
> On ne l'aurait pas mis icy,
> Car sachant que vous l'avez faite
> Le moins équitable interprète
> La nommera d'abord ainsi.

(On the story of M. la Connétable Colonne entitled, truth in its own light./ The
title suits the story/ But if I had been believed/ It would not have been used here/
For knowing that you have written it/ The least equitable interpreter/ Would be
quick to name it thus.)

To entitle the story of one's life simply "the truth" suggests a certain lack of
humility, or an insufficient deference for the role of the reader in judging
whether or not a book is "true". Brémond's revised title announces the kind
of subtle editorial transformations that he will effect on the text: his new
title reminds us that this text is both defensive – an *apologia* – and "written"
by Marie "herself". an assertion that turns out to be less self-evident than it
would appear when Brémond gets around to explaining, in his preface, how
he altered Marie's writing in order to make it more worthy of her true self.
His editorial strategy will be in part to depersonalize the text, to mitigate
the directness of Marie's statements. Where she is forthright, he introduces
indirection; what she states simply, he makes more complex. The precise
and animated style of the original edition is attenuated by Brémond's efforts
to make the author's voice conform to standards of expression found in
seventeenth-century romances such as those he had authored, or manuals of
conduct. He alters her narrative at points when her conduct might be judged
severely, as when she declares in *La Vérité* that she was pleased by the
attentions of another admirer soon after the king had abandoned her.[39] His
changes tend to make her story more coherent, to give it a more classical,
harmonious shape (he divides it into chapters, lengthens phrases, and
multiplies the periodic sentences), and perhaps even to make the text more

effective as an "apology" or piece of testimony to be presented as evidence in a hearing.[40]

Yet Brémond's version of the story eliminates much of its originality, particularly in the manner in which it is repackaged by the addition of a dedicatory letter from the editor to "son altesse sérenissime Monseigneur le Duc de Zell, Brunswick et Lunebourg ... sous la protection de qui le beau sexe a toujours été parfaitement bien reçu" (91). (his most serene highness the duke of Zell, Brunswick and Lunebourg. ... under whose protection the fair sex has always been well received.) Marie's life story is thus presented to the public only indirectly and discreetly, through the mediation of a male writer consigning it to the care of a privileged male reader. Furthermore, Brémond makes the astonishing claim that he has transformed her text into a more perfect expression of *herself*:

> Ce sont ses propres Mémoires, et le portrait que je fais de sa vie est si particulier que Votre Altesse Sérénissime verra bien que c'est d'après l'original que je l'ai tiré. Je puis dire même, sans faire trop l'habile peintre, que *je lui rends jusqu'à la parole*; car, il est vrai que ce ne sont pas seulement ses actions et ses sentiments, mais jusqu'à ses pensées et ses expressions, comme Votre Altesse Sérénissime le reconnaîtra fort bien. On voit un certain caractère naturel et sincère en tout ce qu'elle dit; quelque chose qui sent si fort la noblesse de son âme et le rang qu'elle tient dans le monde, qu'il n'y a qu'elle qui peut s'exprimer de cette manière. (92)

> (These are her own memoirs, and the portrait that I draw of her life is so particular that your Serene Highness will see quite well that I have drawn it from the original. I might go so far as to say, without playing too much the skillful painter, that I portray her down to her voice; for it is true that it is not just her actions and her sentiments that your Highness will recognize, but also her thoughts and her expressions. One sees a certain natural and sincere quality in all that she says; a quality that so strongly shows the nobility of her soul and the rank that she holds in the world, that only she could express herself in this manner.)

Brémond transcends his editorial role here to replace Marie as author of her text. It is Brémond who has become the "painter". *La Vérité dans son jour* merges with the person who wrote it to the point where Brémond can present his work as editor of a text as comparable to the artist who renders the person in a portrait.[41] With this so-called protective gesture Brémond usurps Marie's originality and makes her memoir resemble fictional works in which the female narrator is made presentable to her public by a benevolent male editor. Brémond's version was to be the definitive version of Marie's story for centuries to come.[42]

* * *

If there is one image of Hortense and Marie Mancini that remains with us to this day, it is that of their "adventurous" travels in the years after they moved alone into a world that didn't seem to know how to place their unprecedented life stories in the making. "Quel pays y a-t-il que Madame Mazarin n'a pas vu?" (What country is there that Madame Mazarin has not seen?) writes Saint-Evremond, and Marie's "restless" and "wandering" nature is repeatedly evoked by her biographers. The nomadic quality of the sisters lives is what most profoundly marks them. They inhabited a wider range of countries, cultures, and architectural spaces than did most women of their day. For contemporaries who followed and commented on their movements, these two nieces of Mazarin were destined from the beginning to be vagabonds, having been brought to the court of France from Italy; in leaving, each in her own way was fated to help France exorcise "foreign" influences.[43] Indeed, the picture of Mazarin's nieces reduced to seeking the protection of every minor court in Europe seemed to many to convey a certain poetic justice. In Hortense's 1689 trial this historical distrust of foreignness merged with other trends in public opinion, such as an increasing nationalism, a concern with religious and cultural purity, and an intellectual backlash against the *salonnières*.

Hortense and Marie's own memoirs play along with this legend to a certain extent, invoking the Mazarin family "fate" to account for their exile and perpetual forced travels. At the same time, as their own assertions and the debates they generated make clear, what was at stake in their insistence on freedom of movement was their capacity to achieve personal autonomy in the public sphere. Armand de Mazarin's obsession with keeping her on his own property at all times, however deranged it may have been, was transformed into a sustainable legal position years later by his lawyer Erard, who viewed Hortense's independent travels as the most egregious of her offenses. Travel and the essence of sociability (its virtues or its vices, depending on one's point of view), were linked in arguments presented by parties on both sides of the debate about a woman's rights within marriage. The portraits of Marie and Hortense written by Saint-Evremond, Saint-Réal, and Brémond all draw attention to the ability of the two women to create, with their voices and their presence, a movable salon society wherever their travels landed them. Madame de Villedieu, too, had portrayed a female traveler in her fictional memoir, describing not only the material challenges to her survival but also the challenges to her story posed by the eagerness of other storytellers – and curious listeners – wanting to appropriate and change it. For all three of these writers, the moment that seems best to indicate the control they retained over their own stories is the moment when they move from a circumscribed, intimate or otherwise female-marked space to an open, public, or otherwise male-marked one. It seems crucial for them to establish exactly how they made this move, as important to the fictional Henriette-Sylvie as it is to Hortense and Marie that their readers know that they crossed the border independently and openly. We think of Henriette-Sylvie's ironic correction of the author who reports that she is pining away in a convent, unable to escape, so reminiscent of Marie's angry response to the insinuation that she had been imprisoned in a convent when in fact she had left of her own free will. Or Hortense's correction of a mistake that on its face seems trivial – the claim that she had built a secret door in the wall of her husband's house in order to escape (more than 20 years later, Saint-Evremond would reiterate this correction in his *Remarques sur le plaidoyé*). It is as though by proving not only that they chose to go public but also that they did so freely, and that moreover they were able to navigate the "outside" world once they got there, these women could convince their readers that their lives were not to be read as transgressions, nor were their memoirs to be viewed simply as confessions.

Hortense and Marie Mancini published their life stories, that is, they committed them to print, for specific reasons, which both of them state in the first paragraphs of their books – to defend their reputations, and to claim the right to produce accounts of their own lives, accounts that were already being written, circulated, and published by other writers. Both sisters express their awareness that the patronage ties that they had hoped would sustain them in their flight from their husbands are turning out to be not enough to support their ambition to live independently. In Marie's case, the flat refusal of Louis XIV to act in any way as her protector once she had left her husband was a signal that the political alliance between Colonna and the French court was far stronger than any personal attachment she had formed with Louis in the time before his marriage. In fact, Louis's sacrifice of Marie had already been consecrated in the press and in public conversation as a sign of his new political mastery – his acceptance of the responsibilities of power. Marie Mancini's historical identity was established as that of a victim, a sign of Louis's successful expulsion (from his heart and from his realm) of the Italian, feminine influences that had also encouraged weakness in earlier French monarchs.

It is striking, in reading the memoirs of both Hortense and Marie, that they not only recognize the failure of their reliance on royal patronage but more than that, they de-emphasize that reliance, and try to define their lives on other terms. Hortense, even more than Marie, had tried to claim authority over her life story by excluding the king from the discussion – she seems to be addressing a different court of appeal in her list of grievances against her husband, and she stresses her previous agreement with the king that he stay out of the dispute. In conventional terms, these were not wise moves. Most of their friends called them crazy – *les folles aventurières* – as they passed up opportunities to renew and sustain their former patronage ties and even on occasion seemed to flagrantly disregard those ties. Of the two of them, Hortense displays the more dubious view of the probable consequences of this sort of stance, but she does seem to be aiming for a public judgment that will acknowledge her husband's injustices if not necessarily her own innocence. Later, through her salon in

London and her rejection of invitations to work as a spy for France, she strove to sustain an independent network of alliances not determined by her family or her former connections with Louis XIV's court. In their lives as well as their life writing these women are trying to locate, imagine, or even create a space where their words might circulate freely, unconfined, and where they might be equal participants in the written discussions that were determining both their reputation and their fate.

Notes

1. Other well-known memoirs by women writing at this time and earlier were published posthumously (the memoirs of Madame de Motteville and Madame de Montpensier, for example).
2. Madame d'Aulnoy (1650–1705), whose historical memoirs and works of fiction were published in her lifetime, traveled to Holland, England, and Spain on an itinerary very similar to that of the Mancinis. Her efforts to have her husband brought to trial on charges of treason were highly publicized, and ultimately failed. Marie-Sidonie de Courcelles documented her flight from her husband in the 1670s in memoirs that were published posthumously. On this text and its resemblances to the Mancinis see Mary Christensen Eckman's doctoral dissertation, "Different Accounts: Women's Memoirs in Seventeenth-Century France" (Michigan, 1998), 158–84. Anne-Marguerite Du Noyer and her husband published competing memoir accounts of their marriage in 1709–10; DeJean discusses these in *Tender Geographies: Women and the Origins of the Novel in France* (New York: Columbia University Press, 1991), pp. 145–8.
3. On late seventeenth-century developments in divorce legislation see James Traer, *Marriage and the Family in 18th-Century France* (Ithaca: Cornell University Press, 1980), and Daniel Dessertine, *Divorcer à Lyon sous la Révolution et l'Empire* (Lyon: Presses Universitaires de Lyon, 1981), pp. 8–9, 11, 15, 19–20, 22.
4. For modern biographies, see Georges Mongrédien, *Une Aventurière au grand siècle: La Duchesse Mazarin* (Paris: Amiot-Dumont, 1952); Françoise Mallet-Joris, *Marie Mancini* (Paris: Hachette, 1964); and Claude Dulong, *Marie Mancini: La Première passion de Louis XIV* (Paris: Perrin, 1994). Detailed information on the Mazarin contract and inheritance may be found in Georges Livet, *Le Duc Mazarin, gouverneur d'Alsace* (Strasbourg: Leroux, 1954). The 1896 biography by Lucien Perey (a pseudonym for Clara Herpin) remains valuable, particularly for the extensive use made of private correspondences and other documentary sources: *Une Princesse romaine au XVIIe siècle: Marie Mancini Colonna d'après des documents inédits* (Paris: Calmann Lévy, 1896). Herpin's sources did not, however, include the Colonna family archive in Rome, which was closed to scholars until 1996, when it was moved to a state library. Claude Dulong was granted some access to the archive while it remained private and some letters from the collection are excerpted and appended in her biography. I discuss this material more extensively below.
5. *Mémoires D.M.L.D.M. à M. ****, in *Mémoires d'Hortense et de Marie Mancini*, ed.Gérard Doscot (Paris: Mercure de France, 1987), p. 32; subsequently cited in the text. All translations are my own.

6. Traditionally, authors of memoirs wrote to document a historical period or event. René Démoris, in *Le Roman à la première personne: Du classicisme aux lumières* (Paris: Armand Colin, 1975), has surveyed the development of memoir writing with respect to the author's principal purpose (autobiographical or historical) in the seventeenth century, showing that before the classical era (beginning around 1660) there were almost no memoirs whose principal focus was on the person of the author. Similarly, Faith Beasley classifies Hortense and Marie's memoirs with those of a later generation of women writers who were more interested in "revealing their own lives" than with "exposing the particularities of the public realm". See Beasley's *Revising History: Women's Fiction and Memoirs in Seventeenth-Century France* (New Brunswick, NJ: Rutgers University Press, 1990), p. 64.

7. Démoris, *Le Roman à la première personne*, p. 99.

8. This has been noted by Démoris in his discussion of Hortense's memoirs (ibid., p. 112) and by Micheline Cuénin in the introduction to her edition of Madame de Villedieu's novel, *Mémoires de la vie de Henriette-Sylvie de Molière* (Tours: Université François Rabelais, 1977), p. v.

9. Gustave Dulong presents the most complete summary of opinions concerning Saint-Réal's collaboration in the writing of Hortense's memoirs. Readers familiar with Saint-Réal note that the writing style is unlike his. At the same time, the moral lesson that he sees the narrative communicating (that the "innocent errors" of a noble soul can lead to disaster) is very much in keeping with Saint-Réal's stated project to elicit sympathy and interest from a "common" reader by showing the human weaknesses of grand personages (see Dulong, *Saint-Réal*, pp. 225–30). I do not agree that this is the predominant rhetorical tone in Hortense's text, which I read as much closer to a judicial memoir.

10. Excerpts from this correspondence were published in a commentary by A.D. Perrero, "La Duchessa Ortensia Mazzarino e la Principessa Maria Colonna, Sorelle Mancini, ed il Duca Carlo Emanuele II di Savoia", in *Curiosità e ricerche di storia subalpina* (Torino: Fratelli Bocca, 1876), vol. I, pp. 1–94 and vol. II, pp. 381–443.

11. Andrée Mansau provides some evidence suggesting that the true identity of the translator and author of this prefatory letter was Henry Oldenburg, First Secretary of the Royal Society of London, in *Saint-Réal et l'humanisme cosmopolite* (Paris: Champion, 1976), pp. 141–2.

12. The letter is reproduced in Mansau, p. 145. Based on its resemblance to the style of Saint-Réal, Mansau believes it to be authored by him, while noting also that the letter is designated as having been written in London at a date when Saint-Réal was in Paris.

13. "She is as much mistress of herself while travelling, while hunting, or while in her private study ... While by nature she likes intimate gatherings, almost all hours of the day are public for her, and the most secret places in the house are as open as the common rooms to those who visit ..." This portrait is attributed to Saint-Réal, though, again, the attribution is disputed. See "Lettre touchant le caractère de Madame la Duchesse Mazarin" in *Oeuvres de M. L'Abbé de Saint-Réal* (Amsterdam: François L'Honoré et Fils, 1740), vol. 3, p. 324.

14. Furetière indicates that the term can be used in this sense in either the singular or the plural. Sara Maza describes how the printing and circulation of judicial memoirs would later play an important role in constituting and appealing to the new notion of "public opinion", in her "Le Tribunal de la nation: Les Mémoires judiciaires et l'opinion publique à la fin de l'Ancien Régime", *Annales*, **42**, 1

(January–February 1987): 73–90. The record of the case Hortense's husband was to eventually bring against her in 1689, which I discuss below, is one of the earliest examples of a published judicial memoir.

15. Patricia Cholakian has traced the history of critical commentary on Hortense's memoirs, showing how it has turned a blind eye to the text's focus on material reality – the power of money, for example, and her representation of her complicated legal and social status – in order to insist almost exclusively on the book as a romance suggestive of sexual adventure, in "Sex, Lies, and Autobiography: The Memoirs of Hortense Mancini", in *Women Writers of the Ancien Régime: Strategies of Emancipation*, ed. Donna Kuizenga and Colette Winn (New York: Garland Press, 1997), pp. 17–30.

16. "Je voyais tous les jours disparaître des sommes immenses, des meubles hors de prix, des charges, des gouvernements, et tous les autres débris de la fortune de mon oncle, le fruit de ses travaux, et la récompense de ses services" (p. 48).

17. On laws regarding women and inheritance in the early modern period see Merry E. Wiesner, *Women and Gender in Early Modern Europe* (Cambridge: Cambridge University Press, 1993), pp. 30–35.

18. Hortense attributes the opposing positions taken by the two courts to a generational difference: "M. Mazarin found the same favor with the old [judges] that I had found with the young ones" (*Mémoires*, 61). Both Louis XIV and Colbert attempted to intervene in the Mazarin case at various points. Still, in 1668 Hortense, perhaps encouraged by the first decision, clearly thought that she had a better chance of a sympathetic hearing from the courts than from the king and his ministers (*Mémoires*, 58). In 1670 Colbert officially claimed for the crown the power to adjudicate cases involving marriage contracts. See DeJean's discussion of the importance of this decision for the development of women's writing in *Tender Geographies*, pp. 112–14; 127–34.

19. Jacques Munier-Jolain describes him as a "tombeur de femmes de qualité", and cites his popular appeal in *Procès de femmes* (Paris: Calmann Lévy, 1898), p. 182.

20. The word *divorce* technically signified a legal judgment dividing a couple's wealth between them and allowing them to live separately, but in most cases divorces were informal. Thus, Hortense was said to have divorced her husband simply because they had been living separately for so long.

21. See J.J. Jusserand (ed.), *Recueil des instructions données aux ambassadeurs et ministres de France*, vol. 25, pt 2 (Paris: F. Alcan, 1884), p. 218.

22. Claude Erard, *Plaidoyé prononcée au Grand Conseil pour M. le Duc de Mazarin: contre Mme la Duchesse de Mazarin son épouse* (Paris, 1690), p. 23.

23. Cited in Nicholas Nupied (ed.), *Journal des principales audiences du Parlement* (Paris: Compagnie des libraires associés, 1707), vol. 4, p. 212. Erard's rhetoric here echoes the sort of accusations made in witchcraft trials, which typically described the accused woman's "nocturnal wanderings" and feasts in the company of strange men.

24. Saint-Evremond, "Oraison funèbre de Madame Mazarin", in *Oeuvres choisies* (Paris: Garnier, 1867), pp. 386–98.

25. "On ne saurait faire un bon compte de toute l'extravagance de cet homme; c'est un fou. Il est habillé comme un gueux. La dévotion est tout de travers dans sa tête. Nous voulûmes lui persuader de tirer sa femme d'Angleterre, où elle est en danger d'être chassée, et peut-être pervertie, et où elle est avec les ennemis du Roi. Il en revient toujours à dire qu'elle vienne avec lui – avec lui, bon Dieu! Et il en faut revenir à ce que dit Saint-Evremond: elle est dispensée des règles ordinaires, et

l'on voit sa justification en voyant M. de Mazarin" (Letter to Madame de Grignan, 12 August 1689). (It is difficult to give a good account of all the extravagance of this man; he is a madman. He is dressed like a beggar. Devotion is all twisted around in his head. We wanted to persuade him to remove his wife from England, where she is in danger of being pursued, and even corrupted, and where she is with the enemies of the King. He always comes back to the statement that she may come back with him – with him, dear God! And one has to recall what Saint-Evremond says: she is exempt from the usual rules, and one can see the justification when one sees M. de Mazarin.)

26.   *Réponse de Dame Hortense Mancini Duchesse de Mazarin, aux plaidoyez de Messire Armand Charles Duc de Mazarin son Epoux* (Toulouse: J.J. Boude, n.d.). References in this pamphlet to Saint-Evremond's text, published in 1696, would seem to indicate that it was printed after that date, although of course it is possible that Sachot had seen Saint-Evremond's *Factum* in scribal form. Saint-Evremond does not mention Erard's use of Hortense Mancini's published memoirs.

27.   "Réponse au Plaidoyé de Monsieur Herard, Avocat au Grand Conseil, ou plutôt à l'invective, ou au libelle, que Monsieur le Duc Mazarin a fait imprimer contre Madame la Duchesse son Epouse", in Saint-Evremond, *Oeuvres choisies*, pp. 9–30. The text was first published in 1696.

28.   *Mémoires de M.L.P.M.M. Colonne, G. connétable du royaume de Naples* (Cologne: Pierre Marteau, 1676); subsequently cited in the text. It is extremely unlikely that either book was actually published in Cologne, for Pierre Marteau was a widely used fictitious imprint. See Henri-Jean Martin and Roger Chartier (eds), *Histoire de l'édition française*, vol. 2 (Paris: Promodis, 1984), pp. 114–15.

29.   See Démoris, *Le Roman à la première personne*, pp. 116–18, for an interesting reading of the levels of irony in this text. In my discussion of the apocryphal memoirs, I am following the conventional assumption that they were authored by a man. Thus, I refer to the narrator as female but to the author or impersonator as male.

30.   We know from letters by Marie and others in Madrid in 1677 that the book appeared in French, in that year. The few extant copies indicate no publisher or date of publication. My citations here will be to the new edition I edited with Patricia Francis Cholakian (Delmar, NY: Scholars Facsimiles and Reprints, 1998). It is based on the copy in the Bibliothèque Nationale.

31.   She may have been alluding to two such anonymous "gallant histories" of her affair with Louis XIV: one in *Le Palais-Royal ou les amours de Louis XIV*, published in 1667, and the other in a pamphlet titled *Les Agrémens de la jeunesse de Louis XIV ou son amour pour Mademoiselle de Mancini*, published in 1670. Both are reprinted in D. Boiteau and C.L. Livet (eds), *L'Histoire amoureuse des Gaules suivie des Romans historico-satiriques du XVIIe siècle* (Paris: P. Jannet, 1857).

32.   This correspondence has not been published, although a few letters are excerpted in Claude Dulong's biography, cited above. My own references are to the autograph letters from the Colonna family archive, housed since 1996 in a state library at the Benedictine monastery of Santa Scolastica, Subiaco, Italy. As the letters have not yet been catalogued, I will refer to them by date.

33.   10 January 1672. During the first years of her wanderings, Marie wrote to her husband in Italian, then gradually shifted to Spanish as her residence in Madrid was prolonged. My quotes from these letters, and any others not written in French, will be in English. For the translations of letters written in Spanish I am grateful to have had the assistance of Raphael Cabañas.

34. In the first pages of her memoirs, to which she is referring here, Marie describes her 1660 liaison with the young Louis XIV.
35. Cited by Dulong, *Marie Mancini*, p. 275.
36. Flandrin remarks that discussions of the appropriateness of the "courtly relationship" in marriage, which gain acceptance in the second half of the seventeenth century, are important indications of a challenge to the absolute authority of husbands well before any legislative reforms made divorce a viable option for women. One of the signs of this challenge that he cites is evidence of declining birthrates at the end of the seventeenth century and early eighteenth century. The *"séparation de lit"* that Marie had demanded and been granted by her husband after she had produced the requisite heirs was a challenge to Lorenzo's authority and resulted, she acknowledges in her memoirs, in her own loss of power in the household. See Jean-Louis Flandrin, *Families in Former Times: Kinship, Household, and Sexuality*, trans. Richard Southern (Cambridge: Cambridge University Press, 1979), pp. 224–5.
37. A Spanish translation, *La Verdad en su luz*, was printed in Saragoza in 1677. Like the French original, it has become extremely rare. References I found in letters sent to Lorenzo Colonna from Marie and from Ferdinando Colonna establish that Lorenzo was sent the French and Spanish versions of the memoirs. These letters form part of the Colonna archive described in note 32, above.
38. This version was published in Leyden in 1678; subsequently cited in the text. The modern edition of Marie's memoirs is also based on this version, in *Mémoires d'Hortense et de Marie Mancini*, ed. Gérard Doscot (Paris: Mercure de France, 1987).
39. Brémond has her say the opposite: "I was little disposed to receiving a new passion. The fall from favor that I had just suffered was too great, and I needed time to console myself" (ibid., 114). He further alters Marie's description of her affair with Louis XIV to make the king more sympathetic.
40. Démoris aptly remarks that Brémond's stated objective to render Marie's text more "natural" illustrates the paradox of the classical aesthetic of the natural, which must be cultivated (*Le Roman à la première personne*, 120). I would add that the aesthetic notion of "naturalness" carries a strong prescriptive punch when applied to women. For discussions of the importance of this aesthetic standard in the early history of published writing by women, see my essay, "Authority, Authenticity, and the Publication of Letters by Women", and that of Katherine Jensen, "Male Models of Feminine Epistolarity", in Elizabeth C. Goldsmith (ed.), *Writing the Female Voice: Essays on Epistolary Literature* (Boston: Northeastern University Press, 1989), pp. 46–59; 25–45.
41. Démoris remarks on the striking "ambiguity" of Brémond's preface, which to him is a good illustration of the contradiction implicit in the pose of the memoir writer, who wants to "survive" while also being self-effacing, and producing a faithful historical document (*Le Roman à la première personne*, pp. 120–21). But to me what is striking about this preface is the way in which Brémond substitutes himself for the writer, a move that is not gender neutral.
42. Claude Dulong relies primarily on this edition in her biography, as she erroneously believed that the extant edition of *La Vérité dans son jour* is essentially the same text as *Apologie, ou les véritables mémoires*, and that they were both edited by Brémond. She suggests that an earlier edition of *La Vérité* used in Lucien Pérey's biography has been lost (*Marie Mancini*, pp. 272–3). However, all of Pérey's citations may be found in the edition of *La Vérité* currently at the Bibliothèque

Nationale. It differs significantly from Brémond's reworked text, as our new edition of *La Vérité dans son jour* shows (see note 30 above.)

43. See, for example, Madame de Lafayette's description of Marie's affair with Louis XIV and her subsequent exile in the opening section of *Histoire de Madame Henriette d'Angleterre*.

CHAPTER FIVE

Overheard Conversations: Madame de Villedieu's Autobiographical Fictions

Among the public observers of Hortense and Marie Mancini's real life adventures in the late 1660s was the writer Marie-Catherine Hortense Desjardins, also known as Madame de Villedieu (1640?–83). An ambitious and iconoclastic literary figure, like her friend Hortense Mancini she was also identified as an *aventurière* or scandalous public figure. This was a label that Villedieu, however, had embraced and even incorporated into her artistic credo. Born in Normandy into a bourgeois family, Marie-Catherine moved to Paris with her mother and sister at the age of 16, and she soon became a recognized figure in salon circles, writing and reciting poetry which began appearing in published collections in 1659. She also met and fell in love with a nobleman, Antoine de Villedieu, and began signing her works "Madame de Villedieu", though they never married. The unabashed manner in which she conducted her unconventional private life as well as her career as a writer meant that she had to endure public derision and the painful airing of her periodic breaks with Villedieu (on at least two occasions he filed legal documents renouncing his marriage promises to her). But her novels and poetry were popular, her plays were performed, and she enjoyed an extended, if not always profitable, relationship with the prominent bookseller Claude Barbin.

One of the first French women to openly sign her name to published fiction, she was acutely conscious of her public role as both a literary innovator experimenting in new genres and as a woman refusing to assume the conventionally prescribed mask of anonymity in her published works. Historians as well as novelists, she argued, should draw on their personal experience to explain the events they describe. To be an *aventurière*, then, was inevitable if a woman wanted to be a good writer, for an artist with no experience of the world could not impart knowledge that would be of use to her readers. Writing from experience also meant claiming a new public function for those realms of life already well-charted by women, exposing, for example, the "disorders of love" that had been traditionally left out of historical chronicles. Desjardins' best known work, a collection of stories entitled *Les Désordres de l'amour*, was an early prototype of a new short form of historical fiction called the "*nouvelle historique*". For Desjardins, this new genre offered a means of

Fig. 5.1   Madame de Villedieu

both personalizing and feminizing conventional historical discourse.[1] "Je me cherche moi-même dans tout ce que j'écris," she writes, "c'est pour en avoir fait une parfaite expérience que je me trouve autorisée à le peindre [l'amour] avec de si noires couleurs." (I am searching for myself in all that I write; it is because I have had an exact experience of it that I find I am authorized to depict [love] in such dark colors.)[2]

Madame de Villedieu's modern readers have noted her preoccupation with female speech and her pointed responses to both classical and contemporary renditions of the voice of the abandoned woman in love. As Micheline Cuénin observes, much of her writing is concerned with the process of seduction, of how men make women speak, and also with the writer's project of representing the particular character of women's speech, "comment faire parler une femme".[3] Katherine Jensen has examined how Villedieu reshapes her own unhappy conversations with Antoine de Villedieu in the passionate voices of women in *Les Désordres de l'amour*.[4] But despite her frequent pronouncements on love as the prime mover of both the historical and the particular realms, Villedieu was skeptical, as a writer, of the surge of reader enthusiasm for representations of seduced and abandoned women.

It is somewhat surprising, given her acknowledgment of and even commitment to the need for self-exposure in her writing, that Marie-Catherine Desjardins never published her own memoirs. As an experienced target of printed distortions of her own life, however, she may have wanted to avoid any obvious attempt to set the record straight. In any event, her fictional works strongly suggest her doubts concerning the success of such an endeavor. In 1672, four years after the unauthorized publication of her own life-writing in the form of a collection of her love letters to Antoine de Villedieu, Marie-Catherine did publish a memoir, but a fictional one, titled *Mémoires de la vie de Henriette-Sylvie de Molière*. In many respects a playful and parodic experiment in the memoir genre, it was also a work that was intimately engaged with the lives of real people. Two of these were Hortense and Marie Mancini, whose improbable escapades had already been compared by others to the adventures of novelistic heroines.

In 1662, one year after Hortense Mancini's early marriage, the young Marie-Catherine Desjardins had dedicated her first printed collection of poems to her, evoking in her dedication the hope that the new duchess of Mazarin would favor her verses with patronage and encourage the new author to dedicate future works to her.[5] But while Desjardins' early contacts with Hortense de Mazarin were focused on obtaining the support of the young heiress and her social circle, it soon was apparent that the sort of household the duc de Mazarin had in mind for his wife resembled a convent more than a salon. Like others observing the fanatical efforts of Mazarin's namesake to control his wife's behavior as well as her fortune, Madame de Villedieu must have come to see in

Hortense and her husband figures more fit for fiction than reality.[6] Hortense fled Paris in June of 1668, and just over one year later Madame de Villedieu published the first two parts of a fictional autobiography of the adventures of another woman (whose initials were also 'H.M.') seeking a life not bound by traditional family structures.[7] The *Mémoires de la vie de Henriette-Sylvie de Molière* was published in four more parts between 1672 and 1674, during the same period that Marie and Hortense were continuing their travels and while Hortense was, for a time, enjoying the protection of a foreign court and writing her own memoirs.

Just as Villedieu's fictional work echoes the real life adventures of the Mancinis, so their lives seem to echo the novel's plot turns as they unfold and repeat themselves over the course of the work's publication. This fictional autobiography, moreover, seems to be commenting on the lives of other 'scandalous' women of the decade, including Madame de Villedieu herself.[8] The *Mémoires de la Vie de Henriette-Sylvie de Molière* is, as critics have observed, an important and innovative work in the history of the first-person novel. But it is also a work that casts as fiction some highly publicized contemporary private lives, and creatively explores the ramifications of going public.

Marie-Catherine Hortense's mock memoir

A number of resemblances between the author and her heroine are obvious from the outset. Henriette-Sylvie's marginal status with respect to the aristocratic society she frequents parallels Marie-Catherine's own experiences of exclusion due in part to her modest social origins.[9] Henriette-Sylvie takes up the pen, not as the conventional memorialist would do, to clear her family name, but rather to tell the true story of what she calls "my innocent errors", and to oppose her own version of her private life to the stories being circulated by gossip-mongers, journalists, and novelists. Like Marie-Catherine, Henriette-Sylvie suffers particularly for a lover whose family does everything to oppose their union, and Henriette-Sylvie also tells the story (most unusually, at the time, for a female narrator) of her own lapses into infidelity and eventual indifference. Numerous allusions to historical figures and encounters with real people, events, and places from Mme de Villedieu's life serve further to point to the autobiographical dimension of the memoirs.

But in writing a fictional memoir Villedieu is not simply veiling her own autobiography. As a woman writer exceptionally committed to going public, she is also exceptionally aware of the difficulties of the enterprise. Her novel seems to question the straightforward truth-telling claims made by memoirs. The mock memoirs of Henriette-Sylvie de Molière are largely concerned with the knotty problem of controlling one's social reputation, and with the futility of attempting to do so simply by telling the truth. They are written in the form of six letters to the Duchess of Nemours who has asked her to write a story of her life that would both amuse and convince her readers. The memoirs begin, like Hortense Mancini's, with the narrator expressing her doubts concerning the efficacy of such an enterprise:

> Ce ne m'est pas une légère consolation, Madame, au milieu de tant de médisances qui déchirent ma réputation partout, que Votre Altesse désire que je me justifie. J'en ai les sentiments que je sois, et pour n'en être pas ingrate, j'obéirai volontiers au commandement qu'elle me fait de la divertir, par un récit fidèle de mes erreurs innocentes.
>
> Non que j'espère jamais pouvoir arracher des esprits les cruelles impressions que la calomnie a données de ma conduite: le siècle ne permet pas que je me flatte de cette pensée. Mais pour me servir des termes de Votre Altesse, il viendra un temps, où les hommes ne pourront plus juger si criminellement par eux-mêmes de leurs semblables; parce qu'ils n'auront plus les moeurs si corrompues ni si criminelles; et alors on ajoutera peut-être plus de foi à ce que j'aurai écrit de l'innocence de mes actions, qu'à ce qu'en auront pu dire mes ennemis.[10]

> (It is no small consolation, Madame, in the midst of so many attacks on my reputation, that your highness desires that I justify myself. I feel as I should about this request, and so as not to be ungrateful I will gladly obey your command to amuse you, with a faithful account of my innocent errors. Not that I ever hope to tear from peoples' minds the cruel impressions of my conduct created by the calumny of others. The times do not allow me to flatter myself with such a thought. But in your words, there will come a time when men will no longer be able to judge others so treacherously, because they will no longer be as corrupt nor as criminal in their behavior, and then perhaps people will more readily believe what I have written about my innocent actions than they will believe what my enemies will have been able to say about me.)

Having thus opened her memoir with a dubious acknowledgement of the conventional reason one writes such a text, she begins her story with a phrase that more openly mocks the standard genealogy opening an aristocratic memoir: "Pour commencer, je n'ay jamais bien su qui j'étais …"(7) (To begin, I have never really known who I am). She goes on to tell the story of her illegitimate birth, her ignorance of her parents' identity, her adoption by a wealthy financier family and her idyllic childhood that ends abruptly when she stabs her foster father as he attempts to rape her. For a while it seems as though every event in her life is dictated by her impressive erotic appeal. More often than not, these events are catastrophic: her stepmother denounces her when she perceives that her own lover has fallen for the irresistible Sylvie, Sylvie's young lover the Count of Englesac burns down his own family's château when his mother forbids him to see her, later he kills a rival in a duel and is exiled, and various love-smitten noblemen release her from the bonds of one jealous admirer only to lock her up on their own properties. By the end of Part I,

Henriette-Sylvie has innocently managed to create havoc wherever she goes, and her adventures are being talked of and written about to the point that other characters in the memoirs begin to appear for the purpose of rearranging her life for her. The most benevolent attempt by another character to take control of Henriette-Sylvie's story is by a certain Marquise de Seville, a figure who bears a striking resemblance – both physical and temperamental – to the narrator, and becomes her surrogate mother, establishing her in society and arranging a good marriage for her to a wealthy Spaniard living in Brussels.

The Marquise de Seville is one of several women in the memoirs who try to restore order to Henriette-Sylvie's life, and who clearly serve as models of behavior which the narrator contemplates and admires but inevitably rejects for herself. Her encounters with each of them create moments of stasis in the story, moments which hold out the possibility of two conventional endings for the story of a female life, in marriage or in a convent. But, beginning with her escape from her first, arranged, marriage, the narrator embarks on a series of alternative experiments in creating her own plot.

The boldest of these experiments is the first one, when, like Hortense Mancini, she disguises herself as a man, taking only some jewels with her, and escapes from her jealous husband. But unlike Hortense, who tells us that even far from Paris her disguise fooled no one, Henriette's disguise fools even the sharp-eyed courtiers of Versailles. Here the heroine manages for a time to lead the life of a gallant courtier, orchestrating her own outlandish male plots and discovering their risks and rewards. At Versailles, disguised as a man, Henriette-Sylvie's story is closely interwoven with real historical events. Henriette-Sylvie enters the arena of official (male) history when she arrives at Versailles at the moment of Louis XIV's most celebrated three-day *fête*, and Madame de Villedieu actually interpolates at this point in her narrative a lengthy description of the event taken from one of the official published accounts (92–7). The only happy outcome to Henriette-Sylvie's youthful flight from marriage is to become a man, and so she does for a time. This fantasy is in turn ended by an encounter with the same sort of figure that launched her adventure – a jealous husband, who tries to murder her when he catches her with his wife. Her solution is to switch sexual identities once again – confronted by the sword she is saved when her clothes are torn from her and her adversary sees that she is a woman (106–10).

Time and again, Villedieu launches her heroine's adventures with a reference to a real incident or situation familiar to her readers. During her frequent sojourns in convents she meets other women who are there for the widest variety of reasons, many of them women who, like the Mancinis, are living in convents as a result of family conflicts. Henriette-Sylvie herself seeks refuge in a convent at the beginning of her story, and is befriended by the Abbess who is more "badine" than "dévote". This convent is the only place to which Henriette repeatedly returns voluntarily, for both protection and advice: "elle était ma confidente et j'étais la sienne" (131) (she was my confident and I was hers). Other convents, more austere, are referred to as "*cloîtres*", and these are the prisons to which the heroine is confined against her will. In one such place Henriette befriends a nun who, like Jeanne des Anges, had been placed in a convent as a girl by her family, in order to permit her brother to inherit the family's wealth. This practice was in fact widespread, as the narrator herself notes; it was "la maxime de la plus grande partie de la Noblesse" (43) (the rule amongst most of the nobility). We have seen how certain convents functioned as prisons for Marie Mancini. Such uses were standard during the seventeenth century as marriage legislation treated women with increasing severity.[11] The only way out of a "prison" convent was to escape in secret, using bribery on the inside when possible, and with the help of someone from the outside. In the case of the fictional Henriette, her accomplice is her young friend fleeing with a lover who had courted her, like the Portuguese nun, from the other side of the convent wall.

The long sequence of Henriette-Sylvie's adventures constitute a catalogue of the array of mishaps that brought seventeenth-century women into the legal public sphere. She is abandoned as a baby by an aristocratic mother seeking to hide her illegitimate birth. She kills a man who was trying to rape her, and is blamed for this as well as much of what she does because of her "fatal" beauty. She escapes a marriage that was arranged for her against her will, and when she does choose a clandestine marriage is then pursued for that crime, which as of mid-century was a capital one. She is imprisoned in convents and castles, and voluntarily retreats to other, less grim, convents and abbeys. She is accused of witchcraft following revelry with some of her more libertine friends.

Transcending all of her adventures and misfortunes is her increasing awareness that her life has become the subject not only of scandal but of fiction. At first, she overhears others telling stories about her escapades, then she learns that an article has been published in the *Gazette* about her mysterious origins (51–3). Later, she learns that novels ("romans") about her life had been published and were being distributed by her enemies and presented as the truth about her life (77–8, 141). Scenes in which the narrator finds herself eavesdropping on others' accounts of her own life grow increasingly frequent as the memoirs progress. By the end of the book it is clear that her objective, as she had stated it at the outset, to put an end to other versions of her story by writing the true one, will never be attained.[12] Instead, she opts to participate in this irrepressible circulation of talk and print. The last scene in which Henriette describes herself listening to the public accounts of her own private life is an allusion to gossip about a prank played by Hortense Mancini to protest her confinement in a convent.[13] Disguised as a man, Henriette-Sylvie is travelling with a male companion who, unaware of her true identity, is regaling her with accounts of her notoriety. She is particularly amused by his description of her life in the convent, where, like Hortense Mancini, she had been particularly frustrated by not being able to join the hunting festivities of the feast of St Hubert:

> Il m'en raconta une ... , que je trouvai plaisante, et qui me conviendroit assez, si j'étais retenue dans un Convent où je m'ennuyasse, et où je voulusse lasser les gens de me garder. Il dit que cette Dame, qu'il voulait être moi, aimait fort la chasse, et s'affligeoit beaucoup de passer une S. Hubert sans chasser ... (332).

> (He recounted one to me ... , that I found amusing, and that would well suit me were I detained and bored in a convent and wanting to make people tire of guarding me. He said that this lady, who he claimed was me, loved especially to hunt, and that I was particularly pained to have to spend the St Hubert holiday in a convent instead of hunting.)

Her companion proceeds to recount the tricks that Henriette-Sylvie (and Hortense) had supposedly played on the nuns by arranging for dogs and a rabbit to be let loose in the convent. Bemused, Henriette listens to these well-spun stories and encourages the gentleman to tell her all that he knows of the notorious lady's adventures:

> Les pauvres filles! Elles devaient en effet être bien épouvantées; ... vous eussiez trop ri, Madame, si vous eussiez vu avec quelle ingenuité il m'assurait que tout cela m'était arrivé. ... Il me donnait tous les jours des Comédies semblables, et j'aidais autant que je pouvais à l'entretenir dans son erreur; ... (333).

> (The poor sisters! They must in fact have been very frightened; ... how you would have laughed, Madame, if you had seen the ingenuity with which he assured me that all of this had happened ... He offered me similar comedies every day, and I encouraged him in his error as much as I could.)

In this scene Desjardins offers her readers a lesson in both listening and reading. Henriette-Sylvie maintains an ironic distance when confronted with gossip about her life; she recognizes the inevitability of *médisance* and also its irrepressible, even creative force. She opts for laughter rather than righteous outrage, a response that she also knows will work better than indignation to diminish the power of tall tales.[14] Complicitously addressing her reader, she establishes her superior status with respect to her interlocutor, mocking the pride he took in being "in the know". Addressing her interlocutor, she challenges his claims to knowledge and goads him into sharing it with her: "... il ne voulait point me laisser dans cette opinion, et me donnant la première avanture qui lui revenait dans la mémoire, il me faisait arriver les plus plaisantes choses du monde" (331). (He did not want to leave me with this opinion, and, giving me the first adventure that came into his memory, he had the most amusing things happening to me.)

Hortense and Marie Mancini, in their real memoirs, opted for a more head-on confrontation with the *médisants* and tale-tellers who were publishing their lives. A year after the publication of the last part of *Henriette-Sylvie*, Hortense printed her own response to the same stories about her escapades in a convent. She attempts, like Henriette-Sylvie, to defuse the stories by showing them to be amusing and trivial. She even displays a certain pleasure, as does Desjardins' heroine, in being the subject of gossip in the highest social circles: "On en fit cent contes ridicules au Roi ... Si vous étiez alors à la Cour, il vous souviendra qu'on y conta cet accident comme un franc tour de page."[15] (The King was told a hundred ridiculous tales about this ... If you were at Court at the time, you will remember that this accident was described as a real page's trick.) But the lightly mocking tone that buoys Desjardins' fictional narrative from beginning to end is not sustainable in Hortense Mancini's memoir. Henriette-Sylvie writes of her "amusing" destiny, while Hortense bemoans her "mauvaise destinée" and the "fatalité" that pursues her every move (32). The choice to cast herself more as the tragic victim than the picaresque adventuress *à la Sylvie* is dictated, as we have seen, by the judicial purpose for which she intends her memoirs. *Le badinage* would not have been a suitable tone for a court deposition on behalf of a woman accused of violating her obligations to husband and family.

In her fiction, Marie-Catherine Desjardins is free to explore more daring approaches to going public. An astute observer of the unwitting forays of Hortense and other women into the public sphere, Desjardins well understood the stakes involved in defending one's honor. In her mock memoir she not only shows the project of truth-telling to be inseparable from fiction-making, but she shows her heroine to be strategically engaged in an economy of talk – both written and spoken – in an effort to control her public image. It is not always a winning game, but as long as she remains a player Henriette-Sylvie has not lost.

Scenes in which the narrator seems to be listening in on male accounts of her own female life appear with more frequency as the memoirs progress. By the end of the book such eavesdropping episodes seem to underline the futility of the narrator's purpose as she had stated it at the beginning, to produce one authorized account of her story that would debunk all the others. For outlandish female lives generate not only gossip and envy but they inspire in others the urge to write and read about them, the desire to talk and listen. Madame de Villedieu knew this only too well from her own experience. She also understood the power of publicity and the way that public figures market images of themselves. By opting to write a parodic and playful fictional memoir at a time when real memoirs were first being published by women writers, she managed to explore what it might mean for a woman to publish her own life story, to reveal the political dimensions of self-justification, and to indulge in the pleasures of autobiography while exposing the impossibility of true confession.

Toward the end of her story, Henriette chooses a kind of tactical retreat to the most worldly of the convents she has come to know, where her sophisticated friend and benefactor is the Abbess. Desjardins herself had made precisely this choice in her own life immediately after publishing the first four parts of the book, in 1672, when she "retreated from the world" to a convent for a period of ten months. Although this retreat was undertaken as a flight from the perpetual persecution of her own *médisants*, it was also, as is suggested in the case of Henriette-Sylvie, a time to reflect and write. Henriette is persuaded by her friend's advice that the best form of defense against gossip is to compose oneself, both spiritually and in writing.[16] For Desjardins, the period of retreat was to be productive – she reemerged to publish, in 1673 and 1674, the final part of her memoir novel along with four other short works of fiction. The last of her works published in her lifetime, *Les Désordres de l'amour*, was printed in 1675.

Thus Desjardins' memoir novel tells the story of its own composition and thematizes the conditions of autobiographical publication. Despite her arguments for the value, in literature, of personal revelation, it was through the veil of fiction that she chose to display her own personal stories. Even when openly attacked in a personal way, she had chosen to respond via fiction. In 1667, after a humiliating residence in Brussels during which she was socially ostracized, she had published a sentimental tale (*Anaxandre*) casting a figure much like herself in a courtly intrigue illustrating the cruelty and disorder brought about by prudish and small minds. A year later, after her own lover had sold the letters she had written to him, and having failed in her efforts to prevent them from being printed, she chose to respond in kind, by publishing other private letters that portrayed her in a different light. Against the advice of friends, she opted not to pursue the matter in the courts but instead to print another group of her own letters in which she flamboyantly played the part of the forgiving mistress, bemoaning only the inevitable damage to her lover's reputation that his cynical behavior was bound to bring. In both of these instances Mme de Villedieu had set about reasserting control over her public image only indirectly, by 'repackaging' the fictionalized persona that she had come to represent in society rather than by claiming any authority to state her case more directly and openly.

Epistolary autobiography

The story of both the production and publication of Desjardins' letters to Antoine de Villedieu is a complex and fascinating example of how a woman's private voice could become a commodity over which printers, collaborators, and the woman herself struggled to gain control in the marketplace of readers. Titled *Lettres et billets galants*, the collection was printed in 1668 by Claude Barbin, complete with a *privilège du roi* naming Mademoiselle Desjardins as the author. Two months later another edition of the collection was produced, this time with the author's name removed. Based on information in a cluster of letters that Desjardins wrote to friends and to Claude Barbin during the same year, letters which she subsequently published, it is clear that this was one project that Marie-Catherine had never intended to print, and that the letters were sold to Barbin by Villedieu himself.

The "*galant*" letters that Marie-Catherine sent over a period of six years to Antoine de Villedieu were written as the result of a kind of market exchange proposed by Villedieu. Each written message from her, the two had agreed, would be repaid by a visit from him. In return for her writing, he promised visits. As the letters make clear, Villedieu's attraction to his mistress derived in no small part from his admiration of her as a public figure and a published author. He was eager to receive written messages from her displaying her writerly skills, and was disappointed when she refused to deviate from a repetitive expression of "*tendresses*" that he found both monotonous and stylistically mediocre.

Of all of her published works, the little *Lettres et billets galants* most poignantly evokes the tensions underlying Marie-Catherine's public identity as a woman writer. We can infer from her letters to Villedieu that he repeatedly pressed her for more "beautiful" letters, but Desjardins found that she could not write an expression of her feelings for him that would at the same time be esthetically pleasing. Desjardins resists the notion of writing her love even as she puts pen to paper in this strange contract to which she has agreed. In attempting to describe her feelings she repeatedly stops short, declaring "les grandes douleurs sont muettes, ... il est impossible d'exprimer ce que je ressens pour vous, et ... si quelque chose le pouvait, ce ne serait que le silence, les soupirs et les larmes"[17] (all great pain is silent; it is impossible to express what I feel for you, and ... if anything could express it, it would be silence, sighs, and tears).

The image of her writing self that Marie-Catherine projects in *Lettres et billets galants* is a literary type that Katherine Jensen has called "Epistolary Woman", the suffering, betrayed and abandoned woman who in the seventeenth century became a familiar and popular figure.[18] But while the letters record their author's painful discovery and exploration of unreciprocated love, they communicate nonetheless a sharp writer's awareness of love as a rhetorical experience.[19] It seems that this correspondence was from the outset intended at least in part to help Marie-Catherine's lover understand what a good "*billet galant*" was. He asked for her opinion of his own letters, and that she correct his epistolary style. When Marie-Catherine refused to address these questions of technique, telling him simply that it was clear from his letters that he did not truly love her, Villedieu pressured her to change her own way of writing, to demonstrate more "*esprit*" and less "*amour*". But Marie-Catherine's resistant responses to her lover's demands insist on a different kind of rhetoric, which she seems to discover or invent as their "correspondence" progresses. She tries out a variety of tactics to parry his demands for more pleasing *"billets doux"* and a more moderate expression of tenderness. When her lover objects, she scolds him for his inability to properly interpret the rhetorical turns of passion.[20] While Villedieu had hoped that his mistress's letters would provide him with examples of the rhetoric of gallantry, his expectations were disappointed, for Desjardins insists that *"esprit"* and *"belles expressions"* can only signify an absence of real passion in the writer:

> Ces belles expressions ne persuadent pas bien une violente passion; elles viennent de l'esprit et non pas du coeur. Les grandes douleurs sont muettes: mais je trouve que les vôtres vous laissent bien l'usage de la parole et la liberté de l'esprit toute entière. Néanmoins quoique vos lettres ne me persuadent pas autant que vous le souhaitez, ne laissez pas de me les continuer, et même plus fréquemment que vous n'avez fait. Vous ne me refuserez pas cette complaisance si mes satisfactions ne vous sont pas tout à fait indifférentes, puisque c'est elle seule qui me peut donner toute la joie dont je suis capable en votre absence. (53)

> (These beautiful expressions do not persuade a violent passion; they come from the mind and not the heart. Great pain is mute; but I find that yours leaves you ample use of speech and entire freedom of the mind. Nonetheless, although your letters do not persuade me as much as you would wish, do not stop sending them, and send them even more frequently than you have been. You will not refuse me this indulgence if satisfying me is not entirely a matter of indifference to you, for it is the only thing that can give me all the joy of which I am capable in your absence.)

Marie-Catherine manages, paradoxically, to retain a measure of dominance, if not self-control, in her epistolary contract with Villedieu, even as she complains of the disadvantaged position in which she is placed by the imbalance in their sentiments. Instead of the exemplary *billets galants* that Villedieu had anticipated, he received instead some lessons on how to love. Her early letters to him are dotted with the maxims characteristic of her writing style, reflections which follow her most intimate and personal thoughts, and yet which seem to nudge her reader into an awareness of the superficiality of traditional modes of self-restraint:

> Je hais fort à vous cacher mes sentiments, et pourtant il faut que je vous parle de toute autre chose que de ce que je voudrais vous dire. Sans mentir, quand on ressent de grands maux, c'est une étrange peine que d'être contraint à les dissimuler. (42)

> (I hate to hide my feelings from you, and yet I must speak to you of everything but what I would like to tell you. Without a doubt, when one feels great anguish, it is an extraordinary trial to be obliged to hide it.)

She protests Villedieu's valorization of self-control and dissimulation as a kind of emotional casuistry: "Je sais que vous n'y cherchez que l'esprit et non pas l'amour, dont les témoignages vous sont insupportables ... Votre lettre est la plus galante du monde, mais la moins capable de persuader une forte et sincère passion" (39; 50). (I know that you are looking only for wit and not love, whose expressions are intolerable to you ... Your letter is the most gallant in the world, but the least capable of persuading a strong and sincere passion.) To ask her to write in such a way is tantamount to asking her to betray her faith. Eventually, she simply states that she can no longer indulge in this sort of banter, and she stops writing, before taking up the pen once again to try to explain her position to her increasingly irritated lover.[21]

In her last letters the idea of achieving the kind of restraint Villedieu had been demanding of her no longer is evoked even as an impossibility. Instead, she indulges herself, describing her fantasy of the power she would wish for her letters, and turning the tables on her reluctant correspondent by suggesting to *him* some methods of self-deception that might enable him to see her as the person he wants her to be (p. 74). She tells him how to wishfully "read" her face when he is in her presence. As for her letters, she tells him to take them in his hands, open them, and she will try to assure that they are sufficiently opaque to force him to read them over and over:

> Je ne puis me promettre que vous vous souveniez de moi qu'autant de temps que vous lirez ma lettre, ... je vous la ferai la plus longue qu'il me sera possible. Je serai même bien aise qu'elle ne soit pas de bon sens, afin que vous la trouviez obscure, et que vous soyez contraint de la relire plusieurs fois pour l'entendre. Il faut que je me satisfasse par là, puisque je n'ose espérer que vous la trouviez assez belle pour ne vous lasser jamais de la voir ... (p. 62).

> (I cannot promise myself that you will remember me for more than the time it takes for you to read my letter, ... I will make it as long as possible. I will even be happy if it makes no sense, so that you may find it obscure and be obliged to reread it many times in order to understand it. I must be satisfied in this way, because I dare not hope that you may find it beautiful enough to never tire of seeing it ...)

Furthermore, she seems to think that if her letters are displeasing to Villedieu he will be less likely to share them with others. If he finds them tiresome, surely so would other readers, for only a sincere lover, she writes, can find pleasure in the infinite repetition of the phrase "je vous aime":

> Je ne voudrais pas satisfaire la curiosité de ceux qui souhaiteraient seulement de belles choses, et qui n'auraient pas un plus obligeant motif pour entretenir commerce avec moi. ... Je vois bien que les répétitions ne sont pas ennuyeuses en amour, car vous ne sçauriez lire rien que vous ne m'ayez ouï dire plusieurs fois. ... Si je puis juger de vos sentimens par les miens, je dois croire que la plus parfaite éloquence ne vous serait pas si agréable que la répétition d'un "je vous aime" ... (60).

> (I have no desire to satisfy the curiosity of those who would wish only for beautiful things, and who do not have a more obliging reason to keep commerce

with me … I see that repetitions are not tiresome in love, for you will not be able to read anything that you haven't heard me already say many times. … If I may judge your feelings by my own, I must believe that the most perfect eloquence would be not be as agreeable to you as the repetition of an "I love you" …)

Publishing a passion

When, after breaking off their relationship and announcing his own plans to marry a wealthy young widow, Villedieu took the further step of selling Desjardins' letters to a printer, he was openly flaunting the failure of the epistolary strategies she had proposed to him. The incredibly public nature of his betrayal seems to have taken her by surprise. Learning of the imminent appearance of her "lettres et billets galants" in a letter from a friend, Desjardins at first did not believe it was true.[22] But Villedieu's decision to publish his lover's letters in exchange for money was incontrovertible. It represented, in a sense, his attempt to have the last word on the failure of their contract, an attempt to reposition the letters he had solicited in a context of his own design, and make of himself a kind of author of the private story they told. While Marie-Catherine had refused either to teach him how to write or to heed his editorial admonitions, Villedieu was determined, nonetheless, to profit from her writing. It had been his market proposition that led to the letters being written in the first place, and by publishing them he was reasserting control over a text that he had, in fact, purchased. In addition to the packet of letters, he also sold Barbin a copy of the idealized portrait of himself that Marie-Catherine had written at the beginning of their liaison, as if to underline his own role as originator of the text, and at the same time cynically comment on his lover's failure to accurately capture his character.

Since, by law, Marie-Catherine could not prevent the publication of her letters, she demanded that her name be removed from the *privilège*.[23] First, though, she argued against publication. As we have seen, in her letter to Barbin she tries to persuade him not to print these letters that should not be exposed "à d'autres yeux qu'à ceux de l'amour même" (p. 92) (to any other eyes than those of love itself).

But until she knows for certain that the letters have in fact been published, her arguments seem to apply more to the genre of love letters than to her own particular text. She presents a hypothetical situation that could apply to any woman, and at first evokes her own case only parenthetically: " … si [les lettres tendres] sont trop passionnées, celui qui les reçoit en est assez jaloux (ou au moins le doit être) pour les sauver de l'impression" (p. 92) (If [tender letters] are too passionate, then he who receives them is jealous enough (or at least should be) to save them from being printed). When she finally does refer to her own specific situation, it is to suggest that her letters were inadequately protected, and to reiterate the argument she had made in the letters themselves, that only their addressee, and then only if he were a sincere lover, would find such letters beautiful:

> Mais quand il serait possible que le seul homme qui a des lettres tendres de moi en fût si mauvais ménager qu'il vous fût aisé d'en faire imprimer sans mon consentement, croyez-vous qu'une lettre qui est belle aux yeux d'un amant parût telle aux yeux des gens désintéressés? (92).

> (But while it might be possible that the only man who has tender letters from me has been such a poor keeper of them that you were easily able to print them without my consent, do you believe that a letter that is beautiful in the eyes of a lover could be so in the eyes of disinterested people?)

On this point, it became quickly apparent, Desjardins was dead wrong. Not only was Barbin eager to take his chances on the public's interest, he also understood that in this story it was the plot that would interest his readers at least as much as the style. And it was the audacity of Villedieu's betrayal, together with his lover's response to it, that made the plot most interesting. A year after the appearance of *Lettres et billets galants* Barbin published the letter Desjardins had written to him to protest its publication. This letter and others in which she responds to the news that Villedieu had published her letters in her absence appeared in a collection that, this time, Desjardins herself authorized.

The fact that she continued to publish her works with Barbin after 1667 may be an indication of how common it was for authors to have manuscripts printed without their consent. But if we look closely at the arguments she makes in this second letter collection, we see that Desjardins was reacting to her unauthorized publication by cutting her losses. She counters Villedieu's attempt to control her writing by giving it a new framework. She could thus hope to establish some influence over its reception.

A message written to a friend in Paris who had confirmed for her that her love letters were indeed circulating in print shows Madame de Villedieu's reaction more clearly. Here she addresses the question of how to counter her lover's bad taste with a campaign of her own. She insists that she is not interested in vengeance, but only in regaining control over her own and Villedieu's reputations. Although she had no legal recourse in her complaint against Barbin, she could have brought suit against Villedieu, but she chose instead to do the opposite, she says, and protect his reputation:

> Je suis encore si tendre là-dessus, ou pour mieux dire si peu sensée, que les intérêts propres de cet homme causent ma douleur la plus violente, et je suis plus sensible à la mauvaise réputation qu'il va acquérir qu'à celle qu'il avait entrepris de me donner ... Je veux seulement qu'on le trouve honnête homme, et non pas qu'on le traite comme un méchant; je veux empêcher qu'il ne fasse une action qui doit détruire son honnêteté, et non pas soutenir la mienne ... (94).

(I am still so sensitive on this issue, or I should say so irrational, that the self-interest of this man causes me the most violent pain, and I am more sensitive to the bad reputation that he will acquire than to the one he has undertaken to give me ... I only want him to be seen as a gentleman, and not be treated as a villain; I wish only to prevent him from committing an act that will destroy his good name, rather than try to maintain my own ...)

But by taking this tack it is not at all clear that she will be saving Villedieu from dishonor. Such a dramatic gesture of self-sacrifice on her part underscores his ungallant behavior even more strongly. And by declaring that she is willing to sacrifice her own reputation to his she is reasserting some control over the public reception of her private life. Her letters will be read in the context of her reaction to them, and she will be seen as the woman blinded and betrayed while Villedieu will be the undeserving lover. Don't try to punish him for his injustice to me, she writes, for it is I who have already allowed this damage to be done to me: "et songez qu'on se fait autant de tort en informant le public de l'aveuglement de notre estime que nos faux amis nous en font lorsqu'ils se rendent indignes de la posséder" (94) (and note that one does oneself as much damage in informing the public of the blindness of one's esteem as our false friends do when they show themselves unworthy of having it). In fact, one of her published letters to Villedieu had already indicated how her future readers should interpret any public defense she might make of her false lover's honor. Scolding Villedieu for his attempts to find a pretext for a quarrel, she had assured him that she would always strive to preserve his reputation in the public eye, no matter how unjustified his abandonment of her might be:

Vous cherchez par de continuels reproches un pretexte pour ne me plus voir, sans pouvoir en être blâmé. Mais il n'est pas nécessaire de mettre ces artifices en usage: je consens que vous ne me voyez plus, et je vous promets de vous justifier autant qu'il me sera possible. Ce sera dans l'esprit des personnes qui trouveront étrange que vous vous retiriez ainsi: mais il ne sera pas besoin que dans le mien j'entreprenne de vous justifier. Je vous y détruirai absolument ... (50–51).

(With your continuous reproaches you are seeking a pretext to no longer see me, without being blamed for it. But it is not necessary to use such artifices: I consent that you no longer see me, and I promise to justify you as long as it is within my power. This will be for the minds of those who might find it strange that you take your leave thus: but I will not be obliged to attempt to justify you in my own mind. There I will destroy you absolutely ...)

Her protestations of Villedieu's honor, then, are not to be taken as sincere, but rather as a heroic display of force and self-control in the face of her lover's weakness.

Claude Barbin's active role in determining how the letters were presented to the public makes him a third player in this struggle between Desjardins and Villedieu over how her words would be read. As a publisher, Barbin was exceptionally good at predicting public response. His aggressive marketing

practices were well known, as was his willingness to print anything he thought
would bring him a profit.[24] His purchase from Villedieu may have sparked
his interest in putting other love letters by women on the market, for in the next
year he published *Lettres portugaises* and *Lettres de Babet*, two letter narratives
that initiated the epistolary novel genre in France.[25] Women's love letters, both
real and fictional, but always purporting to be real, were turning out to be easily
saleable. The author of such letters was herself not supposed to be the person
responsible for their publication. For a woman's love letter to be considered
authentic, it was imperative that the writer be innocent of any wish that more
than one reader might see it. This definition of authenticity was to become an
esthetic requirement as well.[26]

Thus the only way to read a good love letter written by a woman, it seemed,
was either to receive one or to read stolen texts. Writers and publishers of letter
novels were quick to exploit this idea in their prefatory remarks to their readers.
The conditions under which Marie-Catherine's letters were published in 1668 –
as a result of a deal struck between the letters' addressee and a publisher – were
to be reenacted as a standard fictional frame for later epistolary novels. Barbin's
1669 preface to *Lettres portugaises* was the text that would set the pattern for
future prefatory statements in letter fiction. In it he writes that he had managed
to acquire a translation of the Portuguese nun's letters and that he is certain
there would be no objection to their publication – coming from either their
recipient or their translator.

The framing of Madame de Villedieu's real-life love story seems to have
many of the elements of a classic epistolary fiction, with some important
differences. Barbin was dealing with the love letters of a professional writer,
and having published this text against her wishes, he still wanted to continue
profiting from her other writings. And Desjardins did go on giving him her
work, beginning with the collection of letters that included her message to
Barbin arguing against publishing the love letters. It is impossible, of course, to
know exactly what motivated her decision, but it is clear that Barbin allowed
her the opportunity to give her own frame to the story and even lay the blame on
him. At the same time this additional publicity could only enhance the public's
interest in the text.

There can be no definitive answer to who, in the end, won this struggle
to control the reception of Marie-Catherine's story.[27] Such control is never
possible beyond a limited point, as she well knew, but she persisted in her
efforts to impose revisions on the way the text would be presented to the public,
first by refusing to openly sign her name to it, then by further illustrating
her theory of unconditional love by continuing to proclaim her passion for
Villedieu. The last sentence of her letter to her Paris friend, in which she
says she leaves justice to the heavens, seems prescient now, for Villedieu was
killed in battle a few months later. After his death and the remarriage of his

wife, Desjardins obtained permission from his family to take his name, thus claiming a symbolic victory in her struggle to unite Villedieu's interests with her own.

Postscript: a packet of letters

From her convent retreat in 1672, Marie-Catherine Desjardins completed *Mémoires de la vie de Henriette-Sylvie de Molière*, and also composed a short work of letter fiction, *Le Portefeuille*. Published in 1674 as part of a collection of her works, it seems to have received very little attention from her contemporaries, who were more attentive to her memoir novel and her popular collection of stories published in 1675, *Les Désordres de l'amour*.[28] The interest of this little work is principally in the way it slyly comments on the production and circulation of "gallant letters", and on the then emergent vogue of epistolary fiction.

The story itself reads like a cynical counter-example to the confessional form and style made popular by works like *Lettres portugaises* and promoted elsewhere in Desjardins' own writings. It is presented as a packet of letters written not by a woman but by a male courtier seeking advice from his correspondent, an older and wiser man living at a distance from the court. The letters, recounting the attempts of their author to refine his own understanding of "gallantry" and advance his amorous ambitions, were found by accident, we are told, by Madame "Desjardins de Villedieu" and sent to another, unnamed woman to whom she addresses a prefatory letter. In this message she expresses her disappointment at being unable to identify the writer of the letters. In fact, she concludes, these letters could have been written by any number of *"gens du grand monde"*:

> J'ai fort raisonné sur l'histoire dont elles traitent, et comme je suis persuadée que les noms en sont supposés, j'ai fait ce qu'il m'a été possible pour deviner les véritables. Mais je n'y ai rien imaginé qui m'ait semblé juste. Ce qu'il y a de vrai, c'est que la manière dont cela est écrit est fort à la mode, et que le caractère des gens qui font les aventures est celui de la plupart des gens du grand monde. (Homand, 3).

> (I have thought a great deal about the story they tell, and as I am persuaded that the names are not real, I have done what was possible to discover the true ones. But I could come up with nothing that seemed right to me. What is true, is that the way in which this is written is very fashionable, and that the character of those who have the adventures is that of most high society people.)

Thus in her own experiment in letter fiction Desjardins de Villedieu turns the tables on an already popular epistolary drama. She gives her readers a packet of letters that she presents, not as the sincere outpourings of passion by an anonymous and singular female voice, but as a rhetoric of gallantry common to all male members of a specific social milieu. To translate into writing a sentimental voice that follows the rhetorical rules for gallant speech, is to lose the uniqueness of that voice, to make of the person speaking a type, identifiable only as one of *des gens du grand monde*. The principal figure in the story is, in the end, disillusioned by the inevitable deceptions of his gallant adventures, and declares he is renouncing life and court and retiring to the country. But Desjardins invites her female correspondent to do the opposite, to return from her retreat and reengage herself in the world. She insists that her correspondent return, in person, to share her thoughts about the text she has offered her through conversation rather than writing:

> Vous m'en direz à votre retour ce que vous en penserez; car, Madame, ne vous avisez pas de ne faire que le mander: il n'y a que trop longtemps que votre absence dure, faites-la cesser comme vous me l'avez promis, et songez que personne ne la supporte avec tant d'impatience que votre très humble et très obéissante servante,
>
> *Desjardins de Villedieu*

> (You will tell me when you return what you think of them; for Madame, don't decide to just send it. Your absence has already lasted too long; bring it to an end as you promised me, and know that no one bears it with as much impatience as your very humble and obedient servant, Desjardins de Villedieu.)

As in her memoir novel, in this epistolary fiction Desjardins examines the failures of communication, the inevitable workings of deception and self-deception that underpin both the written representations of self and the act of reading and receiving those representations. Disillusioned, perhaps, by her failure to compose herself to her satisfaction in both intimate and public spheres, Desjardins reflects in these writings on the serpentine routes by which a singular voice is transposed into print. But with her admonition to her female interlocutor to return, after all is said and done, to a world in which texts are collectively read, talked about, and revised, she invites all of her readers to indulge in the pleasures of vocal participation. With this closing invitation she acknowledges the process of life-writing to be only part of a long conversation, an activity that is always of necessity fragmentary, and to be effective at all a process that can only exist in bits and pieces, as parts of a whole that is never entirely in any individual writer's grasp.

Notes

1. Illuminating discussions of Villedieu's contributions to new ways of writing both history and fiction in the seventeenth century may be found in Faith Beasley, *Revising History: Women's Fiction and Memoirs in Seventeenth-Century France* (New Brunswick and London: Rutgers University Press, 1990), pp. 162–90; and

René Démoris, *Le Roman à la première personne: du Classicisme aux Lumières* (Paris: Colin, 1975), pp. 134–40.

2. *Les Désordres de l'amour*, ed. Micheline Cuénin (Geneva: Droz, 1970), pp. liv–v.

3. *Roman et société sous Louis XIV: Madame de Villedieu* (Paris: Champion, 1979), vol. I, pp. 489.

4. Ibid., I, pp. 58–72.

5. "J'ose espérer que ... mes innocents bergers ... ne laisseront pas de vous être agréable et qu'ils auront assez de bonheur pour m'obtenir la permission de vous consacrer quelque jour des ouvrages plus achevés ... ", cited in ibid., vol. I, pp. 68–9.

6. Madame de Sévigné in her letters to her daughter, and Bussy-Rabutin in his correspondence with Madame de Scudéry, for example, compare the Duc de Mazarin to Tartuffe and Hortense to the romantic but impractical heroines of contemporary novels.

7. Joan DeJean discusses the ways in which this novel may be read as a challenge to the injustices of laws governing women in the ancien régime, particularly as pertaining to marriage and divorce, in *Tender Geographies: Women and the Origin of the Novel in France* (New York: Columbia University Press, 1991), pp. 132–4.

8. Cuénin, in her introduction to the modern facsimile edition of *Henriette-Sylvie*, itemizes a number of allusions to contemporary incidents that are woven through the plot, as well as the autobiographical elements, though she warns against the sort of forced autobiographical reading that Villedieu has traditionally been subjected to. *Mémoires de la vie de Henriette-Sylvie de Molière* (Tours: Université François Rabelais, 1977), pp. vi–xiii. On the tendency toward autobiographical readings of Villedieu and other women writers, and their consequent notoriety, see DeJean, *Tender Geographies*, pp. 127–40.

9. Cuénin suggests that Henriette-Sylvie has a compensatory function for her creator: "Tout se passe comme si Marie-Catherine, en une sorte de psychodrame, se dédommageait de la bassesse de sa naissance et de la cruauté de ses échecs par le biais de la création romanesque", *Mémoires de la Vie*, Introduction, p. vii.

10. Cuénin (ed.), pp. 5–6. All subsequent citations will be from this edition, which is a glossed facsimile of the 1722 printing of Villedieu's *Oeuvres complètes* (Paris, la veuve de Claude Barbin). All English translations are my own.

11. See Sarah Hanley, "Engendering the State: Family Formation and State Building in Early Modern France", *French Historical Studies*, **16**, 1 (Spring 1989), 4–27.

12. This aspect of the novel had been examined most recently by Donna Kuizenga in "Seizing the Pen: Narrative Power and Gender in Villedieu's *Mémoires de la vie de Henriette-Sylvie de Molière* and Manley's *Adventures of Rivella*", in Colette H. Winn and Donna Kuizenga (eds), *Women Writers in Pre-Revolutionary France: Strategies of Emancipation* (New York: Garland Press, 1997), pp. 383–95. She aptly describes how Henriette-Sylvie "transforms herself into a textual commodity, a product designed to compete in the marketplace against the falsified versions of her life story" (385).

13. Cuénin points this out in her gloss on the passage (p. 332).

14. Kuizenga discusses the subversive and liberating force of critical irony in this novel in "Seizing the pen", 385–8. On this point see also Nicole Boursier, "Le Corps de Henriette-Sylvie", in Ronald W. Tobin (ed.), *Le Corps au XVIIe siècle* (Paris: Biblio 17, 1995), pp. 271–80. Deborah Shwartz discusses how Henriette-Sylvie is aided by other female figures in the story in her efforts to combat the force

of *médisance* and reclaim her life story, in "Villedieu, Henriette-Sylvie de Molière, and Feminine Empowerment", in Michel Guggenheim (ed.), *Women in French Literature* (Saratoga: Anima Libri, 1988), pp. 77–90.

15. *Mémoires D.M.L.D.M. à M. ***, in *Mémoires d'Hortense et de Marie Mancini*, ed. Gerard Doscot (Paris: Mercure de France, 1987), pp. 54–5.

16. "... retirez-vous avec moi dans ma solitude, ... faites un peu de reflexion sur tous les incidents de votre vie, ... Il y a de quoi fournir un gros Roman; ne voulez-vous point enfin vous donner un peu de repos, et vous mettre en état que la fortune, et tous vos autres ennemis ne vous puissent nuire?" (301). (Retire with me in my solitude, ... reflect a little on all the events of your life, ... there is enough to fill a huge novel; don't you want to finally take some rest and put yourself in a state such that fortune, and all your other enemies, cannot harm you?)

17. *Lettres et billets galants*, ed. Micheline Cuénin (Paris: Publications de la Société d'Etude du XVIIe Siècle, 1975), pp. 53, 36. All parenthetical references below are to this edition. I have modernized the spelling in the French quotations, and the English translations are my own.

18. *Writing Love: Letters, Women and the Novel in France, 1605–1776* (Carbondale: Southern Illinois University Press, 1995), pp. 36–57.

19. Jensen sees Desjardins' "amorous self" as distinct from her identity as an author (45). I think that Desjardins exhibits more lucidity and self-control than this, deliberately using various rhetorical techniques to resist her lover's demands and suggest his inadequacies as a writer and reader of letters.

20. See, for example, p. 57.

21. "Le désir de conserver votre estime m'a fait dissimuler autant qu'il m'a été possible la cause de mon silence. Mais puisque vous l'avez connue, je vois bien qu'il serait inutile de vous la désavouer. Il est certain que je ne suis plus en pouvoir de vous écrire d'agréables lettres, et que toutes celles qui vous ont plu ne venaient pas de moi. Mon esprit ni mon étude n'y avaient aucune part, et je recevois le plus injustement du monde la gloire que vous m'en donniez" (73–4). (The desire to retain your esteem made me hide the cause of my silence as long as I could. But since you have learned it, I see that it would be useless to deny it. It is certain that it is not in my power to write you agreeable letters, and that all those that pleased you did not come from me. My mind and my education had no part in them, and I most unjustly received the praise that you gave me for them.)

22. The letters exchanged between Desjardins, Barbin, and others concerning the publication of *Lettres et billets galants* are included in an appendix to Cuénin's edition.

23. According to the law, printers had the authority to publish manuscripts without the consent of the author. Alain Viala discusses legislation and codes governing printing practices in *Naissance de l'écrivain* (Paris: Minuit, 1985), pp. 85–122.

24. Gervais Reed discusses this aspect of Barbin's reputation among his contemporaries in *Claude Barbin, 1628–1698: Paris Bookseller During the Reign of Louis XIV* (Geneva: Droz, 1975), pp. 62–5.

25. For discussions of the early history of the letter novel and its connection to women's writing, see the essays by Goldsmith and Jensen in Elizabeth C. Goldsmith (ed.), *Writing the Female Voice: Essays on Epistolary Literature* (Boston: Northeastern University Press, 1989), and Gabrielle Verdier, "Gender and Rhetoric in some Seventeenth-Century Love Letters", *Esprit Créateur*, **23**, 2 (1983), pp. 47–57.

26. For an example of this prescriptive esthetic argument, see La Fevrerie's essay on

epistolary style written in 1683, where he states that the love letter is a genre in which women excel, and goes on to say that fictional examples of the genre are vastly inferior to the real thing: "Du Style épistolaire", numéro extraordinaire du *Mercure galant* (juillet 1683), 35–7.

27. DeJean traces the fascination with Madame de Villedieu's private life and the varying published versions of her biography during her lifetime and immediately following her death in *Tender Geographies*, pp. 130–34.

28. *Le Portefeuille* was originally published as part of a volume of her works entitled *Oeuvres mêlées*, and is now exceedingly rare. A modern edition edited by Jean-Paul Homand was published in 1979 by the University of Exeter.

Conclusion

Madame's goal is to be able to remain at liberty in Madrid, and in her own house ...

(letter from Ferdinando Colonna to Lorenzo Onofrio Colonna, 4 February 1677)

From within the idealized enclosure of the *cabinet* evoked by Madeleine de Scudéry as an alternative to sociability, to the fast-moving public stagecoaches occupied by Madame de Villedieu's runaway women, the writers I have studied here have all been engaged in designing spaces that will adequately contain their reflections and private conversation. None of these writers settled for long in the classical *cabinet*. In fact, committing their life stories to a form of publication was understood by all of them as a kind of break-out, an expression of dissatisfaction with the discursive walls that had previously contained them. In her descriptions of her new life in Canada, Marie de l'Incarnation returned repeatedly to the spatial configurations that had most impressed her: the strangeness of a vast wilderness without borders, and the persistence with which her Indian charges would scale the walls of the convent to return to it.[1] Jeanne Guyon, to satisfy her followers' thirst for her conversation, and to provide them with the material they wanted to commemorate her life, in her last years created a kind of private republic of letters which acknowledged no borders, either national or denominational. Jeanne des Anges wrote a narrative of her life to emphasize the story of her own "cure", which she had first publicly displayed by leaving the convent and making a ceremonial journey across France. Marie Mancini wrote her memoirs as an angry response to another account of her life which had placed her in a prison from which there was no escaping, and her sister Hortense put her life story into circulation to reintroduce her own voice into the discussions concerning her fate taking place in Paris and Versailles, places where she could no longer physically be present.

Madame de Villedieu's fictional autobiographical voices, commenting on the difficulty of bringing a private life out into the open, also offer insightful predictions concerning the future of self-publication. Once Henriette-Sylvie has left the familial enclosure and begun to follow her own itinerary, she learns that there is no going back, for wherever she travels she leaves the mark of her passage, creating the conditions for public "talk" about her private self. Although her forays into the wide world alternate regularly with retreats to castles and cloisters, each time she reemerges she discovers that her public image has continued to grow, hydra-like, in her absence. Villedieu seems to be marveling at the capacity of public conversation to distort and reinvent the spectacle of a woman's private life. Her adventurous heroine, modeled after real escaped ladies such as Hortense and Marie Mancini, is able to maintain an ironic distance from, and even take pleasure in, the drama of her own life even as she loses control of it, and thus suggest to the reader that the risks of going public might be worth taking.[2]

These early examples of women producing and circulating their life stories coincide with two cultural innovations that greatly facilitated both the circulation of personal writing and the freedom of women to travel. In the early seventeenth century, the enclosed, horse-drawn carriage or *carrosse* became the standard means of transportation for wealthy families. Obviously much faster than the sedan chair, and, unlike horseback riding, a socially acceptable way for women to travel, the design of a large enclosed carriage also created a kind of moveable private *cabinet*.[3] Under Mazarin and Colbert, a state postal system was consolidated which offered both regular mail delivery and a scheduled public conveyance system, allowing individual travelers to ride in the postal carriage.[4] The new postal system not only established a routine means of communicating by letter, it also gave a new sense of anonymity to the practice of letter-writing, a consequence that sensitive epistolarians found both fascinating and slightly dangerous. One's letters were no longer carried by one's private servant to their destination, they now rubbed up against the written conversations of any number of unknown private persons; although still private writing, they passed through a more public space before reaching their destination. As for the passengers in the stagecoach, they could find themselves, like Madame de Villedieu's heroine Henriette-Sylvie, engaged in conversation in a kind of miniature salon whose doors were open to anyone who could afford to enter.[5]

All of the women whose writings I have discussed in this book may be said, in their own lives, to have embraced the possibilities of travel. In both their texts and their lives they exploited new modes of self-circulation that were offered to them. Their writings all express the seductive pull of open spaces, while at the same time conveying a kind of panic about how precisely they will manage to negotiate these spaces, and where they will be able to pause and find shelter. A similar anxiety is communicated in their memoirs, as they release them to the world.

Reception of a text, like a person, is difficult to predict outside of one's immediate social circle. But the passage from voice to print required this displacement. In order to write of herself, even to speak of herself, the early modern woman had to dislodge herself from the space she habitually occupied. To write their life stories, all of the women I have studied here had to break free of the household and then identify or invent a space outside that would shelter them, that they could inhabit as private individuals.[6]

Looking back, though, it is interesting to observe that, once their writings were out, the first responses to these women's texts were often more accommodating than the critical reception they were to receive over time. Jeanne Guyon's later influence on the English and German Romantics may have been significant, but it went largely unrecognized in nineteenth-century France, where the response to her effusive devotion was more reactionary. Rousseau's objections to the airing of women's devotional practices outside of the household were to set the tone for subsequent ridicule. On Guyon he has Saint-Preux write Julie:

> Ainsi cette Mme Guyon dont vous me parlez eût mieux fait, ce me semble, de remplir avec soin ses devoirs de mère de famille, d'élever chrétiennement ses enfants, de gouverner sagement sa maison, que d'aller composer des livres de dévotion, disputer avec des évêques, et se faire mettre à la Bastille pour des rêveries où l'on ne comprend rien.[7]

> (Thus that Madame Guyon who you speak about would have done better, it seems to me, to carefully fulfill her duties as a mother, bringing up her children in a Christian manner, wisely managing her household, than to go off composing devotional books and arguing with bishops, getting herself thrown into the Bastille for fantasies that no one understands.)

After Jeanne des Anges was consigned to the annals of hysteria in the nineteenth century, it became impossible to encounter her writing without the inevitable accompanying pseudo-scientific gloss. Marie de l'Incarnation's beatification in the twentieth century may have actually derailed, until very recently, more objective attempts to interpret her writing.

Marie and Hortense Mancini constitute a particularly poignant case study in the editing and reception of women's life writing. Perhaps reacting to the speed with which her published memoirs were sensationalized and imitated, Hortense Mancini refused subsequent requests to defend herself in any written form, preferring to leave the task to more thick-skinned sympathizers like Saint-Evremond, who assumed her voice and wrote letters to Paris in her name during her divorce hearings.[8] Later generations of readers have been less sympathetic, opting quite blindly to accept the claims of her enemies that she wrote her memoirs to disguise the truth of her extramarital transgressions. In a critical gesture that has become typical of commentary on early modern women's autobiography, discussion of Hortense's memoirs has been thus deflected into a debate about whether or not she was telling the truth about her love affairs.[9] Marie Mancini's memoirs have suffered even more editorial abuse. It is perhaps a form of back-handed flattery that her life story continues to offer fodder for scurrilous publication today. The most recent editorial distortion of her autobiography is a re-edition of the apocryphal memoirs of 1676, in which the editor casually insinuates that Mancini herself authored them, ignoring ample published information to the contrary.[10] Modern Italian translations of the memoirs of both Hortense and Marie add sarcastic glosses and subtitles to the text, inviting a receptive stance that Patricia Cholakian has termed that of a "policing reader".[11] Even the newest biography of Marie Mancini by the historian Claude Dulong indulges in a nagging commentary on her flighty character, her impulsiveness, her inexplicable nature, which undermines the otherwise valuable contribution the book makes to document-based studies of Marie's life.[12]

When we consider the dense discursive context within which Marie wrote and published her memoirs, the reasons for her so-called "impulsive" and "rash" behavior in refusing to return to her husband, and then circulating the story of her life, can be seen to be more rationally motivated. As I have shown, Marie wrote her memoirs to counter the publicity that she knew was not only circulating in France in the form of a false autobiography, but also to strengthen her position in her negotiations with her husband and the court of Spain for authorization to live independently. The voluminous correspondence that Lorenzo Colonna maintained with his network of spies attached to the sequence of courts and convents where his wife sought protection demonstrates that Marie's supposed obsession with the idea that she was being followed and watched all the time was in fact a simple acknowledgment of reality. To move about freely, to be able to unlock the doors to one's home and move to another place, to travel accompanied only by companions of one's choice, these are not simply flights of fancy in the minds of spoiled aristocratic women, as some of Hortense and Marie's readers have suggested. They were rather the only reliable indicators of one's liberty. Hortense's husband had literally locked her in their living quarters and sealed off the doors leading from Hortense's apartment to that of her brother Philippe. Lorenzo Colonna's authority extended much further than that of Armand de Mazarin, and during Marie's itinerant journeys he came to view his ability to have her locked up as a standard by which he could measure the extent of his political influence in the country in which she was residing. That she chose finally to remain in Spain has been interpreted by some as a sign of her desperation and faulty logic, since Lorenzo's influence was nominally strong there. But in Spain the one right that Lorenzo did not have was the right to have his wife imprisoned, as letters sent to him from his emissaries attest.

The epistolary messages sent to Marie's husband in Rome during the months that she was writing and publishing her memoirs suggest that she, like her sister, hoped that her text would help her obtain a divorce from her husband. On 4 February 1677, Ferdinando Colonna wrote his brother: "Madame continues to propose a thousand ideas about divorce and other crazy notions; you may be sure that the furies that inhabit her are inspiring such thoughts ..." One month later Marie sent her husband the first pages of her book, and on 19 March a letter to Colonna from the Archbishop di Cesarea in Madrid advised him that it would not be possible to imprison his wife: "I have indicated before to Your Excellency that there would be great difficulty in executing your notion to have Madame shut up in a tower or castle ... here there is great respect for the female sex ..." And again on 2 August the same correspondent replied to Colonna's apparent pursuit of the matter: "That you find it strange that one cannot secure a wife on her husband's orders, and have her shut up in a fortress, I find completely in keeping with Italian practices. Here, though, there are different ways of dealing with the ladies ..."[13]

When we understand how the Mancini memoirs were conceived and published as part of a complicated strategic conversation about their authors' fate, it becomes clearer just how concretely the project of writing them was an effort both to escape confinement and create for the writers an alternative habitable space. To write of one's private life, or even to assume a fictional autobiographical voice, involved both an abandonment of one's "house" or family name and the location of a safe space from which to continue speaking and writing. The goal of "liberty", so persistently evoked in Marie Mancini's memoirs and letters home, is always connected to the idea of shelter or respite from flight.

It is essential, if we are to properly grasp the meaning of the written lives of early modern women, to consider how they were composed, as responses to other versions of their lives that had already been rendered public. The strategies these writers used to circulate their stories in epistolary and manuscript form, and the events that inspired them to go into print, also form crucial parts of the picture. The French attentiveness to the importance of conversation as an aesthetic form as well as a courtly or social skill had a particular bearing on the representation of private voices in first-person writing in this period.[14] The practice of confession and the role of the spiritual advisor in Counter-Reformation Catholicism also embedded the private testimony of French *dévotes* in specific human interactions. The writers I have studied understood their writing projects to be interactive and dialogical. To some extent, this is true of all writers who produced their works before the advent of copyright, before what Roger Chartier terms the "fiction of the integral work", independent of the different material forms it inevitably takes in the world. In the case of women writers of the Old Regime, for whom going public was as yet an uncharted voyage, the practice of publication was one part of an urgent and sustained conversation with others who claimed authority over their lives.

Notes

1. See Marie-Florine Bruneau's discussion of this in *Women Mystics Confront the Modern World: Marie de l'Incarnation (1599–1672) and Madame Guyon (1648–1717)* (Albany: State University of New York, 1998), pp. 114–22.

2. On the strategic value of irony in Villedieu's pseudo-memoir see Donna Kuizenga, "Seizing the Pen: Narrative Power and Gender in Villedieu's *Mémoires de la vie de Henriette-Sylvie de Molière* and Manley's *Adventures of Rivella*", in Colette H. Winn and Donna Kuizenga (eds), *Women Writers in Pre-Revolutionary France: Strategies of Emancipation* (New York: Garland Publishing, 1997), pp. 383–95.

3. László Tarr, *The History of the Carriage* (Budapest: Corvina, 1969), pp. 214–37.

4. On the history of the postal system see A. Belloc, *Les Postes françaises* (Paris: Firmin-Didot, 1886).

5. In an interesting excursus, Joan Landes explores how stagecoach sociability is used as a visual metaphor for more disorienting cultural interactions in Ettore Scola's film *La Nuit de Varennes*, in *Women and the Public Sphere in the Age of the French Revolution* (Ithaca, NY: Cornell University Press, 1988), pp. 94–106.

6. Roger Chartier describes the newly conceived "private" sphere in similar terms in Chartier (ed.), *History of Private Life*, vol. 3 (Cambridge, MA: Harvard University Press, 1989), p. 400.

7. *Julie ou La Nouvelle Héloïse* (Paris: Classiques Garnier, 1988), p. 685.

8. Saint-Evremond, *Works* (1728), vols II and III.

9. See Patricia Francis Cholakian's discussion of this point in "Sex, Lies, and Autobiography: Hortense Mancini's *Mémoires*", in Winn and Kuizenga (eds), 17–30.

10. I refer to Maurice Lever's edition of the pseudo *Mémoires de M.L.P.M.M.* which he retitles *Cendre et poussière, Mémoires* (Paris: Le Comptoir, 1997). Promotional publicity for this edition described it as "Les Mémoires 'non autorisés' du premier amour de Louis XIV" (The unauthorized Memoirs of the first love of Louis XIV).

11. Recent translations of the Doscot edition were published as *I piaceri della stupidità, Ortensia Mancini, duchessa di Massarino* and *I dispiaceri del Cardinale, Maria Mancini, connestabile Colonna* (Palermo: Sellerio, 1987), ed. Daria Galateria. For Cholakian's characterization see "Sex, Lies, and Autobiography".

12. *Marie Mancini, la première passion de Louis XIV* (Paris: Perrin, 1994).

13. Autograph letters to Lorenzo Onofrio Colonna in the Colonna Archive, Biblioteca Statale Santa Scolastica, Subiaco, Italy. I have translated from the original Italian. The project of cataloguing this archive is ongoing and scheduled for completion in 2000.

14. For discussions of this tradition see Elizabeth C. Goldsmith, *Exclusive Conversations: The Art of Interaction in Seventeenth-Century France* (Philadelphia: University of Pennsylvania Press, 1988); Christophe Strosetski, *Rhétorique de la conversation* (Paris: Biblio 17, 1984); and Marc Fumaroli, *Le Genre des genres littéraires français: la conversation* (New York: Oxford University Press, 1992).

Bibliography

Armogathe, Jean-Robert. "Madeleine, ou le corps de Jeanne: Le corps mystique dans l'autobiographie de Jeanne Guyon", in Jean Le Brun (ed.), *La Folie et le corps*. Paris: Presses de l'ENS, 1985. 245–60.

Balsama, George. "Madame Guyon, Heterodox", *Church History*, September 1973, 350–65.

Beasley, Faith. *Revising History: Women's Fiction and Memoirs in Seventeenth-Century France*. New Brunswick and London: Rutgers University Press, 1990.

Belloc, Alexis. *Les Postes françaises*. Paris: Firmin-Didot, 1886.

Beugnot, Bernard. *Discours de la retraite au XVIIe siècle*. Paris: Presses Universitaires de France, 1996.

Boiteau, D. and C.L. Livet (eds). *L'Histoire amoureuse des Gaules suivie des Romans historico-satiriques du XVIIe siècle*. Paris: P. Jannet, 1857.

Bossuet, Jacques Bénigne. *Relation sur le quiétisme*, in *Oeuvres*, ed. Abbé Velat and Yvonne Champailler. Paris: Gallimard, 1970. Vol. 19, 1099–177.

———— *Correspondance*, ed. C. Urbain and E. Levesque. Paris: Hachette, 1920.

Bossy, John. *Christianity in the West, 1400–1700*. Oxford: Oxford University Press, 1985.

Bottereau, Georges. "Jean-Baptiste Saint-Jure S.I., 1588–1657," in *Archivum Historicum Societas IESV*, **XLIX**, 97, pp. 161–202.

Bourignon, Antoinette. *La Vie de Damoiselle Antoinette Bourignon, écrite partie par elle-même, partie par une personne de sa connaissance ...* , ed. Pierre Poiret. Amsterdam: Jean Riewerts et Pierre Arents, 1683.

Boursier, Nicole. "Le Corps de Henriette-Sylvie", in Ronald W. Tobin (ed.), *Le Corps au XVIIe siècle*. Paris: Biblio 17, 1995, 271–80.

Boutauld, Michel. *Méthode pour converser avec Dieu*. Paris: S. Mabre Cramoisy, 1679. New edn, Paris: Ch. Amat, 1899.

Bowman, Frank. "From History to Hysteria: Nineteenth-Century Discourse on Loudun", in *French Romanticism: Intertextual and Interdisciplinary Readings*. Baltimore: Johns Hopkins, 1990. 106–21.

Brémond, Henri. *Histoire littéraire du sentiment religieux en France*. Paris: Bloud and Gay, 1926. New edn, Paris: Armand Colin, 1966.

Bruneau, Marie-Florine. "Marie de l'Incarnation: L'Anthropologie Mystique", in Bernard Beugnot (ed.), *Voyages. Récits et imaginaire*. Paris: Biblio 17 (1984), 181–98.

———— "Le Projet autobiographique: Guyon à l'orée de la modernité," *Papers on French Seventeenth-Century Literature*, **10**, 18 (1983), 59–68.

———— *Women Mystics Confront the Modern World: Marie de l'Incarnation (1599–1672) and Madame Guyon (1648–1717)*. Albany: State University of New York, 1998.

Bynum, Caroline. *Jesus as Mother*. Berkeley: University of California Press, 1982.

Cavallera, Ferdinand. "L'Autobiographie de Jeanne des Anges d'après des documents inédits", in Jeanne des Anges, *Autobiographie d'une hystérique possédée*, eds. Gabriel Legué et Gilles de la Tourette. Grenoble: Jerôme Millon, 1985, 323–32.

Certeau, Michel de. "Surin's Melancholy", in *Heterologies: Discourse on the Other*. Minneapolis: University of Minnesota, 1986.

—— *La Fable mystique: XVIe–XVIIe siècle*. Paris: Gallimard, 1982.

—— *La Possession de Loudun*. Paris, Juillard, 1970.

—— "La Pensée religieuse", in Pierre Abraham and Roland Derné (eds). *Histoire littéraire de la France*, vol. III. Paris: Editions Sociales, 1974.

—— *The Writing of History*, trans. Tom Conley. New York: Columbia University Press, 1988.

—— *The Mystic Fable*, trans. Michael B. Smith. Chicago: University of Chicago Press, 1992.

Chartier, Roger (ed.). *History of Private Life*, vol. 3. Cambridge, MA: Harvard University Press, 1989.

—— *The Order of Books*, trans. Lydia Cochrane. Stanford: Stanford University Press, 1994.

Cholakian, Patricia. "Sex, Lies, and Autobiography: The Memoirs of Hortense Mancini", in Colette H. Winn and Donna Kuizenga (eds), *Women Writers of the Ancien Régime: Strategies of Emancipation*. New York: Garland Press, 1997.

Cognet, Louis. "Dom Claude Martin. (1619–1696) et le mysticisme français", *Revue d'Histoire de l'Eglise de France*, 43 (1957), 125–49.

—— *Crépuscule des Mystiques: Le conflit Fénelon–Bossuet*. Tournai: Desclée, 1958.

—— *De la Dévotion moderne à la spiritualité française*. Paris: Fayard, 1958.

Cuénin, Micheline. *Roman et société sous Louis XIV: Madame de Villedieu*. Paris: Champion, 1979.

Davis, Natalie Zemon. *Women on the Margins*. Cambridge, MA: Harvard University Press, 1995.

DeJean, Joan. *Tender Geographies: Women and the Origins of the Novel in France*. New York: Columbia University Press, 1991.

Démoris, René. *Le Roman à la première personne: Du classicisme aux Lumières*. Paris: Armand Colin, 1975.

Dessertine, Daniel. *Divorcer à Lyon sous la Révolution et l'Empire*. Lyon: Presses Universitaires de Lyon, 1981.

Dulong, Claude. *Marie Mancini: La Première passion de Louis XIV*. Paris: Perrin, 1994.

Dulong, Gustave. *L'Abbé de Saint-Réal*. Paris: E. Champion, 1921.

Eckman, Mary Christensen. "Different Accounts: Women's Memoirs in Seventeenth-Century France." PhD dissertation, Michigan, 1998.

Erard, Claude. *Plaidoyé prononcé au Grand Conseil pour M. le Duc de Mazarin: contre Mme la Duchesse de Mazarin son épouse*. Paris, 1690.

Fénelon, François de Salignac de la Mothe. *Correspondance*, ed. Jean Orcibal. 13 vols. Paris: Klincksieck, 1972.

—— *De l'Education des filles*. *Oeuvres*. Ed. Jacques Le Brun. Paris: Gallimard, 1983.

Flandrin, Jean-Louis. *Families in Former Times: Kinship, Household, and Sexuality*, trans. Richard Southern. Cambridge: Cambridge University Press, 1979.

Fumaroli, Marc. *Le Genre des genres littéraires français: la conversation*. New York: Oxford University Press, 1992.

Garapon, Jean. "Mademoiselle à Saint-Fargeau: la découverte de l'écriture", *Papers on French Seventeenth-Century Literature*, **XXII**, 42. (1995), 37–47.

Goldsmith, Elizabeth C. *Exclusive Conversations: The Art of Interaction in Seventeenth-Century France*. Philadelphia: University of Pennsylvania Press, 1988.
────── "Authority, Authenticity, and the Publication of Letters by Women", in Goldsmith (ed.), *Writing the Female Voice: Essays on Epistolary Literature*. Boston: Northeastern University Press, 1989. 46–59.
Goldsmith, Elizabeth C. and Dena Goodman (eds). *Going Public: Women and Publishing in Early Modern France*. Ithaca: Cornell University Press, 1995.
Gondal, Marie-Louise. *Madame Guyon: Un nouveau visage*. Paris: Beauchesne, 1989.
────── "L'Autobiographie de Madame Guyon (1648–1715): La découverte et l'apport de deux nouveaux manuscrits", *XVIIe siècle*, **164**, 3 (1989), 307–23.
Gordon, Daniel. *Citizens Without Sovereignty: Equality and Sociability in French Thought, 1670–1789*. Princeton: Princeton University Press, 1994.
Greenberg, Mitchell. "Passion Play: Jeanne des Anges, Devils, Hysteria and the Incorporation of the Classical Subject", ch. 3 of *Subjectivity and Subjugation in Seventeenth-Century Drama and Prose*. Cambridge: Cambridge University Press, 1992.
Gunn, Janet. *Autobiography: Toward a Poetics of Experience*. Philadelphia: University of Pennsylvania Press, 1982.
Guyon, Jeanne. *Le "Moyen Court" et autres récits*, ed. Marie-Louise Gondal. Grenoble: Jérôme Millon, 1995.
────── "Lettres au Duc de Chevreuse". Autograph letters, Archives Saint-Sulpice, Paris.
────── *Lettres chrétiennes et spirituelles*. 5 vols. London: n.p., 1768.
────── *Récits de captivité*, ed. Marie-Louise Gondal. Grenoble: Jérôme Millon, 1992.
────── *La Vie de Madame J.M.B. de la Mothe-Guyon, écrite par elle-même*. Paris: Dervy-Livres, 1983.
Hale, Rosemary. "Imitatio Mariae: Motherhood Motifs in Devotional Memoirs". *Mystics Quarterly*, **16** (1990), 193–203.
Hanley, Sarah. "Engendering the State: Family Formation and State Building in Early Modern France". *French Historical Studies*, **16**, 1 (Spring 1989), 4–27.
Harth, Erica. "The Salon Woman Goes Public, … Or Does She?", in Elizabeth C. Goldsmith and Dena Goodman (eds). *Going Public: Women and Publishing in Early Modern France*, 179–93. Ithaca: Cornell University Press, 1995.
────── *Cartesian Women: Versions and Subversions of Rational Discourse in the Old Regime*. Ithaca: Cornell University Press, 1992.
Huxley, Aldous. *The Devils of Loudun*. New York: Harper and Row, 1952.
Jeanne des Anges. *Autobiographie d'une hystérique possédée*, eds. Gabriel Legué and Gilles de la Tourette. Grenoble: Jérôme Millon, 1985.
────── Correspondance. Manuscript copy, dossier *Jean-Joseph Surin* (cote GSu 21), Archives SJ, Vanves, France.
Jelinek, Estelle (ed.). *Women's Autobiography: Essays in Criticism*. Bloomington: Indiana University Press, 1980.
Jensen, Katherine Ann. *Writing Love: Letters, Women, and the Novel in France, 1605–1776*. Carbondale: Southern Illinois University Press, 1995.
Jones, Ann Rosalind. "City Women and Their Audiences: Louise Labé and Veronica Franco", in Margaret W. Ferguson, Maureen Quilligan, and Nancy J. Vickers (eds). *Rewriting the Renaissance: The Discourses of Sexual Difference in Early Modern Europe*. Chicago: University of Chicago Press, 1986. 299–316.
Jusserand, J.J. (ed.). *Recueil des instructions données aux ambassadeurs et ministres de France*, vol. 25, pt 2. Paris: F. Alcan, 1884.

Kolakowski, Lescek. *Chrétiens sans église: La conscience religieuse et le lien confessionnel au 17e siècle.* Paris: Gallimard, 1969.

Kristeva, Julia. "Un Pur silence: La perfection de Jeanne Guyon", in *Histoires d'amour.* Paris: Editions Denoël, 1983. 277–356.

Kuizenga, Donna. "Seizing the Pen: Narrative Power and Gender in Villedieu's *Mémoires de la vie de Henriette-Sylvie de Molière* and Manley's *Adventures of Rivella*", in Colette H. Winn and Donna Kuizenga (eds). *Women Writers in Pre-Revolutionary France: Strategies of Emancipation.* New York: Garland Press, 1997. 383–96.

Lafayette, Marie-Madeleine Pioche de la Vergne. *Histoire de Madame Henriette d'Angleterre.* Paris: Mercure de France, 1988.

La Guette, Catherine Meurdrac, Madame de. *Mémoires de Madame de la Guette, écrits par elle-même.* La Haye: Adrian Moetjens, 1681.

Lalande, Roxanne Decker, ed. *A Labor of Love: Critical Reflections on the Writings of Marie-Catherine Desjardins (Madame de Villedieu).* Madison: Fairleigh Dickinson University Press, 2000.

Landes, Joan. *Women and the Public Sphere in the Age of the French Revolution.* Ithaca, NY: Cornell University Press, 1988.

Le Brun, Jacques. "Expérience religieuse et expérience littéraire", in *La Pensée Religieuse dans la littérature et la civilisation du XVIIe siècle en France.* Paris: Biblio 17, 1984.

———— "Quiétisme", in M. Viller et al. (eds). *Dictionnaire de la Spiritualité ascétique et mystique.* Paris: Beauchesne, 1985. 2805–10.

Leirheimer, Linda. "Female Eloquence and Maternal Ministry: The Apostolate of Ursuline Nuns in Seventeenth-Century France." PhD dissertation, Princeton University, 1994.

Livet, Georges. *Le Duc Mazarin, gouverneur d'Alsace.* Strasbourg: Leroux, 1954.

Loskoutoff, Yvan. *La Sainte et la fée: Dévotion à l'enfant Jésus et mode des contes merveilleux à la fin du règne de Louis XIV.* Geneva: Droz, 1987.

Lougee, Carolyn Chappell. "Reason for the Public to Admire her: Why Madame de la Guette Published her Memoirs", in Goldsmith and Goodman (eds), *Going Public: Women and Publishing in Early Modern France.* Ithaca: Cornell University Press, 1995. 13–29.

Lussan, Marguerite de. *Histoire de la Comtesse de Gondez*, vol. XII of *Bibliothèque de campagne ou amusements de l'esprit et du coeur.* La Haye: Cramer et Philibert, 1749.

Mallet-Joris, Françoise. *Marie Mancini.* Paris: Hachette, 1964.

———— *Jeanne Guyon.* Paris: Flammarion, 1978.

Mancini, Hortense. *Mémoires D.M.L.D.M. à M.* ***, in *Mémoires d'Hortense et de Marie Mancini*, ed.Gérard Doscot. Paris: Mercure de France, 1987.

Mancini, Marie. *Apologie, ou les véritables mémoires de Madame la Connétable de Colonne, Maria Mancini, écrits par elle-même*, in *Mémoires d'Hortense et de Marie Mancini*, ed.Gérard Doscot. Paris: Mercure de France, 1987.

———— Lettere. Collection of autograph letters, Biblioteca Statale Santa Scolastica, Subiaco, Italy.

———— *La Vérité dans son jour*, ed. Patricia Francis Cholakian and Elizabeth C. Goldsmith. Delmar, NY: Scholars Facsimiles and Reprints, 1998.

Mémoires de M.L.P.M.M. Colonne, G. connétable du royaume de Naples. Cologne: Pierre Marteau, 1676. (Reprinted as *Cendre et poussière, Mémoires*, ed. Maurice Lever. Paris: Le Comptoir, 1997.)

Mandrou, Robert. *Magistrats et sorciers en France*. Paris: Plon, 1968.

Mansau, Andrée. *Saint-Réal et l'humanisme cosmopolite*. Paris: H. Champion, 1976.

Marie de l'Incarnation. *Correspondance*, ed. Dom Guy Oury. Solesmes, Abbaye de Saint-Pierre, 1971.

——— *Ecrits spirituels et historiques*, ed. Dom Albert Jamet. Paris: Desclée de Brouwer, 1930.

Martin, Claude, (ed.). *La Vie de la vénérable Mère Marie de L'Incarnation, première supérieure des Ursulines de la Nouvelle France. Tirée des ses Lettres et de ses Ecrits*. Paris: Louis Billaine, 1677. Facsimile edition, Solesmes, 1981.

Martin, Henri-Jean and Roger Chartier (eds). *Histoire de l'édition française*, vol. 2. Paris: Promodis, 1984.

Marvick, Elizabeth Wirth. "Nature Versus Nurture: Patterns and Trends in Seventeenth-Century French Child-Rearing", in Lloyd de Mause (ed.). *The History of Childhood*. New York: Harper & Row, 1974. 259–302.

Mason, Mary. "The Other Voice: Autobiographies of Women Writers", in Bella Brodski and Celeste Schenck (eds). *Life/Lines: Theorizing Women's Autobiography*. Ithaca: Cornell University Press, 1988. 19–44.

Masson, Maurice. *Fénelon et Madame Guyon, documents nouveaux et inédits*. Paris: Hachette, 1907.

Maza, Sarah. "Le Tribunal de la nation: Les Mémoires judiciaires et l'opinion publique à la fin de l'Ancien Régime", *Annales*, **42**, 1 (January–February 1987), 73–90.

McNamara, Jo Ann Kay. *Sisters in Arms: Catholic Nuns Through Two Millennia*. Cambridge, MA: Harvard University Press, 1996.

Mongrédien, Georges. *Une Aventurière au grand siècle: La Duchesse Mazarin*. Paris: Amiot-Dumont, 1952.

Munier-Jolain, Jacques. *Procès de femmes*. Paris: Calmann Lévy, 1898.

Nemours, Marie d'Orléans Longueville de. *Mémoires de M.L.D.D.N.* Cologne, 1709.

Nupied, Nicholas (ed.). *Journal des principales audiences du Parlement*. Paris: Compagnie des libraires associés, 1707.

Nussbaum, Felicity. *The Autobiographical Subject*. Baltimore: The Johns Hopkins University Press, 1989.

Orcibal, Jean. "L'Influence spirituelle de Fénelon dans les pays anglo-saxons du XVIIe siècle", *XVIIe siècle*, 12–14 (1951), 276–87.

Paige, Nicholas B. "Being Interior: French Catholic Autobiographies and the Genesis of a Literary Mentality, 1596–1709." PhD dissertation, University of Pennsylvania, 1996.

Perey, Lucien [pseudonym for Clara Herpin]. *Une Princesse romaine au XVIIe siècle: Marie Mancini Colonna d'après des documents inédits*. Paris: Calmann Lévy, 1896.

Perrero, A.D. "La Duchessa Ortensia Mazzarino e la Principessa Maria Colonna, Sorelle Mancini, ed il Duca Carlo Emanuele II di Savoia", in *Curiosità e ricerche di storia subalpina*. Torino: Fratelli Bocca, 1876.

Rabutin, Roger de, Comte de Bussy. *Mémoires*, ed. Ludovic Lalanne. Paris: Marpon and Flammarion, 1857.

Ranum, Orest. "The Refuges of Intimacy", in Roger Chartier (ed.), *A History of Private Life*, vol. 3. Cambridge, MA: Harvard University Press, 1989. 207–63.

Rapley, Elizabeth. *The Dévotes: Women and Church in Seventeenth-Century France*. Montreal: McGill-Queen's University Press, 1990.

Rayez, André. "Le 'Traité de la contemplation' de Dom Claude Martin", *Revue d'ascétique et de mystique*, 115 (1953), 206–49.

Reed, Gervais. *Claude Barbin, 1628–1698: Paris Bookseller During the Reign of Louis XIV*. Geneva: Droz, 1975.

Représentation et sommaire des signes miraculeux qui ont esté faits à la gloire de Dieu et de son Eglise en la sortie des sept démons qui possédaient le corps de la mère prieure des religieuses ursulines de Loudun. Rouen, D. Ferrand, [1637]).

Rousseau, J.J. *Julie ou La Nouvelle Héloïse*. Paris: Classiques Garnier, 1988.

Saenger, Paul. *Space Between Words: the Origins of Silent Reading*. Stanford, CA: Stanford University Press, 1997.

Saint-Evremond, Charles de Marguetel. *Réponse de Dame Hortense Mancini Duchesse de Mazarin, aux plaidoyez de Messire Armand Charles Duc de Mazarin son Epoux*. Toulouse: J.J. Boude, n.d.

—— *Oeuvres meslees*. Londres: J. Tonson, 1709. 3 vols.

—— *Works*. London: J. and J. Knapton, 1728. 3 vols.

—— *Oraison funèbre de Madame Mazarin*, in *Oeuvres choisies*. Paris: Garnier, 1867. 386–98.

Saint-Jure, Jean-Baptiste. "Lettres inédites", in *Revue d'ascétique et de mystique*, **9**, 34 (1928), 113–39; **11**, 42 (1930), 113–35.

Saint-Réal, César de. *Lettre touchant le caractère de Madame la Duchesse Mazarin* in *Oeuvres de M. L'Abbé de Saint-Réal*. Amsterdam: François L'Honoré et Fils, 1740.

Scudéry, Madeleine de. "De parler trop ou trop peu", in Phillip J. Wolfe (ed.), *Choix de Conversations*. Ravenna: Longo Editore, 1977.

Sévigné, Marie de Rabutin Chantal, Madame de. *Correspondance*, ed. Roger Duchene. Paris: Gallimard, 1973.

Shwartz, Deborah. "Villedieu, Henriette-Sylvie de Molière, and Feminine Empowerment", in Michel Guggenheim (ed.), *Women in French Literature*. Saratoga: Anima Libri, 1988. 77–90.

Slade, Carole. "Saint Teresa's *Meditaciones sobre los cantares*: The Hermeneutics of Humility and Enjoyment", *Religion and Literature*, **18**, 1 (1986), 27–44.

Stefanofska, Malina. "Strolling through the Galleries, hiding in a Cabinet: Clio at the French Absolutist Court", *The Eighteenth Century, Theory and Interpretation*, **35**, 3 (1994), 261–79.

Strosetski, Christophe. *Rhétorique de la conversation*. Paris: Biblio 17, 1984.

Surin, Jean-Joseph. *Correspondance*, ed. Michel de Certeau. Paris: Desclée de Brouwer, 1965.

—— *Triomphe de l'amour divin sur les puissances de l'Enfer*. Grenoble: Jérôme Millon, 1990.

Tarr, Lázló. *The History of the Carriage*. Budapest: Corvina, 1969.

Timmermans, Linda. *L'Accès des femmes à la culture, 1598–1715*. Paris: Champion, 1993.

Traer, James. *Marriage and the Family in 18th-Century France*. Ithaca: Cornell University Press, 1980.

Verdier, Gabrielle. "Gender and Rhetoric in some Seventeenth-Century Love Letters", *Esprit Créateur*, **23**, 2 (1983), 45–57.

Viala, Alain. *Naissance de l'écrivain*. Paris: Minuit, 1985.

Villedieu, Marie-Catherine Desjardins, Madame de. *Anaxandre*. Paris: Jean Ribov, 1667.

—— *Les Désordres de l'amour*, ed. Micheline Cuénin. Geneva: Droz, 1970.

—— *Lettres et billets galants*, ed. Micheline Cuénin. Paris: Publications de la Société d'Etude du XVIIe Siècle, 1975.

———— *Mémoires de la vie de Henriette-Sylvie de Molière*, ed. Micheline Cuénin. Tours: Université François Rabelais, 1977.

———— *Le Portefeuille*, in *Oeuvres mêlées*, ed. Jean-Paul Homand. Exeter: University of Exeter, 1979.

Weber, Alison. *Teresa of Avila and the Rhetoric of Femininity*. Princeton: Princeton University Press, 1990.

Weinstein, Donald and Rudolph M. Bell. *Saints and Society: Two Worlds of Western Christendom, 1000–1700*. Chicago: University of Chicago Press, 1982.

Weintraub, Karl Juachim. *The Value of the Individual: Self and Circumstance in Autobiography*. Chicago: University of Chicago Press, 1978.

Wiesner, Merry, E. *Women and Gender in Early Modern Europe*. Cambridge: Cambridge University Press, 1993.

Wright, Wendy. *Bond of Perfection: Jeanne de Chantal and François de Sales*. New York: Paulist Press, 1985.

Index